Frommer's

PORTABLE
Las Vegas for Non-Gamblers

2nd Edition

by Mary Herczog

Here's what critics say about Frommer's:

"Amazingly easy to use. Very portable, very complete."

—*Booklist*

"Detailed, accurate, and easy-to-read information for all price ranges."

—*Glamour Magazine*

Wiley Publishing, Inc.

Published by:

WILEY PUBLISHING, INC.

111 River St.
Hoboken, NJ 07030-5774

ISBN-13: 978-0-7645-8338-4
ISBN-10: 0-7645-8338-7

Editor: Kitty Jarrett
With: Naomi Kraus
Production Editor: Donna Wright
Photo Editor: Richard Fox
Cartographer: Liz Puhl
Production by Wiley Indianapolis Composition Services

For information on our other products and services or to obtain technical support, please contact our Customer Care Department within the U.S. at 800/762-2974, outside the U.S. at 317/572-3993 or fax 317/572-4002.

Wiley also publishes its books in a variety of electronic formats. Some content that appears in print may not be available in electronic formats.

Manufactured in the United States of America

5   4   3   2

Contents

List of Maps

About the Author

Mary Herczog writes a great many books for Frommer's (*Frommer's Las Vegas, Frommer's New Orleans, California For Dummies,* and *Las Vegas For Dummies,* among others) and lives in the hopes of writing a great many more. When she is not traveling or writing, she lives in Los Angeles and works for Hollywood. She has spent upwards of a week in Vegas and not so much as touched a slot machine.

Acknowledgments

Gracious thanks to Frommer's, and especially to Naomi Kraus, who always makes me look better than I am—kind of like a showgirl's wig. Thanks to my Designated Drinkers Arlene and Caroline, and to Fact Finders Rick and Lisa. Going to Vegas with Steve Hochman is a jackpot.

An Invitation to the Reader

In researching this book, we discovered many wonderful places—hotels, restaurants, shops, and more. We're sure you'll find others. Please tell us about them, so we can share the information with your fellow travelers in upcoming editions. If you were disappointed with a recommendation, we'd love to know that, too. Please write to:

> *Frommer's Portable Las Vegas for Non-Gamblers,* 2nd Edition
> Wiley Publishing, Inc. • 111 River St. • Hoboken, NJ 07030-5774

An Additional Note

Please be advised that travel information is subject to change at any time—and this is especially true of prices. We therefore suggest that you write or call ahead for confirmation when making your travel plans. The authors, editors, and publisher cannot be held responsible for the experiences of readers while traveling. Your safety is important to us, however, so we encourage you to stay alert and be aware of your surroundings. Keep a close eye on cameras, purses, and wallets, all favorite targets of thieves and pickpockets.

FROMMER'S STAR RATINGS, ICONS & ABBREVIATIONS

Every hotel, restaurant, and attraction listing in this guide has been ranked for quality, value, service, amenities, and special features using a **star-rating system.** In country, state, and regional guides, we also rate towns and regions to help you narrow down your choices and budget your time accordingly. Hotels and restaurants are rated on a scale of zero (recommended) to three stars (exceptional). Attractions, shopping, nightlife, towns, and regions are rated according to the following scale: zero stars (recommended), one star (highly recommended), two stars (very highly recommended), and three stars (must-see).

In addition to the star-rating system, we also use **seven feature icons** that point you to the great deals, in-the-know advice, and unique experiences that separate travelers from tourists. Throughout the book, look for:

Finds	Special finds—those places only insiders know about
Fun Fact	Fun facts—details that make travelers more informed and their trips more fun
Kids	Best bets for kids and advice for the whole family
Moments	Special moments—those experiences that memories are made of
Overrated	Places or experiences not worth your time or money
Tips	Insider tips—great ways to save time and money
Value	Great values—where to get the best deals

The following **abbreviations** are used for credit cards:

| AE | American Express | DISC | Discover | V | Visa |
| DC | Diners Club | MC | MasterCard | | |

FROMMERS.COM

Now that you have the guidebook to a great trip, visit our website at **www.frommers.com** for travel information on more than 3,000 destinations. With features updated regularly, we give you instant access to the most current trip-planning information available. At Frommers.com, you'll also find the best prices on airfares, accommodations, and car rentals—and you can even book travel online through our travel booking partners. At Frommers.com, you'll also find the following:

- Online updates to our most popular guidebooks
- Vacation sweepstakes and contest giveaways
- Newsletter highlighting the hottest travel trends
- Online travel message boards with featured travel discussions

Introducing Las Vegas

Las Vegas is the city of sin and illusion, the town that Bugsy built, and it's like nothing you've seen before—a facade of a facade with some neon on it. And you're here! And you—don't gamble! Egads!

But don't despair. Las Vegas is many, many things—Sin City, Disneyland for Adults, A Stopover on a Drive Through the West, Convention Central—and just because you aren't all that interested in the main attraction doesn't mean you can't have a whale of a good time. Sure, Vegas would still prefer that you lighten your pockets the traditional way, and so you will still find casinos and slot machines nearly everywhere you go. But with our guidance, not only will you be able to avoid a great deal of exposure to the one-armed bandit, you will also find plenty to otherwise fill your time.

As a non-gambler, your biggest problem will be finding a hotel where the emphasis isn't on gambling. There are a few of these, most of them chain hotels without casinos, although the posh Four Seasons also remains unsullied by craps. But even the official casino hotels have come around to the idea that gambling may not be everyone's first reason for coming to Vegas, with two of them (Mandalay Bay's THEhotel and The Venetian's Venezia tower) built recently specifically as alternatives to casino hotels, though still attached to casino hotels. And so visitors now have swell pools, lush spas, and some of the best restaurants in the country—and if all that doesn't spell vacation, well, then you've also got access to some marvelous hiking in Red Rock Canyon, water fun on Lake Mead, stunning desert visits in Valley of the Fire State Park, and the engineering and architectural marvels at Hoover Dam. And back in town, there are shows—some hokey, and some on the level of the best in the world. There are even a few real museums, with actual masterpieces.

But there are some things to bear in mind while navigating Vegas and avoiding the temptation of the dice or the cards or the slot machines. First of all, the casinos aren't easy to avoid. They generally stand between you and, well, anything you want. When staying inside a hotel, a casino can sometimes be between you and the entire outside world. In chapter 4, we will let you know how obtrusive the casino in question (if there is one) is and how much of a hindrance it can be. Anyone traveling with children should take special note of those descriptions; kids aren't allowed in casinos, though if the only way through the facility is through the gambling area, obviously that rule is relaxed. But kids are expected to stick to walkways between machines, and many a child who has stopped (and who can blame them?) because their attention was caught by noise or flashing lights, have found themselves descended upon by security, who hustle them right along. If this sounds like the opposite of fun, you might want to avoid a casino hotel.

Second, the days of Vegas bargains are, for the most part, gone. Sure, hotel prices can dip quite low (provided that you travel during the off season or want a room Sun–Thurs nights), but the cost of everything else is high. The best restaurants are the expensive ones, with prices hitting nearly New York City levels. The better museums charge a bundle. Spa treatments? Ouch. And the best shows charge outrageous ticket prices.

But then again, you are on vacation. Or maybe you are in town for a convention. Either way, you deserve some foie gras. Or a little massage. See Cirque du Soleil and marvel. Then go outside and look at the lights of Las Vegas. Ever seen anything like it? Of course not. Remember, that's really why you are here.

1 Favorite Vegas Experiences

- **Taking a stroll on the Strip:** Sure, it's a skyline made up entirely of the skylines of other cities, but where else can you see a glowing pyramid, a gleaming giant brass lion, a mini version of New York City, a volcano, the sights of Paris and Venice, and more, all in one day? The Strip, known officially as Las Vegas Boulevard South, is where it's at—and by "it" we mean "huge enormous hotels, most with a theme," and by "theme" we mean "copies, sometimes faithful, of some of the great sights of the world, plus some other stuff just for Vegas."

  So walk down the Strip during the day and giggle. And then do it again at night, when the lights turn it all into something magical. Get in your car and cruise, for maximum effect.

- **Checking out the inside of the hotels:** Remember the part about the theme? Well, in many cases, it's continued inside—and how! Egypt, Rome, Venice, Paris, just to name a few—all lovingly and cartoonishly evoked within.

- **Free shows and attractions:** To further lure you, many of the hotels provide free entertainment, of varying degrees of worth.

The best, and not to be missed, are the fountains of Bellagio, which rise and fall in choreographed rhythms to tunes from Sinatra to opera during the day and part of the night. The Mirage's volcano "explodes" (spews light and fire). Treasure Island's pirates battle scantily clad "sirens" in a really stupid show. One of Siegfried & Roy's white tigers is usually hanging out at The Mirage, and the MGM Grand lets you get up close to a lion or two. And every hotel has at least one lounge with free music every night.

- **The Dolphin Habitat at The Mirage:** Dolphins in the desert? Don't worry, these Atlantic bottlenose dolphins have one of the finest (admittedly manufactured) habitats in the world, and they get cosseted and coddled and stimulated by some marvelous handlers. Watching them frolic—leap, flop, and even toss balls around—is an utter delight. It's the best attraction in Vegas.

- **Eating out:** No longer the joke of the foodie scene, Vegas has attracted many of the most prominent chefs in the country, from Food Network favorites such as Puck and Emeril, to Jean-Georges, Julian Serrano, and more. You may well have one of the meals of your life here.

- **Binging at buffets:** Of course, buffets are quality over quantity, but nothing says "vacation" to us like unlimited mounds of shrimp and an endless flow of prime rib.

- **Cirque du Soleil:** It's a costly ticket, but it's also world-class entertainment. Cirque has four shows as we write this, with more on the way. The magical *Mystère* (at The Mirage); the almost-cinematic *KÀ* (at the MGM Grand); and the other-worldly *O* (at Bellagio), where the troupe's trademark acrobatics and surreal theatrics take place on, above, around, and in water, are the best, while you can skip *Zumanity.*

- **Red Rock Canyon and Valley of the Fire State Park:** When visiting this Wonder of the Artificial World, it's important to remind yourself of the Natural World, and what better way to do it than with awe-inspiring desert rock formations? No money-grubbing businessperson caused these to be built, and they will be standing long after Vegas.

- **Shopping:** The above doesn't mean we don't have our materialistic side, and while Vegas has little in terms of unique shops, it does have pretty much every store you could want, and while shopping at a Gap is nothing special, shopping at a Gap set in a Roman coliseum or a mock Venice is.

- **Liberace museum:** While much fuss—some of it even justified—has been made about Vegas's additions to the cultural scene, you probably should not miss the most Vegas of Vegas attractions, the Liberace Museum. Who needs masterworks when you've got rhinestones?

2 Best Hotel Bets

- **Best for Business Travelers:** If you have a good expense account, head over to the **Four Seasons,** 3960 Las Vegas Blvd. South (✆ 877/632-5000), and let them soothe and pamper you. Otherwise, you can join the other business travelers who have made the **Las Vegas Hilton,** 3000 Paradise Rd. (✆ 800/732-7117), their stop for many years, or you can stretch out in the comfort of the mini-apartments found at the **Residence Inn,** 3225 Paradise Rd. (✆ 800/331-3131).
- **Best for families:** The **Four Seasons** (see above for contact info) is the only hotel in town that truly rolls out the red carpet for Junior (they will provide cribs, toys, and treats, and even baby-proof a room), plus guests have access to Mandalay Bay's ultra-kid-friendly pool area. If you want lower prices and little or no exposure to the Strip, try the **Hawthorn Suites,** 5051 Duke Ellington Way (✆ 800/527-1133), just a couple blocks away, with a free breakfast buffet, a good pool, and basketball and volleyball courts; and they allow pets.
- **Best luxury resorts:** It's a toss-up between the **Four Seasons** (see above for contact info) and **Ritz-Carlton, Lake Las Vegas** (1610 Lake Las Vegas Pkwy., Henderson, NV; ✆ 800/241-3333), with the more moderately priced **Green Valley Ranch Resort** also getting a nod (2300 Paseo Verde Dr., Henderson, NV; ✆ 866/782-9487). The Four Seasons sits atop Mandalay Bay but seems like a world away, whereas the Ritz-Carlton really is (it's about 30 min. away, in Henderson)—so much so (and now we are referring to gestalt, not geography) that once you arrive, it's very hard to leave. Green Valley Ranch is a winning combo of Ritz-Carlton posh and W Hotel hip. If you want Strip proximity and brand-name comfort, the Four Seasons is for you. If you want a genuine luxury resort experience, then it's the Ritz. If you want a bargain as well, try Green Valley Ranch.
- **Best swimming pool:** The winner is the 11 acres of water fun (including a beach pool with regular waves, plus a long lazy river) at **Mandalay Bay,** 3950 Las Vegas Blvd. South

(☎ **877/632-7800**). But second is a tossup between the jungle fantasy at **The Mirage,** 3400 Las Vegas Blvd. South (☎ **800/627-6667**), and the one at **The Flamingo Las Vegas,** 3555 Las Vegas Blvd. South (☎ **888/308-8899**). Both are full of slides and waterfalls, plus lots of lush foliage.

- **Best spa:** The designers of **Elemis Spa** at the **Aladdin,** 3667 Las Vegas Blvd. South (☎ **702/785-5555**), were sent to Morocco for inspiration, and the result is the most beautiful spa in Vegas. We hope the new Planet Hollywood owners keep their mitts off it. The greatest number of services can be found at the highly regarded (and highly expensive) **Canyon Ranch Spa** at **The Venetian,** 3355 Las Vegas Blvd. South (☎ **877/283-6423**), which also has the best health club.

- **Best rooms: THEhotel at Mandalay Bay,** 3950 Las Vegas Blvd. South (☎ **877/632-7800**), with full one-bedroom suites with impressive bathrooms, beats out **The Venetian,** 3355 Las Vegas Blvd. South (☎ **888/283-6423**), whose rooms include sunken living rooms. For over-the-top Vegas style, **Luxor,** 3900 Las Vegas Blvd. South (☎ **800/288-1000**), helps you sleep like an Egyptian.

- **Best beds: Ritz-Carlton, Lake Las Vegas** and **Green Valley Ranch Resort** (see contact info above) both have plush beds, high-thread-count sheets, and down comforters; and it all comes together in a cocoon you will be hard-pressed to leave. **Palms Resort & Casino,** 4321 W. Flamingo Rd. (☎ **866/942-7770**), has a similar philosophy toward nighttime comfort.

- **Best bathrooms: THEhotel at Mandalay Bay** (see contact info above) heads a pack (which includes Mandalay Bay, the Ritz, the Four Seasons, Green Valley Ranch, Bellagio, and The Venetian) of hotels with marble tubs and large glass-and-marble showers, but THEhotel adds a flat-screen plasma TV and a chin-deep soaking tub.

- **Best hotel dining:** On one hand, it's hard to beat the line-up at **Bellagio; Picasso, Le Cirque, Circo, Prime Steakhouse**—these represent some important names in the restaurant world. But **Mandalay Bay's** wattage—**Fleur de Lys, Aureole, Border Grill,** even the amusing **Red Square**—may thrill us even more.

3 Best Dining Bets

- **Best buffet:** You get what you pay for, so in the expensive category, try the incredible assortment offered at Bellagio's **Buffet**

(© 877/234-6358), or the buffet at the French-regional-themed **Le Village Buffet** (© 888/266-5687) at Paris. In the moderate category, try local favorite **Rio's Carnival World Buffet** (© 702/252-7777). And at the low end, head Downtown, where **Main Street Station's Garden Court** (© 702/387-1896) offers a well-priced and quite good buffet.

- **Best for families:** Buffets work well for feeding bottomless-pit teenagers, but **Monte Carlo Pub & Brewery** (© 702/730-7777) has mounds of family-friendly food (Buffalo wings, pizza, ribs, large salads) for even better prices. **Cypress Street Marketplace** in Caesars Palace (© 702/731-7110) has such a wide variety of food booths (salads to fat Chicago hot dogs, to wraps, to Vietnamese noodle bowls) that there should be something there for even the most varied family tastes.

- **Best for a romantic dinner:** It's hard to beat the view found at **Alizé** (© 702/951-7000)—at the top of the Palms, with no other tall buildings around to obscure the twinkling city lights from three walls of windows. It's a wow.

- **Best for sexy food and dining:** We mean this in a grown-up way, not in a tummy-bearing, Sin-Is-In way. The playful, teasing concoctions at the luscious **Fleur de Lys** (© 877/632-9200) make other attempts at fine dining in town look feeble. Food here is sensual in all ways.

- **Best wine list:** Mandalay Bay's **Aureole** (© 877/632-5300) is renowned for its "wine angels," the catsuit-clad gals who rise to the top of a four-story tower of wine bottles to retrieve a patron's selection. It's a gimmick that may be misleading; they have a wonderful selection, as well as handheld computers that guide you through the selections.

- **Best steak:** Fighting words for many. Not for us, though. We think it's at **Charlie Palmer Steak,** in the Four Seasons (© 702/632-5120). But others think it can be found in **Austins Steakhouse** (© 702/631-1000).

- **Best bistro:** Thomas "Best Chef in America" Keller has finally succumbed and gotten himself a Vegas restaurant. **Bouchon** in The Venetian (© 702/414-6200) surpasses the original in Napa. Not a misstep on the menu.

- **Best decor:** Genuine works from the master on the wall (and the most lovely casual floral arrangements possible) at **Picasso** (© 877/234-6358) or the over-the-top-of-the-Iron-Curtain satirical fun of Mandalay Bay's **Red Square** (© 877/632-5300).

2

Planning Your Trip to Las Vegas

Before any trip, you need to do a bit of advance planning. You'll need to decide whether a package tour makes sense for you, when to go, and more. In the pages that follow, you'll find everything you need to know to handle the practical details of planning your trip to Las Vegas in advance: airlines and area airports, a calendar of events, a list of major conventions you may want to avoid, resources for those with special needs, and much more.

We also suggest that you check out chapter 8, "Las Vegas After Dark," before you leave home; if you want to see the most popular shows, it's a good idea to call ahead and order tickets well in advance to avoid disappointment. (Ditto if you want to dine in one of the city's top restaurants; head to chapter 5, "Where to Dine," for full reviews and contact information.)

1 Visitor Information

For information, contact the **Las Vegas Convention and Visitors Authority,** 3150 Paradise Rd., Las Vegas, NV 89109 (© **877/ VISITLV** or 702/892-7575; www.lvcva.com). They can send you a comprehensive packet of brochures, a map, a show guide, an events calendar, and an attractions list; help you find a hotel that meets your specifications (and make reservations); and tell you if a major convention is scheduled during the time you would like to visit Las Vegas. They're open daily from 8am to 5pm.

Another excellent information source is the **Las Vegas Chamber of Commerce,** 3720 Howard Hughes Pkwy., #100, Las Vegas, NV 89109 (© **702/735-1616;** www.lvchamber.com). Their *Visitor's Guide* contains extensive information about accommodations, attractions, excursions, children's activities, and more. They can answer all your Las Vegas questions, including those about weddings and divorces. They're open Monday to Friday 8am to 5pm.

Tips Winning Websites

When you consider the enormous popularity of Las Vegas, it should come as no surprise that there are hundreds of websites devoted to the destination. There is a lot of good—and bad—information about everything from the casino hotels to dining suggestions.

Start your online journey to Sin City at **www.vegas4 visitors.com**. This small, family-run endeavor is packed full with information; unbiased reviews; contact info; maps; photos; and links to hotels, restaurants, and more. There's also a weekly news and events column.

If you want to pick the brains of the local populace—and who better to ask about life in Las Vegas?—head over to **www.lasvegasweekly.com**. You'll find out where locals go for fun, and you can browse through reviews of bars, cafes, nightclubs, restaurants, and amusement parks.

For the most comprehensive Vegas dining resource on the Web, go to **www.nightonthetown.com**. The site arranges its plethora of restaurants by cuisine and location so you can find what you want, where you want it.

If you like your information with a side order of humor, then head to **www.cheapovegas.com**. This fun site offers lots of sassy reviews and unbiased opinions, especially on the Las Vegas casino hotels. There's also a small section on getting freebies while you're in town.

For information on all of Nevada, including Las Vegas, contact the **Nevada Commission on Tourism** (© 800/638-2328; www.travelnevada.com). If you call or visit their website, they'll send you a comprehensive information packet on Nevada.

2 Money

ATMs linked to both the **Cirrus** (© 800/424-7787; www.master card.com) and **PLUS** (© 800/843-7587; www.visa.com) networks can be found everywhere in Las Vegas; no one wants you to find yourself without cash you could lose in a slot! Beware of withdrawal charges, though, which can often run as high as $2 or $3 (the highest charges are usually for commercial machines in convenience stores and hotel lobbies). Also be aware that your own bank may impose a fee every time you use your card at an ATM in a different city or bank. To compare banks' ATM fees within the U.S., use **www.bankrate.com**.

At most banks, you don't even need to go to a teller; you can get a cash advance at an ATM with your credit card if you know your PIN. If you've forgotten your PIN, or didn't even know you had one, call the number on the back of your credit card and ask the bank to send it to you.

Almost every credit card company has an emergency toll-free number that you can call if your wallet or purse is stolen. **Visa**'s U.S. emergency number is © **800/847-2911.** American Express cardholders and traveler's check holders should call © **800/221-7282. MasterCard** holders should call © **800/307-7309.**

3 When to Go

Since most of a Las Vegas vacation is usually spent indoors, you can have a good time here year-round. The most pleasant seasons are spring and fall, especially if you want to experience the great outdoors.

Weekdays are slightly less crowded than weekends. Holidays are almost always a mob scene and are accompanied by high hotel prices. Room rates also skyrocket when big conventions and special events are taking place. The slowest times of year are June and July, the week before Christmas, and the week after New Year's.

If a major convention is to be held during your trip, you might want to change your date. Contact the **Las Vegas Convention and Visitors Authority** (© **877/VISITLV** or 702/892-7575; www.lvcva. com), since convention schedules often change.

THE WEATHER

First of all, Vegas isn't always hot, but when it is, it's *really* hot. One thing you'll hear again and again is that even though Las Vegas gets very hot, the dry desert heat is not unbearable. This is true (we know this because we spent a couple days there in 104° weather and lived to say "It wasn't all that bad, not really"), except in most of the hotel pool areas; they are surrounded by massive buildings covered in mirrored glass, which act like a giant magnifying glass on the antlike people below. Still, generally the humidity averages a low 22%, and even on very hot days, there's apt to be a breeze. Also, except on the hottest summer days, there's relief at night, when temperatures often drop by as much as 20°.

Las Vegas's Average Temperatures (°F/°C) & Precipitation

	Jan	Feb	Mar	Apr	May	June	July	Aug	Sept	Oct	Nov	Dec
Average Temp. (°F)	47	52	58	66	75	86	91	89	81	69	55	47
(°C)	8	11	14	19	24	30	33	32	27	21	13	8
Avg. High Temp. (°F)	57	63	69	78	88	99	104	102	94	81	66	57
(°C)	14	17	21	26	31	37	40	39	34	27	19	14
Avg. Low Temp. (°F)	37	41	47	54	63	72	78	77	69	57	44	37
(°C)	3	5	8	12	17	22	26	25	21	14	7	3
Average Precip. (in.)	.59	.69	.59	.15	.24	.08	.44	.45	.31	.24	.31	.40
(cm)	1.5	1.8	1.5	.4	.6	.2	1.1	1.1	.8	.6	.8	1.0

But this is the desert, and it's not hot all year round. It can get quite cold, especially in the winter, when at night it can drop to 30°F (–1°C) and lower. (In the winter of 1998–99, it actually snowed in Vegas, dropping nearly 2 in. on the Strip. There's nothing quite like the sight of Luxor's Sphinx covered in snow.) The breeze can also become a cold, biting, strong wind of up to 40 mph or more. And so there are entire portions of the year when you won't be using that hotel swimming pool at all (and even if you want to, be advised that most of the hotels close huge chunks of those fabulous swimming pool areas for "the season," which can be as long as from Labor Day to Memorial Day). If you aren't traveling in the height of summer, bring a wrap. Also, remember your sunscreen and hat—even if it's not all that hot, you can burn very easily and very fast. (You should see all the lobster-red people glowing in the casinos at night.)

LAS VEGAS CALENDAR OF EVENTS

You may be surprised that Las Vegas does not offer as many annual events as most tourist cities. The reason is Las Vegas's very raison d'être: the gaming industry. This town wants its visitors spending their money in the casinos, not at Renaissance fairs and parades.

When in town, check the local paper and call the **Las Vegas Convention and Visitors Authority** (© 877/VISITLV or 702/892-7575; www.lvcva.com), or the **Chamber of Commerce** (© 702/735-1616; www.lvchamber.com) to find out about other events scheduled during your visit.

June

World Series of Poker. This famous event used to take place at Binion's Horseshoe Casino in late April and early May, but now that Harrah's has bought Binion's—and the Horseshoe name, and the WSOP—they've moved it and changed the date. The 2005 WSOP will be held June 2 to July 15 at the Rio. An estimated 5,000 players are expected to participate in the buy-in, no-limit Texas Hold 'em Championship, hoping for the $1 million purse, double the number that competed in 2004. Chalk that up to increased profile for the event via popular TV poker shows. Between that and the celebrities who will turn out, trying to test their acting abilities on a bluff, it may be tough to get a seat to watch the action, though it costs nothing should you do so. With high-stakes gamblers and show-biz personalities competing for six-figure purses, there are daily events with entry stakes ranging from $125 to $5,000. Check out **www.worldseriesofpoker.com**.

CineVegas International Film Festival. This annual event, usually held in early June, is growing in both popularity and prestige with film debuts and competitions from both independent and major studios, plus lots of celebrities hanging around for the big parties. Call ℭ **702/992-7979**or visit **www.cinevegas.com**.

Las Vegas Jazz Festival. World-class jazz musicians are invited to this relatively new but growing festival held at the Fremont Street Experience for 3 days, usually in early June. For details, schedules, and tickets call ℭ **800/249-3559** or visit **www.vegas experience.com**.

September

International Mariachi Festival. This worldwide Mariachi music festival, held the first week in September, has become one of the city's most eagerly anticipated events. Call **Aladdin** at ℭ **877/333-9474.**

Oktoberfest. This boisterous autumn holiday is celebrated from mid-September through the end of October at the **Mount Charleston Resort** (ℭ **800/955-1314** or 702/872-5408; www.mtcharlestonlodge.com), about a 35-minute drive northwest of Las Vegas, with music, folk dancers, singalongs around a roaring fire, special decorations, and Bavarian cookouts.

October

Michelin Championship at Las Vegas, PGA Tour. This 4-day championship event is played on three local courses in early October. For details, call ℭ **702/242-3000.**

December

National Finals Rodeo. This is the Super Bowl of rodeos, attended by about 200,000 people each year. The top 15 male rodeo stars compete in calf roping, steer wrestling, bull riding, team roping, saddle bronco riding, and bareback riding. And the top 15 women compete in barrel racing. An all-around "Cowboy of the Year" is chosen. In connection with this event, hotels book country stars into their showrooms, and a cowboy shopping spree—the **NFR Cowboy Christmas Gift Show,** a trade show

Moments   New Year's Eve in Las Vegas

Over the last couple years, more and more people have been choosing Las Vegas as their party destination for New Year's Eve. In fact, some estimates indicate that by the time you read this, there will be more people ringing in the New Year in Nevada than in New York City's Times Square.

From experience, we can tell you that there are a lot of people who come here on December 31. We mean a *lot* of people. During the Y2K festivities, almost *all* the 120,000 hotel rooms were sold out to 250,000 visitors. In 1997, nearly 400,000 total jammed the Strip to watch the Hacienda implode. Another 25,000 paid $100 apiece to experience New Year's Eve at the Fremont Street Experience. Traffic is a nightmare, parking is next to impossible, and there is not a square inch of the place that isn't occupied by a human being.

A major portion of the Strip is closed down, sending the masses and their mass quantities of alcohol into the street. Each year's celebration is a little different but usually includes a streetside performance by a major celebrity, confetti, the obligatory countdown, fireworks, and, if you're lucky, maybe even a building implosion. This has become one of the city's biggest annual events.

for Western gear—is held at Cashman Field. The NFR runs for 10 days during the first 2 weeks of December at the Thomas and Mack Center of UNLV. Order tickets as far in advance as possible at ℂ **866/388-3267** or www.nfrexperience.com.

Las Vegas Bowl Week. A championship football event in late December pits the winners of the Mid-American Conference against the winners of the Big West Conference. The action takes place at the 32,000-seat Sam Boyd Stadium. Call ℂ **866/388-3267** for ticket information or visit www.lvbowl.com.

New Year's Eve. This is a biggie (reserve your hotel room *early*). Downtown, at the Fremont Street Experience, there's a big block party with two dramatic countdowns to midnight (the first is at 9pm, midnight on the East Coast). The Strip is usually closed down to street traffic, and hundreds of thousands of people pack the area for the festivities. Of course, there are fireworks.

4 Money-Saving Deals

Before you start your search for the lowest airfare, you may want to consider booking your flight as part of a travel package.

Package tours are not the same as escorted tours. They are simply a way to buy airfare and accommodations (and sometimes extras like sightseeing tours and hard-to-get show tickets) at the same time. When you're visiting Las Vegas, a package can be a smart way to go. In many cases, a package that includes airfare, hotel, and a rental car will cost you less than your hotel bill alone would have, had you booked it yourself. That's because packages are sold in bulk to tour operators, who then resell them to the public at a cost that drastically undercuts standard rates.

Packages, however, vary widely. Some offer a better class of hotels than others. Some offer the same hotels for lower prices. With some packagers, your choice of accommodations and travel days may be limited. Which package is right for you depends entirely on what you want. Prices vary according to the season, seat availability, hotel choice, whether you travel midweek or on the weekend, and other factors. But since even an advance-purchase round-trip fare between New York and Las Vegas can easily be $100 or $200 more than the figures quoted below, it seems almost insane *not* to book a less expensive package that includes so many extras.

Just to give you a couple of examples, at press time, a **Delta Vacations** package leaving from New York cost as little as $378 per person, based on double occupancy, including round-trip coach air transportation, 2 nights at your choice of several major casino hotels, a rental car, airport transfers, and bonus discounts and admissions. At press time, **Southwest Airlines Vacations** was offering round-trip airfare from Los Angeles with 2 nights at several different hotels; cost per person, based on double occupancy, was $199 for the Mirage (before applicable taxes and fees).

Here are a few tips to help you tell one package from another and figure out which one is right for you:

- **Read this guide.** Do a little homework. Compare the rates that we've published to the discounted rates being offered by the packagers to see what kinds of deals they're offering—if you're actually being offered a substantial savings, or if they've just gussied up the rack rates to make their offer *sound* like a deal. If you're being offered a stay in a hotel we haven't recommended, do more research to learn about it, especially if it isn't a reliable franchise. It's not a deal if you end up at a dump.

- **Read the fine print.** Make sure you know *exactly* what's included in the price you're being quoted and what's not. Are hotel taxes included, or will you have to pay extra? Before you commit to a package, make sure you know how much flexibility you have, say, if your kid gets sick or your boss suddenly asks you to adjust your vacation schedule. Some packagers require ironclad commitments, while others will go with the flow, charging only minimal fees for changes or cancellations.
- **Use your best judgment.** Stay away from fly-by-nights and shady packagers. If a deal appears to be too good to be true, it probably is. Go with a reputable firm with a proven track record. This is where your travel agent can come in handy; he or she should be knowledgeable about different packagers, the deals they offer, and the general rate of satisfaction among their customers.

So how do you find a package deal? Perhaps the best place to start is with the airlines themselves, which often package their flights together with accommodations. **Southwest Airlines Vacations** (© 800/243-8372; www.swavacations.com) has dozens of flights in and out of Las Vegas every day, so the sheer volume allows them to offer some relatively inexpensive vacation deals with lots of options in terms of travel time and hotels.

Other airlines that offer air/land packages include **American Airlines Vacations** (© 800/321-2121; http://aav1.aavacations.com), **Delta Vacations** (© 800/654-6559; www.deltavacations.com), **Continental Airlines Vacations** (© 800/301-3800; www.cool vacations.com), **United Vacations** (© 888/854-3899; www.united vacations.com), and **US Airways Vacations** (© 800/422-3861; www.usairwaysvacations.com).

Reservations Plus, 2275-A Renaissance Dr., Las Vegas, NV 89119 (© 800/805-9528; www.resplus.com), runs a free room-reservation service, but they can also arrange packages (including meals, transportation, tours, show tickets, car rentals, and other features) and group rates.

The biggest hotel chains, casinos, and resorts also offer package deals. If you already know where you want to stay, call the resort itself and ask if they can offer land/air packages.

Another place to start your search is the travel section of your local Sunday newspaper. Also check the ads in the back of national travel magazines like *Travel Holiday, National Geographic Traveler,* and *Arthur Frommer's Budget Travel.*

One of the biggest packagers in the Northeast, **Liberty Travel** (© **888/271-1584;** www.libertytravel.com) boasts a full-page ad in many Sunday papers. You won't get much in the way of service from them, but you can get a good deal. **American Express Vacations** (© **800/346-3607;** http://travel.americanexpress.com) is another option.

For one-stop shopping, **Vacation Together** (© **800/839-9851;** www.vacationtogether.com) allows you to search for and book Las Vegas packages offered by a number of tour operators and airlines.

Finally, another good source for money-saving deals is online travel-planning sites, which frequently offer discounted packages to Las Vegas. The most longstanding and reputable sites, **Travelocity** (www.travelocity.com or http://frommers.travelocity.com) and **Expedia** (www.expedia.com), offer excellent selections and searches for complete vacation packages. Travelers search by destination and dates coupled with how much they are willing to spend.

Orbitz (www.orbitz.com), a site launched by United, Delta, Northwest, American, and Continental airlines, offers a huge range of airfares and hotel rooms, as well as complete vacation packages.

5 Tips for Travelers with Special Needs
TRAVELERS WITH DISABILITIES

On the one hand, Las Vegas is fairly well equipped for those with disabilities, with virtually every hotel having accessible rooms, ramps, and other requirements. On the other hand, the distance between hotels (particularly on the Strip) makes a vehicle of some sort virtually mandatory for most travelers with disabilities, and it may be extremely strenuous and time-consuming to get from place to place (even within a single hotel because of the crowds). Even if you don't intend to gamble, you still may have to go through the casino, and casinos can be quite difficult to maneuver in, particularly for a guest in a wheelchair. Casinos are usually crowded, and the machines and tables are often laid out close together, with chairs, people, and such blocking easy access. You should also consider that it is often a long trek through larger hotels between the entrance and the room elevators (or, for that matter, anywhere in the hotel), and then add a crowded casino to the equation.

Southern Nevada Center for Independent Living, 6039 Eldora St., Suite F, Las Vegas, NV 89146 (© **800/870-7003** or 702/889-4216; www.sncil.org) can recommend hotels and restaurants that meet your needs, help you find a personal attendant, advise about transportation, and answer all sorts of other questions. The **Nevada Commission on Tourism** (✆ **800/638-2328;** www.travelnevada. com) offers a free accommodations guide to Las Vegas hotels that includes access information.

GAY & LESBIAN TRAVELERS

For such a licentious, permissive town, Las Vegas has its conservative side, and it is not the most gay-friendly city. This will not manifest itself in any signs of outrage toward open displays of gay affection, but it does mean that the local gay community is largely confined to the bar scene. This may be changing, with local gay pride parades and other activities gathering steam each year, including the first-ever nighttime parade through Downtown with the mayor in attendance in 2001. See listings for gay bars in chapter 8, "Las Vegas After Dark." Also, if you're on the Web, check out **GayLasVegas,** at **www. gaylasvegas.com**, or **Gayvegas.com,** at **www.gayvegas.com**, both of which have helpful advice on lodging, restaurants, and nightlife.

QVegas, a monthly magazine serving the gay community, provides information about bars, workshops, local politics, support groups, shops, events, and more. A subscription costs $25 for 12 issues. You can find the magazine in bars, music stores, and most libraries and bookstores. For details, call ✆ **702/650-0636** or check their online edition at **www.qvegas.com**.

SENIORS

Seniors, don't be shy about asking for discounts, but always bring an ID card, especially if you've kept your youthful glow. Mention the fact that you're a senior when you first make your travel reservations. Most of the major domestic airlines offer discount programs for senior travelers, as does **Greyhound** (✆ **800/229-9424;** www.greyhound.com).

Members of **AARP** (formerly known as the American Association of Retired Persons), 601 E St. NW, Washington, DC 20049 (✆ **888/ 687-2277;** www.aarp.org), get discounts on hotels, airfares, and car rentals. AARP offers members a wide range of benefits, including *AARP The Magazine* and a monthly newsletter. Anyone 50 or over can join.

FAMILY TRAVEL

Vegas is a city that caters to the over-21 set and isn't the best destination to bring the kids to. For one thing, kids are not allowed in casinos at all. Since most hotels are laid out so that you have to frequently walk through their casinos, you can see how this becomes a headache.

Some casino hotels will not allow the children of nonguests on the premises after 6pm—and this policy is seriously enforced. If you choose to travel here with the children, see the "Especially for Kids" section in chapter 6 and look for the hotels, restaurants, and shows bearing the Kids icon in chapters 4, 5, and 8.

If you do bring your children to Las Vegas during the summer, you'll definitely want to book a place with a pool. Many hotels also have enormous video arcades and other diversions.

WOMEN TRAVELERS

Thanks to the crowds, Las Vegas is as safe as any other big city for a woman traveling alone. Take the usual precautions and be wary of hustlers or drunken businessmen who may mistake a woman on her own for a "working girl." (Alas, million-dollar proposals, a la Robert Redford, are a rarity.) Many of the big hotels (most MGM-Mirage hotels, for example) have security guards stationed at the elevators at night to prevent anyone other than guests from going up to the room floors. Ask when you make your reservation. If you're anxious, ask a security guard to escort you to your room. *Always* lock your door *and* deadbolt it to prevent intruders from entering.

6 Getting There

BY PLANE

The following airlines offer regularly scheduled flights into Las Vegas's **McCarran International Airport,** 5757 Wayne Newton Blvd. (© **702/261-5211;** www.mccarran.com; some of these are regional carriers, so they may not all fly from your point of origin): **AeroMexico** (© 800/237-6639; www.aeromexico.com), **Air Canada** (© 888/247-2262; www.aircanada.com), **Alaska Airlines** (© 800/426-0333; www.alaskaair.com), **Allegiant Air** (© 877/202-6444; www.allegiant air.com), **Aloha Air** (© 800/367-5250; www.alohaairlines.com), **America West** (© 800/235-9292; www.americawest.com), **American/American Eagle** (© 800/433-7300; www.aa.com), **American Trans Air** (© 800/435-9282; www.ata.com), **Champion Air** (© 800/387-6951; www.championair.com), **Continental** (© 800/525-0280; www.continental.com), **Delta/Skywest** (© 800/221-1212; www.delta.com), **Frontier Airlines** (© 800/432-1359; www.fly frontier.com), **Harmony Airways** (© 866/248-6789; www.hmy airways.com), **Hawaiian Airlines** (© 800/367-5320; www.hawaiian air.com), **Japan Airlines** (© 800/525-3663; www.jal.co.jp/en), **Jet-Blue Airways** (© 800/538-2583; www.jetblue.com), **Mexicana**

(© 800/531-7921; www.mexicana.com), **Midwest Airlines** (© 800/452-2022; www.midwestairlines.com), **Northwest** (© 800/225-2525; www.nwa.com), **Philippine Airlines** (© 800/435-9725; www.philippineairlines.com), **Song Airlines** (© 800/359-7664, www.flysong.com), **Southwest** (© 800/435-9792; www.southwest.com), **Spirit Air** (© 800/772-7117; www.spiritair.com), **United** (© 800/241-6522; www.united.com), **US Airways** (© 800/428-4322; www.usair.com), and **Virgin Atlantic Airways** (© 800/862-8621; www.virgin-atlantic.com).

We've always enjoyed Southwest's relaxed attitude, and their service leaves few complaints.

BY CAR

The main highway connecting Las Vegas with the rest of the country is I-15; it links Montana, Idaho, and Utah with southern California. The drive from Los Angeles is quite popular, and thanks to the narrow two-lane highway, can get very crowded on Friday and Sunday afternoons with hopeful weekend gamblers making their way to and from Vegas. (By the way, as soon as you cross the state line, there are three casinos ready to handle your immediate gambling needs, with two more about 20 min. up the road, 30 miles before you get to Las Vegas.)

From the east, take I-70 or I-80 west to Kingman, Arizona, and then U.S. 93 north to Downtown Las Vegas (Fremont St.). From the south, take I-10 west to Phoenix and then U.S. 93 north to Las Vegas. From San Francisco, take I-80 east to Reno and then U.S. 95 south to Las Vegas. If you're driving to Las Vegas, be sure to read the driving precautions in "Getting Around" in chapter 3.

Vegas is 286 miles from Phoenix, 759 miles from Denver, 421 miles from Salt Lake City, 269 miles from Los Angeles, and 586 miles from San Francisco.

BY TRAIN

Amtrak (© **800/872-7245;** www.amtrak.com) does not currently offer direct rail service to Las Vegas, although plans have been in the works to restore the rails between Los Angeles and Las Vegas for years now. It probably won't ever happen, but here are the dream plans: a European-designed "Casino Train" will complete the trip from Los Angeles in about 5½ hours, with a wholesale seat price of $99 round-trip. Ah, it sure does sound nice.

In the meantime, you can take the train to Los Angeles or Barstow, and Amtrak will get you to Vegas by bus.

3

Getting to Know Las Vegas

Located in the southernmost precincts of a wide, pancake-flat valley, Las Vegas is the biggest city in the state of Nevada. Treeless mountains form a scenic backdrop to hotels awash in neon glitter. Although it is one of the fastest-growing cities in America, for tourism purposes, the city is quite compact.

1 Orientation

ARRIVING AT THE LAS VEGAS AIRPORT

Las Vegas is served by **McCarran International Airport,** 5757 Wayne Newton Blvd. (© **702/261-5211;** www.mccarran.com). It's just a few minutes' drive from the southern end of the Strip. This big, modern airport—with a relatively new $500-million expansion and more on the way—is rather unique in that it includes several casino areas with more than 1,000 slot machines. You non-gamblers will save lots of money bypassing the machines (they are avoidable), which are reputed to offer lower payback than the casinos.

Getting to your hotel from the airport is a cinch. **Bell Trans** (© **702/739-7990;** www.bell-trans.com) runs 20-passenger minibuses between the airport and all major Las Vegas hotels and motels daily from 7:45am to midnight. Several other companies run similar ventures—just stand outside on the curb, and one will be flagged down for you. Buses from the airport leave about every 10 minutes. When you want to check out of your hotel and head back to the airport, call at least 2 hours in advance to be safe (though often you can just flag down a shuttle outside any major hotel). The cost is $4.75 per person each way to the Strip and Convention Center area hotels, $6 to Downtown or other Off-Strip properties (any place north of the Sahara Hotel and west of I-15). Other similarly priced shuttles run 24 hours daily and can be found in the same place.

Less expensive than shuttles are **Citizen's Area Transit (CAT)** buses (© **702/CAT-RIDE;** www.catride.com). The no. 108 bus departs from the airport and will take you to the Stratosphere, where you can transfer to the no. 301, which stops close to most Strip and

> **Tips Help for Troubled Travelers**
>
> The **Traveler's Aid Society** is a social-service organization geared to helping travelers in difficult straits. Their services might include reuniting families separated while traveling, feeding people stranded without cash, or even providing emotional counseling. If you're in trouble, seek them out. In Las Vegas, there is a Traveler's Aid office at McCarran International Airport (© 702/798-1742). It's open daily 8am to 5pm. Similar services are provided by **Help of Southern Nevada,** 953-35B E. Sahara Ave. (Suite 208), at Maryland Parkway in the Commercial Center (© 702/369-4357). Hours are Monday to Friday 8am to 4pm.

Convention Center area hotels. The no. 109 bus goes from the airport to the Downtown Transportation Center at Casino Center Boulevard and Stewart Avenue. The fare is $1.25, 60¢ for seniors (62 and older) and children 5 to 17, and free for those under 5. (Strip routes cost $2, $1 for seniors and children 5–17.) *Note:* You might have a long walk from the bus stop to your door (even if it's right in front of your hotel); keep this in mind if you have heavy luggage.

All the major car-rental companies are represented in Las Vegas. For a list of agencies and more information on getting a good deal on a rental, see "Getting Around," later in this chapter.

VISITOR INFORMATION
All major Las Vegas hotels provide comprehensive tourist information at their reception and/or sightseeing and show desks.

Other good information sources are the **Las Vegas Convention and Visitors Authority,** 3150 Paradise Rd., Las Vegas, NV 89109 (© **877/VISITLV** or 702/892-7575; www.lvcva.com), open daily from 8am to 5pm; the **Las Vegas Chamber of Commerce,** 3720 Howard Hughes Pkwy., #100, Las Vegas, NV 89109 (© **702/735-1616;** www.lvchamber.com), open Monday to Friday 8am to 5pm; and, for information on all of Nevada, including Las Vegas, the **Nevada Commission on Tourism** (© **800/638-2328;** www.travel nevada.com), open 24 hours.

CITY LAYOUT
There are two main areas of Las Vegas: the **Strip** and **Downtown.** For many people, that's all there is to Las Vegas. But there is actually more to the town than that; maybe not as glitzy and glamorous— okay, definitely not—but you will find still more casino action on

Las Vegas at a Glance

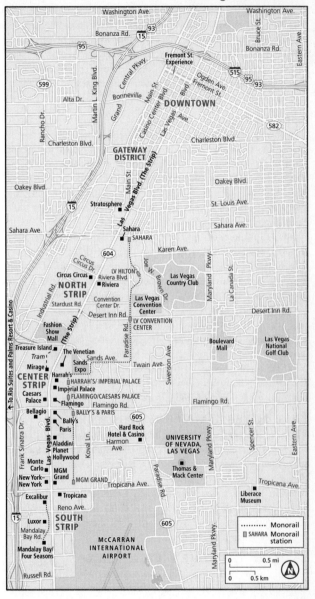

Washington Ave. · Washington Ave.
Bonanza Rd. · Bonanza Rd.
93 · 15 · Bruce St. · Eastern Ave.
95 · Central Pkwy. · Fremont St. Experience
599 · Bonneville · Ogden Ave. · Fremont St. · 515 · 95 · 93
Alta Dr. · Grand · Main St. · Casino Center Blvd. · Las Vegas Ave. · DOWNTOWN
Rancho Dr. · Martin L. King Blvd. · Charleston Blvd. · Charleston Blvd. · 582
GATEWAY DISTRICT
Oakey Blvd. · Main St. · Oakey Blvd. · St. Louis Ave.
15 · Stratosphere · Las Vegas Blvd. (The Strip)
Sahara Ave. · Sahara · Sahara Ave.
SAHARA
604 · Karen Ave.
Circus Circus Dr. · LV HILTON · Maryland Pkwy. · Joe W. Brown Dr. · La Canada St.
Circus Circus · Riviera Blvd. · Las Vegas Country Club
NORTH STRIP · Riviera
Industrial Rd. · Stardust Rd. · Convention Center Dr. · Las Vegas Convention Center · Desert Inn Rd.
Desert Inn Rd. · LV CONVENTION CENTER
(The Strip) · Fashion Show Mall · Paradise Rd. · Boulevard Mall · Las Vegas National Golf Club
Treasure Island · The Venetian
Tram · Sands Ave. · Swenson Ave.
Mirage · Sands Expo · Twain Ave.
CENTER STRIP · Harrah's
Caesars Palace · HARRAH'S/ IMPERIAL PALACE
Imperial Palace
Bellagio · FLAMINGO/CAESARS PALACE · Flamingo Rd.
Flamingo · Flamingo Rd. · 605
Las Vegas Blvd. · Bally's · BALLY'S & PARIS · Spencer St. · Eastern Ave.
Paris · Hard Rock Hotel & Casino
Frank Sinatra Dr. · Aladdin/ Planet Hollywood · Harmon Ave. · UNIVERSITY OF NEVADA, LAS VEGAS
Monte Carlo · Koval Ln. · Maryland Pkwy.
New York–New York · MGM Grand · Thomas & Mack Center
Excalibur · MGM GRAND · Tropicana Ave. · Tropicana Ave.
Tropicana · Paradise Rd. · Liberace Museum
15 · Reno Ave. · SOUTH STRIP
Luxor · 605
Mandalay Bay Rd. · McCARRAN INTERNATIONAL AIRPORT · Maryland Pkwy.
Mandalay Bay/ Four Seasons
Russell Rd.

←To Rio Suites and Palms Resort & Casino

········· Monorail
SAHARA Monorail station

0 · 0.5 mi
0 · 0.5 km
N

Paradise Road and in east Las Vegas, mainstream and alternative culture shopping on Maryland Parkway, and different restaurant choices all over the city. Confining yourself to the Strip and Downtown is fine for a first-time visitor, but repeat customers should get out and explore. Las Vegas Boulevard South (the Strip) is the originating point for addresses; any street crossing it starts with 1 East and 1 West at its intersection with the Strip.

THE STRIP

The Strip is probably the most famous 4-mile stretch of highway in the nation. Officially called Las Vegas Boulevard South, it contains most of the top hotels in town and offers almost all of the major showroom entertainment. First-time visitors will, and probably should, spend the bulk of their time on the Strip. If mobility is a problem for you, then we suggest basing yourself in a South or Mid-Strip location.

For the purposes of organizing this book, we've divided the Strip into three sections. The **South Strip** is roughly defined as the portion of the Strip south of Harmon Avenue and north of Russell Road. It's home to the MGM Grand, Mandalay Bay, the Monte Carlo, New York–New York, Luxor, and many more hotels.

Mid-Strip is a long stretch of the street between Harmon Avenue and Spring Mountain Road. Hotels you'll find here include Bellagio, Caesars, The Mirage and Treasure Island, Bally's, Paris Las Vegas, the Flamingo Las Vegas, and Harrah's, among others.

North Strip stretches north from Spring Mountain Road all the way to the Stratosphere Tower and features the Wynn Las Vegas, Stardust, Sahara, Riviera, and Circus Circus, to name a few.

EAST OF THE STRIP/CONVENTION CENTER

This area has grown up around the Las Vegas Convention Center. Las Vegas is one of the nation's top convention cities, attracting more than 2.9 million conventioneers each year. The major hotel in this section of town is the Las Vegas Hilton, but in recent years, Marriott has built Residence Inn and Courtyard properties here, and a Hard Rock Hotel has opened. You'll find many excellent smaller hotels and motels southward along Paradise Road. All of these offer proximity to the Strip.

BETWEEN THE STRIP & DOWNTOWN

The area between the Strip and Downtown is a seedy stretch dotted with tacky wedding chapels, bail-bond operations, pawnshops, and cheap motels.

However, the area known as the **Gateway District** (roughly north and south of Charleston Blvd. to the west of Las Vegas Blvd. South) is slowly but surely gaining a name for itself as an actual artists' colony. Studios, small cafes, and other signs of life are springing up, and we hope this movement will last.

DOWNTOWN

Also known as **"Glitter Gulch"** (narrower streets make the neon seem brighter), Downtown Las Vegas, which is centered on Fremont Street between Main and 9th streets, was the first section of the city to develop hotels and casinos. With the exception of the Golden Nugget, which looks like it belongs in Monte Carlo, this area has traditionally been more casual than the Strip. But with the advent of the **Fremont Street Experience** (p. 111), Downtown has experienced a revitalization. The area is clean, the crowds are low-key and friendly, and the light show overhead is as silly as anything on the Strip. Don't overlook it. Las Vegas Boulevard South runs all the way into Fremont Street Downtown.

2 Getting Around

It shouldn't be too hard to navigate your way around Las Vegas. But keep in mind that, given the huge hotel acreage, increased and very slow traffic, and lots and lots of people like you, getting around takes a lot longer than you might think. Heck, it can take 15 to 20 minutes to get from your room to another part of your hotel! Always allow for plenty of time to get from point A to point B.

At press time, the **Las Vegas Monorail** (www.lvmonorail.com) was back up and running—and nicely, too—after two mishaps shut it down for a length of time. Ideally, this will end its woes, but don't be overly surprised if more mechanical problems prevent if from operating when you are there. When it does work, it runs from the Sahara Hotel, zigzagging out to the Hilton and the Convention Center, and then back down the east side of the Strip, making several stops along its 4-mile journey before ending at the MGM Grand and turning around. It's a fabulous idea, and we hope the bugs get worked out permanently. Prices are $3 one-way, $5.75 round-trip.

BY CAR

If you plan to confine yourself to one part of the Strip (or one cruise down to it) or to Downtown, your feet will suffice. Otherwise, we highly recommend that visitors rent a car. The Strip is too spread out for walking (and is often too hot or too cold to make strolls pleasant),

Downtown is too far away for a cheap cab ride, and public transportation is ineffective, at best (at least until the monorail is running consistently). Plus, further visits call for exploration of still more parts of the city, and a car brings freedom (especially if you want to take any side trips—bus tours are available, but a car lets you explore at your own pace rather than according to a tour's schedule).

You should note that places with addresses some 60 blocks east or west from the Strip are actually less than a 10-minute drive—provided there is no traffic.

Having advocated renting a car, we should warn you that the growing population of Vegas means a proportionate increase in the number of cars. Traffic is getting worse, and it's harder and harder to get around town with any certain swiftness. A general rule of thumb is to avoid driving on the Strip whenever you can, and avoid driving at all during peak rush hours, especially if you have to make a show curtain.

Parking is usually a pleasure because all casino hotels offer valet service. That means that for a mere $1 to $2 tip, you can park right at the door (though the valet usually fills up on busy nights).

RENTING A CAR

National car-rental companies with outlets in Las Vegas include **Alamo** (© 877/227-8367; www.alamo.com), **Avis** (© 800/230-4898; www.avis.com), **Budget** (© 800/527-0700; www.budget.com), **Dollar** (© 800/800-3665; www.dollar.com), **Enterprise** (© 800/736-8227; www.enterprise.com), **Hertz** (© 800/654-3131; www.hertz.com), **National** (© 800/227-7368; www.nationalcar.com), **Payless** (© 800/729-5377; www.paylesscarrental.com), and **Thrifty** (© 800/847-4389; www.thrifty.com).

Car-rental rates vary even more than airline fares. The price you pay will depend on the size of the car, where and when you pick it up and drop it off, the length of the rental period, where and how far you drive it, whether you purchase insurance, and a host of other factors. A few key questions could save you hundreds of dollars.

- Are weekend rates lower than weekday rates? Ask if the rate is the same for pickup Friday morning, for instance, as it is for pickup Thursday night.
- Is a weekly rate cheaper than the daily rate? Even if you need the car for only 4 days, it may be cheaper to keep it for 5.

- Does the agency assess a drop-off charge if you don't return the car to the same location where you picked it up? Is it cheaper to pick up the car at the airport than at a Downtown location?
- Are special promotional rates available? If you see an advertised price in your local newspaper, be sure to ask for that specific rate; otherwise, you may be charged the standard cost. Terms change constantly, and reservations agents are notorious for not mentioning available discounts unless you ask.
- Are discounts available for members of AARP, AAA, frequent-flier programs, or trade unions? If you belong to any of these organizations, you may be entitled to discounts of up to 30%.
- How much tax will be added to the rental bill? local tax? state use tax?
- What is the cost of adding an additional driver's name to the contract?
- How many free miles are included in the price? Free mileage is often negotiable, depending on the length of your rental.
- How much does the rental company charge to refill your gas tank if you return with the tank less than full? Though most rental companies claim these prices are "competitive," fuel you purchase yourself is almost always cheaper. Try to allow enough time to refuel the car yourself before returning it.

Some companies offer "refueling packages," in which you pay for an entire tank of gas up front. The price is usually fairly competitive with local gas prices, but you don't get credit for any gas remaining in the tank. If a stop at a gas station on the way to the airport will make you miss your plane, then by all means take advantage of the fuel purchase option. Otherwise, skip it.

Many packages are available that include airfare, accommodations, and a rental car with unlimited mileage. Compare these prices with the cost of booking airline tickets and renting a car separately to see if these offers are good deals. (See "Money-Saving Deals" in chapter 2.)

Internet resources can make comparison shopping easier. An excellent car-rental website is Breezenet, at **www.bnm.com**.

Demystifying Renter's Insurance
Before you drive off in a rental car, be sure you're insured. Hasty assumptions about your personal auto insurance or a rental agency's additional coverage could end up costing you tens of thousands of dollars—even if you are involved in an accident that was clearly the fault of another driver.

If you already hold a **private auto insurance** policy, you are most likely covered in the United States for loss of or damage to a rental car and liability in case of injury to any other party involved in an accident. Be sure to find out whether you are covered in the area you are visiting, whether your policy extends to all persons who will be driving the rental car, how much liability is covered in case an outside party is injured in an accident, and whether the type of vehicle you are renting is included under your contract. (Rental trucks, sports utility vehicles, and luxury vehicles such as a Jaguar may not be covered.)

Most **major credit cards** provide some degree of coverage as well—provided that they were used to pay for the rental. Terms vary widely, however, so be sure to call your credit card company directly before you rent.

If you are **uninsured,** the credit card you use to rent a car may provide primary coverage as long as you decline the rental agency's insurance. This means that the credit card company will cover damage or theft of a rental car for the full cost of the vehicle. If you already have insurance, your credit card may provide secondary coverage— which basically covers your deductible. *Credit cards will not cover liability* or the cost of injury to an outside party and/or damage to an outside party's vehicle. If you do not hold an insurance policy, you may want to seriously consider purchasing additional liability insurance from your rental company. Be sure to check the terms, however: Some rental agencies cover liability only if the renter is not at fault; even then, the rental company's obligation varies from state to state. Bear in mind that each credit card company has its own peculiarities; call your own credit card company for details before relying on a card for coverage.

The basic insurance coverage offered by most car rental companies, known as the **loss/damage waiver (LDW)** or **collision damage waiver (CDW),** can cost as much as $20 per day. It usually covers the full value of the vehicle with no deductible if an outside party causes an accident or other damage to the rental car. In all states except California, you will probably be covered in case of theft as well. Liability coverage varies according to the company policy and state law, but the minimum is usually at least $15,000. If you are at fault in an accident, however, you will be covered for the full replacement value of the car—but not for liability. Some states allow you to buy additional liability coverage for such cases. Most rental companies require a police report in order to process any claims you file, but your private insurer will not be notified of the accident. Check your own policies and credit cards before you shell out money for this extra insurance because you may already be covered.

BY TAXI

Since cabs line up in front of all major hotels, an easy way to get around town is by taxi. Cabs charge $3 at the meter drop and 20¢ for each additional ⅙ mile, with an additional $1.20 fee for all fares originating from the airport. A taxi from the airport to the Strip will run you $10 to $15, from the airport to Downtown $15 to $20, and between the Strip and Downtown about $10 to $12. You can often save money by sharing a cab with someone going to the same destination (up to five people can ride for the same fare).

If you want to call a taxi, any of the following companies can provide one: **Desert Cab Company** (② 702/386-9102), **Whittlesea Blue Cab** (② 702/384-6111), and **Yellow/Checker Cab** (② 702/873-2000).

BY PUBLIC TRANSPORTATION

The no. 301 bus operated by **CAT** (② 702/CAT-RIDE; www.cat ride.com) plies a route between the Downtown Transportation Center (at Casino Center Blvd. and Stewart Ave.) and a few miles beyond the southern end of the Strip. The fare is $2 for adults, $1 for seniors (62 and older) and children 5 to 17, and free for those under 5. CAT buses run 24 hours a day and are wheelchair-accessible. Exact change is required, but dollar bills are accepted.

Or you can hop aboard a classic streetcar replica run by **Las Vegas Strip Trolley** (② 702/382-1404). These old-fashioned dark green vehicles have interior oak paneling and are comfortably air-conditioned. Like the buses, they run northward from Hacienda Avenue, stopping at all major hotels en route to the Sahara, and then looping back via the Las Vegas Hilton. They do not, however, go to the Stratosphere or Downtown. Trolleys run about every 15 minutes daily between 9:30am and 2am. The fare is $1.75 (free for children under age 5), and exact change is required.

There are also a number of free transportation services, courtesy of the casinos. A free monorail connects Mandalay Bay with Luxor and Excalibur, and a free tram shuttles between The Mirage and Treasure Island. Given how far apart even neighboring hotels can be, thanks to their size, and how they seem even farther apart on really hot days, these are blessed additions—and the more tourists who take them, the less traffic there might be on the Strip.

FAST FACTS: Las Vegas

American Express There are about a dozen offices in town, but the closest one to the Strip is located inside the MGM Grand, at 3799 Las Vegas Blvd. South (corner of Tropicana; ✆ 702/739-8474).

Babysitters Contact **Around the Clock Child Care** (✆ 800/798-6768 or 702/365-1040). In business since 1987, this reputable company clears its sitters with the health department, the sheriff, and the FBI, and it carefully screens references. Charges are $50 for 4 hours for one or two children, and $10.50 for each additional hour, with surcharges for additional children and on holidays. Sitters are on call 7 days a week, 24 hours a day, and they will come to your hotel. Call at least 3 hours in advance.

Banks Banks are generally open 9 or 10am to 5 and sometimes 6pm, and most have Saturday hours. ATMs are plentiful all around town. When the banks are closed, note that most casino cashiers will cash personal checks and can exchange foreign currency.

Car Rentals See "Getting Around," earlier in this chapter.

Conventions Las Vegas is one of America's top convention destinations. Much of the action takes place at the **Las Vegas Convention Center,** 3150 Paradise Rd., Las Vegas, NV 89109 (✆ 702/892-7575), which is the largest single-level convention center in the world. Its 1.3-million square feet house 89 meeting rooms. And this immense facility is augmented by the **Cashman Field Center,** 850 Las Vegas Blvd. North, Las Vegas, NV 89101 (✆ 702/386-7100). Under the same auspices, Cashman provides another 98,100 square feet of convention space. Additionally, there are massive convention facilities at many of the big hotels, including the MGM Grand, The Mirage, Mandalay Bay, The Venetian, and more.

Dentists & Doctors Hotels usually have lists of dentists and doctors. In addition, they are listed in the Centel Yellow Pages. See also "Hospitals," below.

For dentist referrals, you can call the **Southern Nevada Dental Society** (✆ 702/733-8700), weekdays 9am to noon and 1 to 5pm; when the office is closed, a recording will tell you who to call for emergency service.

For physician referrals, call **Desert Springs Hospital** (© 702/ **388-4888;** www.desertspringshospital.net). Hours are Monday to Friday 8am to 8pm, and Saturday from 9am to 3pm.

Dry Cleaners Things spill, and silk stains. When in need, go to **Steiner Cleaners,** 1131 E. Tropicana Ave., corner of Maryland Parkway, in the Vons Shopping Center (© **702/736-7474**), open Monday to Friday 7am to 6:30pm, Saturday 8am to 6pm. Not only did they clean all the costumes for the movie *Casino,* but they were Liberace's personal dry cleaner for years.

Emergencies Dial © **911** to contact the police or fire departments or to call an ambulance.

Highway Conditions For recorded information, call © **702/ 486-3116.**

Hospitals Emergency services are available 24 hours a day at **University Medical Center,** 1800 W. Charleston Blvd., at Shadow Lane (© **702/383-2000**); the emergency room entrance is on the corner of Hastings and Rose streets. **Sunrise Hospital and Medical Center,** 3186 Maryland Pkwy., between Desert Inn Road and Sahara Avenue (© **702/731-8080**), also has a 24-hour emergency room.

For more minor problems, try the **Harmon Medical Urgent Care Center,** the closest to The Strip, with doctors and X-ray machines; it's located at 105 E. Harmon at Koval, near the MGM Grand (© **702/796-1116**). It's open 24 hours, and there is a pharmacy on-site.

Hot Lines Emergency hot lines include the **Rape Crisis Center** (© 702/366-1640), **Suicide Prevention** (© 702/731-2990), and **Poison Emergencies** (© 800/446-6179).

Liquor & Gambling Laws You must be 21 to drink or gamble; proof of age is required and often requested at bars, nightclubs, and restaurants, so it's always a good idea to bring ID when you go out if you look young. There are no closing hours in Las Vegas for the sale or consumption of alcohol, even on Sunday. Don't even think about driving while you're under the influence or having an open container of alcohol in your car. Beer, wine, and liquor are all sold in all kinds of stores pretty much around the clock; trust us, you won't have a hard time finding a drink in this town. It's even legal to have an open container outside on the Strip (but not Downtown).

Newspapers & Periodicals There are two Las Vegas dailies: the *Las Vegas Review-Journal* and the *Las Vegas Sun*. The *Review-Journal*'s Friday edition has a helpful "Weekend" section with a comprehensive guide to shows and buffets. A free alternative paper—the *Las Vegas Weekly*—has club listings and many unbiased restaurant and bar reviews. And at every hotel desk, you'll find dozens of free local magazines, such as *Vegas Visitor, What's On in Las Vegas, Showbiz Weekly,* and *Where to Go in Las Vegas,* that are chock-full of helpful information—although probably of the sort that comes from paid advertising.

Parking Valet parking is one of the great pleasures of Las Vegas and well worth the dollar or two tip (given when the car is returned) to save walking a city block from the far reaches of a hotel parking lot, particularly when the temperature is over 100°F (38°C). Another summer plus: The valet will turn on your air-conditioning so that you don't have to get in an "oven on wheels."

Pharmacies There's a 24-hour **Walgreens** (which also has a 1-hr. photo) at 3763 Las Vegas Blvd. South (© 702/739-9638) almost directly across from the Monte Carlo. **Sav-On** is a large 24-hour drugstore and pharmacy close to the Strip at 1360 E. Flamingo Rd., at Maryland Parkway (© 702/731-5373 for the pharmacy, 702/737-0595 for general merchandise). **White Cross Drugs,** 1700 Las Vegas Blvd. South (© 702/382-1733), open daily 7am to 1am, will make pharmacy deliveries to your hotel during the day.

Police For non-emergencies, call © 702/795-3111. For emergencies, call © **911**.

Post Office The most convenient post office is immediately behind the Stardust Hotel at 3100 Industrial Rd., between Sahara Avenue and Spring Mountain Road (© 800/297-5543). It's open Monday to Friday 8:30am to 5pm. You can also mail letters and packages at your hotel, and there's a full-service U.S. Post Office in the Forum Shops in Caesars Palace.

Safety In Las Vegas, vast amounts of money are always on display, and criminals find many easy marks. Don't be one of them. At gaming tables and slot machines, men should keep wallets well concealed and out of the reach of pickpockets, and women should keep handbags in plain sight (on laps). If you win a big jackpot, ask the pit boss or slot attendant to cut you a check rather than give you cash—the cash may look nice, but flashing it can attract the wrong kind of attention. Outside casinos, popular spots for pickpockets and thieves are restaurants and outdoor shows, such as the volcano at The Mirage or the Treasure Island pirate battle. Stay alert. Unless your hotel room has an in-room safe, check your valuables in a safe-deposit box at the front desk.

Taxes Clark County hotel room tax is 9%, and in Henderson, it's 10%; the sales tax is 7%.

Time Zone Las Vegas is in the Pacific time zone, 3 hours earlier than the East Coast, 2 hours earlier than the Midwest.

Veterinarian If Fido or Fluffy gets sick while traveling, go to the **West Flamingo Animal Hospital,** 5445 Flamingo Rd., near Decatur Boulevard (© **702/876-2111**). They're open 24 hours; they take Discover, MasterCard, and Visa; and they have an ATM.

Weddings Las Vegas is one of the easiest places in the world to tie the knot. There's no blood test or waiting period, the ceremony and license are inexpensive, chapels are open around the clock, and your honeymoon destination is right at hand. More than 101,000 marriages are performed here each year. Get a license Downtown at the **Clark County Marriage License Bureau,** 200 S. 3rd St., at Bridger Avenue (© **702/ 455-4415**), which is open Monday to Thursday 8am to midnight, and from 8am Friday through midnight Sunday. On legal holidays, they're open 24 hours. The cost of a marriage license is $55; the cost of the ceremony varies depending on where you go to have it done. See "Getting Married," in chapter 6, for details on the local wedding chapels.

4

Where to Stay

Accommodations in Vegas, if gambling is not your priority, are perhaps the trickiest part of a visit. Not because Vegas lacks for space. Goodness no; at last count, the city had nearly 130,000 hotel rooms and rising. It's because you aren't there specifically to indulge in the usual pastime of gaming, and the hotel owners, by and large, are going to do their darnedest to make you change your mind.

Everywhere else in the world, hotels are built near the top attractions. Here, they *are* the top attractions. A hotel's designers are considered failures if they have not made leaving the premises unnecessary, if not outright impossible, so you can see that your choice of lodging is going to be a challenge. Because as fantastical as these behemoths are, they exist for one reason: to trap their customers into using slot machines. Or blackjack tables. Whatever.

Consequently, the most common design of a casino hotel makes sure that all guests have to skirt, if not cross, the casino floor on their way from their room to anywhere else. Many make the layout as confusing as possible, in the hopes that you will grow so exhausted trying to find the exit, you will just give up and eat/play/gamble there. Why go find a curious little ethnic place when there is Chinese food right there? Why go see a show at some other hotel when they've got a circus act right there? And hey, I've got these quarters in my hand, I might as well play them instead of carting them around. . . . There are alternatives: Can you say *chain hotel?* Name one, any one, and Vegas has it. They're designed for the comfort and anonymity of the business traveler. They're fine, for sure, but nothing special, and certainly offer no dazzle. On the other hand, they are without casinos, which brings their noise and chaos quotients way down. We list the best; figure that any we don't list may have hookers living (though not working) in them.

There are a number of things to keep in mind when booking accommodations in Vegas. The first and most significant is that rack rates have little to do with real rates. No one ever pays rack rates in Vegas. Ever. Vegas hotels change their prices at the drop of a hat.

Tips **A Web Wonder**

A little-known gem, **Travelaxe (www.travelaxe.com)** offers a free, downloadable price-comparison program that will make your Las Vegas hotel search infinitely easier. The program searches the hotels and a host of discount travel websites for the best prices for your travel dates. Click on the price you like, and the program will send you straight to the website offering it. And, unlike most websites, Travelaxe prices include hotel tax, so you actually see the total price of the room.

The same room can cost $39 one night and two nights later cost $239 if there is a convention, the Super Bowl, or a holiday going on. This is why the rates listed in this chapter in some cases fluctuate wildly. What to do? Keep your eyes open for deals; the Internet will be your friend, with websites such as **www.lodging.com** and **www.hotels.com** offering a roundup of low prices on rooms. Newspapers often have ads offering terrific room rates. And you can also just call up a hotel and beg the person who answers to help you out. Note that for some reason, casino hotels are often considerably more affordable than the chains; though the days of rock-bottom room prices, figuring guests will then feel comfortable dropping more at the tables, are gone, that basic incentive is still at the back of the casino hotel's minds. Chain hotels, *sans* casino, don't have that kind of motivation. Web clearance sites, however, can often let you know if Marriott or whomever is offering a special.

If you have the chance, when booking your room, request a corner unit, for they tend to be larger and have more windows. Also, the higher up the room, the better the view; nearly every Strip hotel in Vegas has some special view to offer (The Mirage of the exploding volcano, Treasure Island of its siren-and-pirate battle, The Venetian of Treasure Island's sirens-and-pirates battle, and for all, the bright lights that are the Strip in all its nightly glory). A room on a low floor will often net you only a view of other buildings.

Note also that while we will tell you if there are any differences in Vegas rooms, it can sometimes be hard to spot any such differences. There seem to be a few basic categories—okay; somewhat better than okay; somewhat nicer than that—but within those categories, with a few exceptions, there isn't that much to distinguish one room from another. After all, again we are talking cookie-cutter chain hotels or big giant enormous hotels—individuality is just difficult to produce when you are talking upward of 3,000 rooms. Speaking of which, if you are coming to Vegas because you've heard it's now focusing on being a luxury resort town, remind yourself that full service and Egyptian cotton sheets are not found in bulk. If you agree with us that those are not insignificant components in the concept of "luxury," head toward the smaller complexes.

The resorts are pretty smashing, in terms of all they offer, but there are hidden potholes. Like how those glorious spas cost dearly (p. 57). How the pools are shallow and the newer ones generally don't have much tree cover or other shade. There are usually cabanas, but there's a charge for using them. Actually, there's a charge for everything after the basic cost of your room, and it adds up.

The location of your hotel is also worth taking into consideration. All the Downtown hotels are totally skewed toward gamblers and would not be good choices for non-gamblers, so we have not reviewed any of them here. If you aren't going to gamble, but you do want to engage in the second most popular Vegas pastime, cruising the Strip uttering variations on "Wow!," you need to either rent a car (cabs add up, and while many off-Strip hotels have shuttle service, it may not be often enough for comfort and flexibility) or stay at a centrally located hotel, either at the corner of Tropicana Avenue and the Strip or no farther north than The Venetian. The Strip is long, the properties are bigger than they seem, and it gets really hot in the summer and cool and windy in the winter. On the other hand, if you want peace, stay away from the Strip, and in a non-casino hotel; the hustle-bustle factor goes way, way down.

Note: The star ratings we assign in this chapter reflect *the hotel's suitability for non-gamblers.* Thus, a hotel that might rate three stars for gamblers may rate only two stars for you.

1 The Top Hotels

The following are our absolute favorites for non-gambler accommodations, thanks to either layout or services.

SOUTH STRIP

Four Seasons Las Vegas ⭐⭐⭐ *Kids*   We love the four three-star hotels in this section just about equally; each has something to recommend it over the others. But we give a slight edge to the Four Seasons because of the combination of location and service; it is right on the Strip (as opposed to the Ritz and Green Valley Ranch,

Accommodations on the Strip

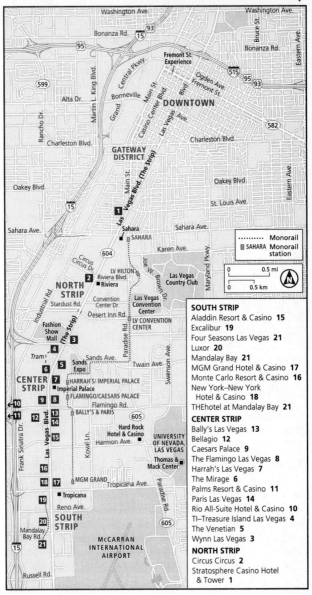

Monorail

▇ **SAHARA** Monorail station

0		0.5 mi
0		0.5 km

SOUTH STRIP
Aladdin Resort & Casino **15**
Excalibur **19**
Four Seasons Las Vegas **21**
Luxor **20**
Mandalay Bay **21**
MGM Grand Hotel & Casino **17**
Monte Carlo Resort & Casino **16**
New York–New York
  Hotel & Casino **18**
THEhotel at Mandalay Bay **21**

CENTER STRIP
Bally's Las Vegas **13**
Bellagio **12**
Caesars Palace **9**
The Flamingo Las Vegas **8**
Harrah's Las Vegas **7**
The Mirage **6**
Palms Resort & Casino **11**
Paris Las Vegas **14**
Rio All-Suite Hotel & Casino **10**
TI–Treasure Island Las Vegas **4**
The Venetian **5**
Wynn Las Vegas **3**

NORTH STRIP
Circus Circus **2**
Stratosphere Casino Hotel
  & Tower **1**

both of which are in nearby Henderson), and the Four Seasons is one of the world's premier hotel conglomerates, so these people know all about pampering—from the moment you hit the portico, everyone is looking out for you.

Located on the top floors of Mandalay Bay, the entrance is located on the other side of that hotel, so you need never hear the clang of a slot if you so choose. The rooms are heavy on neutral tones and quiet good taste. The bathrooms are lush, stocked with pricey L'Occitane amenities. The hotel has all its own facilities, including a medium-size pool and a fully equipped health club with no fee (unique in Vegas). Despite the grown-up atmosphere, children are welcome; rooms can be baby-proofed, kids get a welcome gift of toys and goodies, and on it goes. Of the hotels in this category, it's the best place for children (provided that their parents have deep pockets).

Service is impeccable; one guest recalls asking for a Christmas tree during a holiday stay and finding said tree, fully decorated, waiting for her. The restaurants, Charlie Palmer Steak and Veranda Café, are good to even superlative. Plus, all those hidden extras at the other hotels—health club usage, cabanas at the pool, and so forth—are included in the room rate, which makes it at times even cheaper than the other fancy hotels. And should you get tired of the hush, Mandalay Bay and all its delights are just a hallway away.

3960 Las Vegas Blvd. South, Las Vegas, NV 89119. ℂ 877/632-5000 or 702/632-5000. Fax 702/632-5105. www.fourseasons.com. 424 units. $200–$500 double; $400 and up suite. Extra person $30. Children 17 and under stay free in parent's room. Crib/rollaway free. AE, DC, DISC, MC, V. Free self- and valet parking. Pets under 25 lb. accepted. **Amenities:** 2 restaurants; heated outdoor pool; health club (free to guests); spa; concierge; car-rental desk; courtesy car; full 24-hr. business center w/faxing, delivery, and secretarial service; 24-hr. room service; in-room massage; babysitting; overnight laundry service; overnight dry cleaning; executive-level rooms. *In room:* A/C, TV w/pay movies, dataport, minibar, fridge, coffeemaker, hair dryer, iron/ironing board, safe.

Mandalay Bay 🏨🏨   Of all the true Strip casino hotels, this may be the one best suited for non-gamblers. Alone of all the Strip casino-hotels, here guests do not have to enter the casino to reach the guest elevators, though the casino lies between them and all the good clubs and restaurants. There are an awful lot of the latter, and within them are some of the most fanciful interiors in a town lousy with bland dining settings. The rooms are decent and basic, but the bathrooms are the largest on the Strip in this price range.

The pool area is superb: The 11-acre pool zone has a large lazy river, a regular pool, and a wave pool that sends junior-size tubes out at regular intervals for wannabe Surfer Joes (boogie board rentals extra). For an extra (and exorbitant) fee, you can stroll through the soothing Shark Bay Reef. Between the hot scenes at rumjungle and the House of Blues, nightlife is well served. While we do know some families who have stayed here happily, note that an extra person, regardless of size or time spent on the planet, costs an additional $35.

3950 Las Vegas Blvd. South (at Hacienda Ave.), Las Vegas, NV 89119. ℂ **877/632-7000** or 702/632-7000. Fax 702/632-7228. www.mandalaybay.com. 4,427 units. From $99 double; $149 and up suite; $149 and up House of Blues Signature Rooms; $159 and up THEhotel suites. Extra person $35; no discount for children. AE, DC, DISC, MC, V. Free self- and valet parking. **Amenities:** Casino; 12,000-seat events center; 1,700-seat performing arts theater; aquarium; 16 restaurants; outdoor pool w/lazy river and wave pool; health club; spa; Jacuzzi; sauna; watersports equipment/rental; concierge; tour desk; business center; 24-hr. room service; in-room massage; babysitting; laundry; dry cleaning; executive-level rooms. *In room:* A/C, TV w/pay movies, dataport, hair dryer, iron/ironing board, safe.

THEhotel at Mandalay Bay ⭑⭑⭑   A smashing, sophisticated "wow" of a hotel, contemporary and classy; the only thing that keeps it from being our no. 1 choice for the non-gambler—or possibly anyone—is that, unlike the Four Seasons or the Ritz, this is still Vegas-size. Which means that even though it *looks* like a boutique hotel and *acts* like a boutique hotel, it simply can't *run* like a boutique hotel. Pare this puppy down and add some of that cosseting service you find at the Ritz or the Four Seasons, and you would have something that could compete with any fancy-pants Manhattan lodgings. And to be fair, with all rooms true one-bedroom suites, containing no fewer than three flatscreen plasma TVs, bathrooms with tubs so deep most can soak up to their chins, robes and slippers, and even decent sheets, the experience is so unlike anything else in Vegas that we aren't even sure we need much else.

THEhotel is set up in an entirely different building than the rest of Mandalay Bay, though they are connected by a long hallway. So you, the non-gambling guest, can stay in a hushed, mature environment, though you are within easy walking of all that traditional Vegas has to offer. Though you might not be all that tempted; for once, these glossy accommodations (separate living room, wet bar, even a half-bathroom), despite an excess of mirrors and some rather dim lighting, are designed to make you want to stay in your room.

Prices are high; the state-of-the-art health club will cost you $30 a day, and the sleek cafes make you pay for their marvelous decor. But still, if this place does anywhere near the business it ought, watch the rest of Vegas to take a cue—and about time.

3950 Las Vegas Blvd. South (at Hacienda Ave.), Las Vegas, NV 89119. ✆ **877/632-7800** or 702/632-7777. Fax 702/632-7228. www.thehotelatmandalaybay.com. 1,120 units. $189 and up suite. AE, DC, DISC, MC, V. Free self- and valet parking. **Amenities:** 2 restaurants; bar; access to Mandalay Bay restaurants, pool, and casino; health club; spa; tour desk; car-rental desk; business center; 24-hr. room service; laundry service. *In-room:* A/C, 3 flatscreen plasma TVs w/pay movies, DVD player, CD player, high-speed Internet access (for a fee), printer/fax, minibar, hair dryer, iron/ironing board, safe.

EAST OF THE STRIP

Green Valley Ranch Resort ☆☆☆   In a town that persists in boasting that it's now offering "true resort" options in contrast to the traditional view of Vegas being, well, just for gamblers, it's nice to know that at least *one* place isn't exaggerating. Of course, the resort in question is in Henderson, but you can see the Strip from the pool area, and it's only a 15-minute drive, depending on traffic.

So what makes it worth the (really insignificant unless it's rush hour) drive? Green Valley's odd and oddly successful merging of the Ritz-Carlton luxury with W and the Hard Rock Hotel's style. Inside all is posh and stately, a dignified classy lobby, large rooms with the most comfortable beds in town (high-thread-count linens, feather beds, plump down comforters), and luxe marble bathrooms. Outside is the hippest pool area this side of the Hard Rock Hotel and our favorite for sheer relaxation. It's part lagoon, part geometric, with shallow places for reading and canoodling, and your choice of poolside lounging equipment, ranging from teak lounge chairs to thick mattresses strewn with pillows, plus drinks served from the trendy Whiskey Beach. Use of the tiny health club is free, and the charming spa is modern and hip. At night, Whiskey Sky heats up—more mattresses and couches, strewn with pillows and the fittest bodies in Vegas—while DJs spin tunes and poor souls try to get past the velvet rope. You can, because you stay here.

The entirely separate casino area (it's off in another, adjoining building) offers an assortment of restaurants, from a small Stage Door deli, to the Pancake House, to Bull Shrimp, with its fine steaks and fried goodies. Add in a multiscreen movie theater, and this is a resort that has something for every demographic.

2300 Paseo Verde Dr. (at I-215), Henderson, NV 89012. ✆ **866/782-9487** or 702/617-7704. Fax 702/617-6885. www.greenvalleyranchresort.com. 400 units. Sun–Thurs $109 and up double; Fri–Sat $159 and up double. Extra person $12. Children under 12 stay free in parent's room. Crib/rollaway free. AE, DC, DISC, MC, V. Free self- and valet parking. **Amenities:** Casino; nightclub; movie theater; 10 restaurants; outdoor pool; health club; spa; Jacuzzi; sauna; concierge; business

(*Tips* **So Your Trip Goes Swimmingly . . .**

Part of the delight of the Vegas resort complexes is the gorgeous pools—what could be better for beating the summer heat? But there are pools and there are *pools,* so you'll need to keep several things in mind when searching for the right one.

During the winter, it's often too cold or windy to do much lounging, and even if the weather is amenable, the hotels often close part of their pool areas during winter and early spring. The pools are also not heated for the most part, but they largely don't need to be.

Most hotel pools are shallow, chest-high at best (the hotels want you gambling, not swimming). Diving is impossible—not that a single pool allows it anyway.

And finally, during those hot days, be warned that sitting by pools next to heavily windowed buildings such as The Mirage and Treasure Island will allow you to experience the same thing a bug does under a magnifying glass with a sun ray directed on it. Regardless of time of year, be sure to slather on the sunscreen; there's a reason you see so many lobster-red people roaming the streets. Many pool areas don't offer much in the way of shade.

At any of the pools, you can rent cabanas (which often include TVs, special lounge chairs, and special poolside service), but these should be reserved as far in advance as possible, and with the exception of the Four Seasons and the Ritz, where they are complimentary, most cost a hefty fee. If you are staying at a chain hotel, you will most likely find an average pool, but if you want to spend some time at a better one, be aware that most of the casino-hotel pool attendants will ask to see your room key. If they are busy, you might be able to sneak in or at least blend in with a group.

center; 24-hr. room service; in-room massage; laundry service; dry cleaning; executive-level rooms. *In room:* A/C, TV w/pay movies, dataport, high-speed Internet access (for a fee), coffeemaker, hair dryer, iron/ironing board, safe.

Ritz-Carlton, Lake Las Vegas ✦✦✦ *(Kids)* Say you are coming to Vegas not for a convention or to visit relatives, both of which may require a stay in town, but for a genuine getaway. Consider this:

Don't stay in Vegas. Stay outside of town. About a half-hour and a whole different attitude away is the manmade but still comely Lake Las Vegas, bridged at one end by this striking hotel, modeled after the Ponte Vecchio. It's our hands-down favorite in the area. There is very little incentive to leave the premises. Ever. The setting—fire-blue lake, ring of austere mountains, all serenity—is polar opposite Vegas hectic overwhelming. The result is a true resort of great appeal. It's not a bit snobby, as the well-trained and solicitous staff coddle every guest, regardless of their dress or wallet.

With a swimming pool and shady beach pool (both with cabanas as well as umbrellas), free yoga and aerobics classes, hikes, bike rides, star gazing, watersports and other activities for additional fees, and a nice gym and even nicer spa, this is an excellent choice for couples looking for romance or friends on a bonding weekend. All kinds of wholesome activities (albeit usually for an extra fee) and the distance from Vegas mayhem make this a fine choice for families as well. Rooms are well sized, done in pleasing muted pastels with nicely squishy beds, and all have lake or mountain views. Consider the extra nightly fee for the Club Level (about $100), which will be more than worth it for the four daily food services and unlimited drinks. The adjacent village offers some adequate dining options, but the food at the Ritz is (if pricey) superior. The casino in that same complex is so-so, so if gambling urges overwhelm, you may prefer to drive to Vegas or take the regular shuttles to the Strip (they run until 2am).

1610 Lake Las Vegas Pkwy., Henderson, NV 89011. ℂ **800/241-3333** or 702/567-4700. Fax 702/567-4777. www.ritzcarlton.com. 349 units. $229 and up. Children stay free in parent's room. Additional charge for rollaway bed. AE, DC, DISC, MC, V. Pets accepted. **Amenities:** Restaurant; bar; concierge; 2 pools; health club; spa; some free exercise classes; business center; shuttle to Strip; water taxis to nearby attractions; 24-hr. room service; in-room massage; babysitting; laundry; dry cleaning; executive-level rooms. *In room:* A/C, TV w/pay movies, Nintendo, dataport, high-speed Internet access (for a fee), minibar, coffeemaker, hair dryer, iron/ironing board, safe.

2 Best Casino Hotels

Each of the following has something to recommend it, whether it's a preponderance of non-gambling activities, or an easy-to-handle layout, or just a particularly swell Vegas motif. They each have their own drawbacks as well. Choose based on your own needs.

SOUTH STRIP

Aladdin Resort & Casino ⟨ᴿ⟩   Planet Hollywood has bought this hotel and has big plans for the place, not one of which has been formalized, much less put into place. So by the time you read this, it may have undergone a partial or total makeover, possibly changing to a theme to better reflect the new owners. Or it just may have a blue Planet Hollywood globe out front. Or . . . nothing. It's frustrating, we know. But here's the place as it stands while we write this:

The Arabian Nights theme translates into a complex full of northern-Africa-by-Way-of-Disneyland architecture, fake sultans' jewels, and real Moroccan tile. But the large casino, while in the middle of things, is easy to skirt—restaurants, lobby, and shopping are all in a separate section. Expect generic Vegas rooms of decent size and mediocre beds; even the deluxe accommodations have spacious marble bathrooms with generous soaking tubs and spice-scented amenities.

The Desert Passage shopping area is our favorite in town, though the slightly exotic rooftop pool area is something of a disappointment. The spa is run by London-based Elemis Spa, and it is the most gorgeous in Vegas (though the workout room is on the small side), thanks to architects who went to Morocco and came back with lamps, arches, and other smashing details, plus specialists who give a heck of a hydro-treatment. Some of the nicest restaurants in town, including a branch of New Orleans's venerable Commander's Palace (see review on p. 66), are also here.

3667 Las Vegas Blvd. South, Las Vegas, NV 89109. ℂ **877/333-9474** or 702/785-5555. Fax 702/785-5558. www.aladdincasino.com. 2,567 units. $99 and up double. Extra person $30. Children under 12 stay free in parent's room, depending on season. Crib/rollaway free. AE, DC, DISC, MC, V. Free self- and valet parking. **Amenities:** Casino; performing arts center; showroom; 21 restaurants; 7 bars/lounges; 2 outdoor pools; health club; spa; Jacuzzi; sauna; watersports equipment/rental; concierge; tour desk; car-rental desk; business center; shopping arcade; 24-hr. room service; in-room massage; babysitting; laundry service; dry cleaning; executive-level rooms. *In room:* A/C, TV w/pay movies, dataport, high-speed Internet access (for a fee), hair dryer, iron/ironing board, safe.

Excalibur You may be tempted to stay here because it's shaped like a big castle and you have King Arthur fantasies. Good enough, but be warned that it's huge, sprawling, and they've taken out much of the charming kitsch and replaced it with nothing much. Kids swarm the place, hoping to run into Merlin; grown-ups who left their families at home are there because they got a comfortable but unassuming room for under $40, thus saving some cash for the slots. Note that none of the bathrooms have tubs, just showers. In addition to finding the smoky casino area hard to avoid, you aren't going to find much in the way of interesting shopping or eating, though they do have a Krispy Kreme on-site. And the pool is unremarkable, at best.

On the other hand, if you want a fantasy Camelot wedding, they rent the costumes needed to properly dress such an event.

3850 Las Vegas Blvd. South (at Tropicana Ave.), Las Vegas, NV 89109. ℭ **800/937-7777** or 702/597-7700. Fax 702/597-7163. www.excalibur.com. 4,008 units. $49–$119 double. Extra person $15. Children under 13 stay free in parent's room. Crib/rollaway free. AE, DC, DISC, MC, V. Free self- and valet parking. **Amenities:** Casino; showrooms; wedding chapel; 11 restaurants; outdoor pool; video arcade; concierge; tour desk; car-rental desk; shopping arcade; 24-hr. room service; laundry service; dry cleaning. *In room:* A/C, TV w/pay movies, dataport, hair dryer.

Luxor ⌀   We wish more of the theme resorts would make like the Luxor and gussy up the rooms to match the over-the-top shenanigans going on out in the lobby. Here, you've got your giant Ramses statues, talking camels, and other bits of Egypt relics, and here you can stay in rooms that similarly have the Egyptian theme spread among the decorated furniture, Tut-embossed bedspreads, and the like.

The Pyramid rooms, accessible by a slanting elevator known as an "inclinator" (a cheap thrill ride itself), are slightly cheesy (though we do like them); they do have those slanted outside walls, plus shower-only bathrooms, so guests with space issues may have problems. On the other hand, corner Pyramid rooms are larger and have a Jacuzzi tub tucked into the nook of the walls, a nice tip for romance-seekers. Pyramid rooms are also arranged around the perimeter of the casino, though, of course, that will be many floors below unless you get a room on the first floor or two. Tower rooms are more spacious and away from all the hustle and bustle (you can pretty much avoid the casino if you stay in these rooms), and they have better bathrooms. Be careful, however, that you don't get one on a low floor because your view might be of a wall.

The buffet here is the best in its price range. The pool area offers five pools and an Egyptian theme but is still kind of shabby; the health club is small but well stocked (and is open 24 hr.—unique for Vegas), and there are simulator rides and a surprisingly nicely done replica of Tut's tomb. All in all, the Luxor is good cheesy Vegas fun.

3900 Las Vegas Blvd. South (between Reno and Hacienda aves.), Las Vegas, NV 81119. ℭ **800/288-1000** or 702/262-4000. Fax 702/262-4478. www.luxor.com. 4,400 units. Sun–Thurs $49 and up double; Fri–Sat $99 and up double; $149 and up whirlpool suite, $249–$800 other suites. Extra person $25. Children under 12 stay free in parent's room. Crib $15; rollaway $25. AE, DC, DISC, MC, V. Free self- and valet parking. **Amenities:** Casino; showrooms; 10 restaurants; 5 outdoor pools; health club; spa; 18,000-sq.-ft. video arcade w/latest Sega games and more; concierge; tour desk; car-rental desk; courtesy car or limo; business center; shopping arcade; 24-hr. room service; dry cleaning; executive-level rooms. *In room:* A/C, TV w/pay movies, hair dryer, iron/ironing board.

MGM Grand Hotel & Casino ⌘   We've grown very fond of this hotel, as it has gradually shed its "family fun" skin for something more mature. This mostly translates into several naughty shows, clubs, and bars, which in turn translates into a clientele that is a mix between giggly gals who find Paris and Britney superior role models and middle-age Jimmy Buffett fans in town for a concert. The hotel can be a horror for anyone not interested in gaming; between you and the outside world stands the largest casino in Vegas, and navigating it would make Magellan cry. Having said that, should you find yourself here, you will unearth some comforts: The rooms are a delight—pale pastels or earth tones evoking '30s Hollywood curvy elegance, with black-and-white matinee-idol photos on the walls. It's the best style and floor space for the price, for sure.

The pool area is also marvelous in the summer months—four large pools, plus a lazy river—but is likely to be shut down otherwise. If you're sans kids and care to avoid those belonging to others, be advised that packs of children are always likely to be present in the pool area. The spa is a Zen-Asian retreat dripping with ambience, complete with a decent-size workout room. The restaurant section has a better variety than many of the other hotels, and there is Studio 54, which still isn't the nightclub we hoped it to be. The glass Lion Exhibit is pretty swell; different lions lounge about within for a few hours a day. Shows include the racy *La Femme* and the newest Cirque du Soleil production, *KÀ*.

3799 Las Vegas Blvd. South (at Tropicana Ave.), Las Vegas, NV 89109. © **800/ 929-1111** or 702/891-7777. Fax 702/891-1030. www.mgmgrand.com. 5,034 units. $69–$329 double; $99–$2,500 suite. Extra person $25. Children under 13 stay free in parent's room. Crib free; rollaway $25 per night. AE, DC, DISC, MC, V. Free self- and valet parking. **Amenities:** Casino; events arena; showroom; cabaret theater; 2 wedding chapels; 16 restaurants; 4 outdoor pools and lazy river; health club; spa; Jacuzzi; sauna; game room/video arcade; concierge; tour desk; car-rental desk; business center; 24-hr. room service; in-room massage; babysitting; laundry service; dry cleaning; executive-level rooms. *In room:* A/C, TV w/pay movies, dataport, hair dryer, iron/ironing board, safe.

Monte Carlo Resort & Casino   Once meant to evoke the grand style of the real Monte Carlo, it still does, sort of, with its gleaming marble lobby, nicely separate from the James Bond–style casino. But the rooms need a massive redo—they are borderline dingy these days, and the bathrooms are dinky. The pool area features a couple desultory pools plus an itty wee lazy river—and you have to pay $10 for an inner tube. Kids run rampant in the pool area, which ends up looking rather dirty. The health club is nothing to speak of. There are, however, some good-value restaurants and a wonderful food court. And Lance Burton is one of the best shows in town.

3770 Las Vegas Blvd. South (between Flamingo Rd. and Tropicana Ave.), Las Vegas, NV 89109. ℂ **800/311-8999** or 702/730-7777. Fax 702/730-7250. www.monte carlo.com. 3,002 units. Sun–Thurs $59 and up double; Fri–Sat $109 and up double; $149 and up suite. Extra person $25; no discount for children. AE, DC, DISC, MC, V. Free self- and valet parking. **Amenities:** Casino; showroom; wedding chapel; 7 restaurants; outdoor pool, wave pool, lazy river, and kiddie pool; 3 night-lit tennis courts w/full services and equipment rental; health club; spa; Jacuzzi; sauna; watersports equipment/rental; video arcade; concierge; tour desk; business center; shopping arcade; 24-hr. room service; in-room massage; babysitting; laundry service; dry cleaning; executive-level rooms. *In room:* A/C, TV w/pay movies, dataport, hair dryer, iron/ironing board.

New York–New York Hotel & Casino ✿   If you are in Vegas for the hoot value, you could do far worse than this hilarious theme hotel. But if you really want to stay away from gaming, this is not for you; it's another maze-trap, where utility is subverted in the name of over-the-top style. Sure, the casino is funny at first, with each section modeled after an iconic part of New York (Greenwich Village, complete with faux brownstones; Central Park, complete with faux trees; Times Square, complete with nightly faux New Year's Eve), but it's smoky, crowded, large, and meandering. Walking anywhere here is a navigational nightmare. (They seem to have forgotten the lesson of the real Manhattan's user-friendly grid.)

The restyled rooms are no longer as striking as they once were (and, yes, they are housed in the towers that make up the faux skyline, and no, that skyline never did include the World Trade Center), though they remain comfortable, but some can be quite cramped and, oddly, the style goes down the larger the room gets. The roller coaster (oh, yeah) passes right over the pool area, which borders the parking garage, so you wouldn't catch us swimming there. The health club is fine, and there are lots of quite decent restaurants (including reliable chains such as Il Fornaio and Chin Chin), though breakfast anywhere comes at a dear price, and there is no excuse for a hotel modeled on the city that never sleeps to have no food available at midnight. There is a fabulous arcade area for the kids, while grown-up children won't find a more fun bar than Coyote Ugly.

3790 Las Vegas Blvd. South (at Tropicana Ave.), Las Vegas, NV 89109. ℂ **800/693-6763** or 702/740-6969. Fax 702/740-6920. www.nynyhotelcasino.com. 2,033 units. Sun–Thurs $59 and up double; Fri–Sat $109 and up double. Extra person $30; no discount for children. AE, DC, DISC, MC, V. Free self- and valet parking. **Amenities:** Casino; showrooms; roller coaster; 10 restaurants; outdoor pool; small health club and spa; Jacuzzi; sauna; video arcade w/carnival midway games; concierge; tour desk; 24-hr. room service; laundry service; dry cleaning; executive-level rooms. *In room:* A/C, TV w/pay movies, dataport, hair dryer, safe.

MID-STRIP

Bellagio 🌟🌟 Recalling that no place with more than 3,000 rooms can be as chic and pampering as the image Bellagio wants to present, this is decidedly the place where the grown-ups stay in town. It's still mostly about the gambling—it's hard to avoid the massive casino, but routes through the hotel are plainly marked and mostly accessible around the perimeter—but there are still enough genuine resort elements here, and the superlatives just pile up. Rooms are the poshest of the bigger casino hotels; take a basic room at The Mirage, but jump everything up a notch or two in quality and size—linens are nicer, beds softer, and bathrooms are larger, gleaming with marble and glass. And by the time you read this, the Spa Tower, with an additional 900 rooms plus more restaurants and shops, will be open.

The pool area is the most sophisticated on the Strip, with a trio of elegant Roman villa-esque pools (we ruin our own pretensions of cool by standing underneath the fountains in the center of each pool). The spa and health club are marvelous but pricey. You'll find one of the better collections of restaurants in town, run by such celebrity chefs as Julian Serrano and Jean-Georges. The show is Cirque de Soleil's *O*, an expensive ticket that is worth the money. The nightclub, Light, is grown-up but not stodgy, while Petrossian has the most knowledgeable bartenders in town. And the Conservatory right off the lobby is full of seasonal flowers and plants—the best hotel-based antidote to the artificial Vegas you are likely to find.

3600 Las Vegas Blvd. South (at the corner of Flamingo Rd.), Las Vegas, NV 89109. ✆ **888/987-6667** or 702/693-7111. Fax 702/693-8546. www.bellagio.com. 3,005 units. $139–$499 double. Extra person $35; no discount for children. AE, DC, DISC, MC, V. Free self- and valet parking. **Amenities:** Casino; showrooms; art gallery; wedding chapel; 16 restaurants; 6 outdoor pools; health club; spa; concierge; tour desk; car-rental desk; business center; shopping arcade; 24-hr. room service; in-room massage; laundry service; dry cleaning; executive-level rooms. *In room:* A/C, TV w/pay movies, dataport, high-speed Internet access (for a fee), hair dryer, iron/ironing board, safe.

Caesars Palace 🌟 Once the sine non qua of romantic but schlocky Vegas, Caesars still has a great deal going for it, but easy it's not in the maneuvering department. One of the most sprawling hotel complexes, you'll need a compass to navigate it, and once you get outside, it's set so far back from the street—and by then you are so exhausted—you may rethink the whole "leaving" idea. Having said that, there is ample reason to stay here, most of it found in The Forum Shops (recently expanded yet again), where a number of fine restaurants, snack places (still more in the food court, though you have to navigate the tortuous casino yet again to get there), rides, and stores, plus ridiculous animatronic statues, are there to amuse you.

The rooms are no longer the over-the-top glorious whacked-out orgies of "Roman" statues, but the ones in the main complex still have bits of silliness, while rooms in the Tower feature nearly floor-to-ceiling windows and lots of regular hotel room space. And yet another 1,000-room tower, complete with more restaurants, will be open by the time you read this. The Greco-Roman pool area is so grown-up, it even has a topless pool (protected with walls) so you can avoid tan lines. The spa is small, but we've had some of the best facials, massages, and eyebrow waxes of our lives there. Caesars is an excellent choice for someone wanting to experience the Vegasness of Vegas, but you'll need to bring sturdy walking shoes.

3570 Las Vegas Blvd. South (just north of Flamingo Rd.), Las Vegas, NV 89109. ✆ 877/427-7243 or 702/731-7110. Fax 702/731-6636. www.caesars.com. 2,471 units. $99 and up standard double; $109–$500 "run of house deluxe" double; $549–$1,000 suite. Extra person $20. Children under 18 stay free in parent's room. Crib free; rollaway $20. AE, DC, DISC, MC, V. Free self- and valet parking. **Amenities:** Casino; wedding chapel; 24 restaurants; 3 outdoor pools; health club; spa; concierge; tour desk; car-rental desk; business center; shopping arcade; 24-hr. room service; laundry service; dry cleaning; executive-level rooms. *In room:* A/C, TV w/pay movies, dataport, hair dryer, iron/ironing board, safe.

The Mirage ✸   There is lots to like here, but all of it is arranged so that, at all times, you must navigate the most twisting casino in Vegas. While it's not the largest (the MGM Grand is), it is so exhausting that it might as well be. And the rooms simply can't compare to newer ones around town, particularly the cramped bathrooms. Still, one of the best pools in Vegas is here, a tropical, curvy monster complete with slides and waterfalls. The health club features attendants handing you iced towels and smoothies, while the spa is pretty in the same neutral-heavy way the guest rooms are.

On the premises is a free exhibit of one of Siegfried & Roy's white tigers (don't worry, each beast hangs in the small enclosure for only a couple hours daily), while an extra fee gets you into one of the best attractions in Vegas, the Siegfried & Roy's Secret Garden and the Dolphin Habitat (p. 119). Restaurant row has several high-priced basics, plus the recently renovated buffet, looking quite snazzy. A major production show, Danny Gans, is here, but "major" comes with an indefensible price tag. And don't forget that volcano out front, with its regular (if anticlimactic) explosions, the soothing front-desk aquarium, and the vanilla-smelling rainforest at the opening to the casino. Now, about that casino. . . .

3400 Las Vegas Blvd. South (between Flamingo Rd. and Sands Ave.), Las Vegas, NV 89109. ✆ 800/627-6667 or 702/791-7111. Fax 702/791-7446. www.mirage.com. 3,044 units. Sun–Thurs $79–$399 double; Fri–Sat and holidays $159–$399 double; $250–$3,000 suite. Extra person $30; no discount for children. AE, DC, DISC, MC, V. Free self- and valet parking. **Amenities:** Casino; showrooms; 14 restaurants; beautiful outdoor pool; health club; spa; concierge; tour desk; car-rental desk; business center; shopping arcade; 24-hr. room service; laundry service; dry cleaning; executive-level rooms. *In room:* A/C, TV w/pay movies, dataport, high-speed Internet access (for a fee), hair dryer, iron/ironing board, safes.

Palms Resort & Casino 🐱🐱   The hip and the happening wouldn't dream of staying anywhere else—unless they are at the Hard Rock, that is—and so if you are one of them, fancy you are one of them, want to be one of them, or want to hang out with them, you should stay here, too. It's Hard Rock hip with the sort of nebulous architecture/ design only found in Vegas—swoops and circles on the ceiling that are not quite Miami, not quite Jetsons space age. Not everyone here is as aggressively young as the target demographic, and good for them. Rooms have the second-nicest beds in town (the first are over at Green Valley Ranch), with high-quality linens and soft mattresses. Some of the best views in town are from the windows here because there are no other tall buildings near enough to obstruct said view. The elevators are watched constantly, lest The Wrong Sort board them and get into the wonderful (one of the best in town) restaurant Alizé or the ultratrendy Ghost Bar. That sort of diligence in black Armani can feel intimidating. The Palm-Springs–influenced pool area—with an above-ground glass pool and hammocks—is also a place to see and be seen, so you might seek refuge across the casino at either the surprisingly good buffet or the food court, where regular-folk places such as McDonald's and Coffee Bean & Tea Leaf are represented. And who needs Ghost Bar when you've got actual movie theaters on the premises?

4321 W. Flamingo Rd. (at I-15), Las Vegas, NV 89103. ✆ 866/942-7777 or 702/942-7777. Fax 702/942-6859. www.palms.com. 400 units. Sun–Thurs $79 and up double; Fri–Sat $119 and up double. Extra person $12; no discount for children. AE, DC, DISC, MC, V. Free self- and valet parking. **Amenities:** Casino; nightclub/showroom; movie theater; 8 restaurants; outdoor pool; health club; spa; Jacuzzi; sauna; concierge; business center; 24-hr. room service; in-room massage; laundry service; dry cleaning; executive-level rooms. *In room:* A/C, TV w/pay movies, dataport, high-speed Internet access (for a fee), coffeemaker, hair dryer, iron/ironing board, safe.

Paris Las Vegas ⚐   An in-between hotel—just right if you're going to feel cheated if your stay in Vegas doesn't include some Vegas theme—but laid out to be user-friendly. The casino is right there, to be sure, in the lobby like a good casino should be, but all paths to all things (registration, concierge, rooms, shops, food) skirt around it, making it an easy place to navigate, if you don't mind signage in Franglais ("le car rental" indeed!) or employees who will "Bonjour, Madam!" you to death. Of course, you are going to do a lot of neck craning at this Disney version of gay Paree. It's all here, all boiled down to an iconic essence, starting with that half-size replica Eiffel Tower out front with what appears to be the five or six most famous buildings from the City of Light shrunk to play-piece size and all crammed into the courtyard of the Louvre. The fleur-de-lis–bedecked rooms are pretty, if not particularly extraordinary, with deep tubs in the bathrooms. The rooftop pool is small and dull. There are reasonably authentic and terribly overpriced pastries and fresh bread in several locations, plus the charming Mon Ami Gabi restaurant and the terrific buffet. *Viva la France!*

3655 Las Vegas Blvd. South, Las Vegas, NV 89109. ℰ 888/266-5687 or 702/946-7000. Fax 702/967-3836. www.parislv.com. 2,916 units. $119–$269 double; $350 and up suites. Extra person $30. Children under 18 stay free in parent's room. Crib free; rollaway $10. AE, DC, DISC, MC. V. Free self- and valet parking. **Amenities:** Casino; showrooms; 2 wedding chapels; 11 restaurants; outdoor pool; health club; spa; concierge; tour desk; business center; shopping arcade; 24-hr. room service; laundry service; dry cleaning; executive-level rooms. *In room:* A/C, TV w/pay movies, dataport, hair dryer, iron/ironing board, safe.

TI–Treasure Island Las Vegas ⚐⚐   In many ways, this hotel is interchangeable with The Mirage, though each has its own fans. It's easier to navigate the TI (note name alteration, an attempt to give the place a coolness factor like the Palms), thanks to an actual lobby that isn't carved grudgingly out of casino space, and pathways that skirt a square (rather than amorphous) casino. You do have to look hard for any pirate lore these days (apart from the free battle that wages a few times nightly outside), so anxious is the hotel's management to rid itself of all kid-friendly elements. This includes various homages to the scantily clad leggy gals of the *Sirens of TI* "show" that replaced the beloved pirate battle, including a gia-normous bare-breasted ship head's gal that greets you when you walk in from the Strip. Despite this, it still remains a top family choice, and many kids are often running about, which some vacationers may not find desirable and we think probably poor planning, considering the shift in target demographic.

Rooms are superior to those at The Mirage, with actual signed art on the walls, plus other nice touches, including comfy beds (though not much drawer space) and nice marble bathrooms with deep tubs. Like the one at The Mirage, there are more visually interesting spas in town, but again, the workout room is decent sized and the attendants ready with smoothies. Given how well The Mirage formula has otherwise worked here, it's odd that the TI's pool is so dull and the restaurants not much better. But they do have one of the best shows in town in Cirque de Soleil's *Mystère*.

3300 Las Vegas Blvd. South (at Spring Mountain Rd.), Las Vegas, NV 89177. © **800/ 944-7444** or 702/894-7111. Fax 702/894-7446. www.treasureisland.com. 2,885 units. $69 and up double; $109 and up suite. Extra person $30; no discount for children. Crib/rollaway free. AE, DC, DISC, MC, V. Free self- and valet parking. **Amenities:** Casino; showrooms; 11 restaurants; outdoor pool; health club; spa; very well equipped game and video arcade; concierge; tour desk; car-rental desk; business center; shopping arcade; 24-hr. room service; laundry service; dry cleaning; executive-level rooms. *In room:* A/C, TV w/pay movies, fax, dataport, high-speed Internet access (for a fee), hair dryer, iron/ironing board, safe.

The Venetian ✦✦ This hotel is a mixed bag for a non-gambler's purposes. The giggle factor for a good Vegas theme hotel actually transforms here into something approaching awe; we hate to admit it, but they did a nice job of replicating the real Venice for the facade, which is the only one you can stroll through in Sin City. Inside you'll find, hands down, the best rooms on the Strip (except perhaps for the comfort level offered over at the Four Seasons)—true "junior" suites complete with a sunken living room and marvelous marble bathrooms. Better still, check into the slightly higher-priced new tower, the Venezia, where the rooms are even bigger, and the casino-free ambience is more like that at the Ritz—on steroids.

The spa is run by Canyon Ranch, so the health club is better than the one you will find at your gym, the treatments outstanding, and the prices for either so high they undo any good the place might have done for your stress level. (The high health club charge does include a number of daily exercise classes, which is unique among the local health clubs.) The shopping area has its own Venice canal, plus gondoliers and strolling costumed actors. There is a collaboration between the venerable Guggenheim and Hermitage museums, so you can have some actual culture. And the restaurants are a terrific assortment at all prices, from the divine Bouchon to the mammoth-size menu at the Grand Luxe Café, a division of the reliable Cheesecake Factory.

So what's not to love? Well, after you get through that grand colonnade, loaded with marble and preposterous copies of Italian art, you have to endure a mazelike wander through the noisy casino to get to the guest elevators. Signage is poor, so good luck with that. The rooftop pool area is strangely hideous for such an otherwise great hotel, and, like everything else here, it's really hard to find. And you'll feel nickel-and-dimed to death, thanks not just to the health club charges but also to other hidden tricks, such as a minibar that charges you if you so much as touch a bottle within (computer sensors) and the boasted fax machine/printer in each room that also costs dearly. The price-gouging is the one item reminiscent of the real Venice that we could do without.

3355 Las Vegas Blvd. South, Las Vegas, NV 89109. ℰ **888/283-6423** or 702/414-1000. Fax 702/414-4805. www.venetian.com. 4,029 units. $125–$399. Extra person $35. Children under 13 stay free in parent's room. Crib free; no rollaways. AE, DC, DISC, MC, V. Free self- and valet parking. **Amenities:** Casino; showroom; wedding chapel; 19 restaurants; 6 outdoor pools; health club; spa; video arcade; concierge; tour desk; car-rental desk; business center; shopping arcade; 24-hr. room service; laundry service; dry cleaning; executive-level rooms. *In room:* A/C, TV w/pay movies, fax (for a fee), dataport, fridge, hair dryer, iron/ironing board, safe.

EAST OF THE STRIP

Hard Rock Hotel & Casino ✮   Now, you're thinking, "I'm a rock fan, I oughta stay here," and we're saying "yes, probably, BUT." Not a lot of buts, actually—more like caveats. Like many a Vegas hotel, this one is a bit more interested in the high rollers and the highly recognizable than it is in tourists with basic budgets; it just may be a bit more obvious here because of its smaller size, which means it's clear that they are ignoring you in favor of Britney (or someone who looks an awful lot like her) over there.

The smaller size works in your favor, too, as this is an easy property to navigate, if a noisy one. For a small casino, the Hard Rock's is the loudest, thanks to the constant (if catchy) music, and it is plopped down in the middle of the hotel, though all your activity will skirt it on a raised walkway. The hopping restaurants and bars teem with noise and activity, and then there is the pool area—a beach blanket bikini bonanza (yeah, it's got sand), with a constant surfin' soundtrack and loads of women inspired by the tasteful looks of Pamela Anderson. Rooms are a mix of some odd attempts at no-tell motel and more primary-color-based styles, with bathrooms that use stainless steel like other places in town use marble. (The whole thing is supposed to be getting another redo any minute now.) Truth be told, while certainly standing out more than the usual generic Vegas hotel, the rooms aren't that comfortable. But why be in your room when you could be standing on the edge of the casino/pool/nightclub Baby's, trying to see if that really *was* Britney after all?

4455 Paradise Rd. (at Harmon Ave.), Las Vegas, NV 89109. ℭ **800/473-7625** or 702/693-5000. Fax 702/693-5588. www.hardrockhotel.com. 657 units. Sun–Thurs $79 and up double; Fri–Sat $145 and up double; $250 and up suite. Extra person $35. Children 12 and under stay free in parent's room. Crib $25; rollaway free, available in suites only. AE, DC, MC, V. Free self- and valet parking. **Amenities:** Casino; showroom; 6 restaurants; 2 outdoor pools w/lazy river ride and sandy beach bottom; small health club; small spa; concierge; tour desk; 24-hr. room service; laundry service; dry cleaning; executive-level rooms. *In room:* A/C, TV w/pay movies, dataport, high-speed Internet access (for a fee), hair dryer, iron/ironing board.

Las Vegas Hilton ☉☉   The LV Hilton (as it's known locally) is largely preferred by businesspeople, thanks to its proximity to the behemoth Convention Center. It doesn't quite have the same savoir-faire elegance it once did, but you may be pleased by the sunken, and thus out of the way (and rather petite), casino; or if you are of that bent, that there is still more casino to be found around the most enjoyable *Star Trek* ride. Rooms are standard business—pun intended—with touches of marble that aren't as swell-elegant as those found at, say, The Mirage. The restaurants are all reliable and forgettable (unless you've never experienced the knife shows at a Benihana), the rooftop pool and health club are similarly businesslike, and the shows are often better than the larger extravaganzas on the Strip (perhaps one faint reminder of Elvis, who called the Hilton his Vegas home for so many years).

3000 Paradise Rd. (at Riviera Blvd.), Las Vegas, NV 89109. ℭ **888/732-7117** or 702/732-5111. Fax 702/732-5805. www.lvhilton.com. 3,174 units. $49 and up double. Extra person $30. Children under 18 stay free in parent's room. Crib free; rollaway $30 if you are not paying the extra person charge. AE, DC, DISC, MC, V. Free self- and valet parking. **Amenities:** Casino; showrooms; 13 restaurants; outdoor pool; golf course adjacent; 6 tennis courts (4 night-lit); health club; spa; Jacuzzi; car-rental desk; business center; shopping arcade; 24-hr. room service; laundry service; dry cleaning; executive-level rooms. *In room:* A/C, TV w/pay movies, dataport, hair dryer, iron/ironing board.

The Westin Casuarina Las Vegas Hotel and Spa ☉   While not the kicky Vegas boutique hotel we still dream of (and may get with the new MGM Grand project), this transformation of the seedy and unlamented Maxim nonetheless is perfect for the business traveler who wants a little panache on top of the basic needs. The rooms are in good, subdued taste, nothing compared to the overwhelming flash found at, say, THEhotel, but considerably more pleasant than the generic bores found in many high-profile chains elsewhere in Vegas. The Westin boasts about its "Heavenly Beds," to which we shrug and say "Eh. The ones at the Palms, Green Valley Ranch, Ritz, Four Seasons, and THEhotel are better." But then again, we are mattress and thread count snobs. Bathrooms are small but sparkling, and there is a small but serviceable (and free!) gym. The casino area alone has not had a face-lift and feels dated. Boring by Vegas standards, nonetheless it's professional, yet personal.

160 E. Flamingo Rd., Las Vegas, NV 89109. ☎ 702/836-9775. fax 702/836-9776. www.starwood.com. 825 units. $139–$269. Children stay free in parent's room. Cribs free. AE, DC, DISC, MC, V. Free self- and valet parking. Pets accepted. **Amenities:** Casino; showroom; 2 restaurants; 1 bar; small outdoor heated pool; small health club; concierge; tour desk; business center; 24-hr. room service; in-room massage; laundry service; dry cleaning. *In-room:* A/C, TV w/pay movies, high-speed Internet access (for a fee), minibar, hair dryer, iron/ironing board, safe.

3 Best Casino-Free Hotels

Despite the preponderance of hotels in Vegas, there is one accommodations area where the city is sorely lacking—regular hotels. Not that there aren't any, but every single one of them is a chain hotel. If you earn points in a chain or if you are fond of the various ways a Marriott can be configured, you're in luck. But if you are looking for quirky lodgings with distinct character, or a bed-and-breakfast, or anything other than a hotel identical to the one with the same name in Phoenix or Boston, you are in for a disappointment. And if you want a room with flavor, you simply must go back to the theme hotels.

Normally, this doesn't matter. A large part of the fun of coming to Vegas is for the hotels that are Vegas-specific. But, in glancing over the above listings, you may discover that they may not suit your purposes at all. At least with a non-casino hotel, you've eliminated a lot of noise, and possibly a great deal of rowdy drunks (if they are staying at one of the following, then surely by the time they've stumbled home, they are nearly done for the night). But don't expect much that is particularly special, though some chains and styles are better than others. And in a quirk particular to Vegas, it may not be much cheaper (or cheaper at all) to stay at one of the following than it would be to stay on the Strip in a high-profile destination.

Note: All hotels in this section are located east of the Strip and can be found on the map on p. 35.

AmeriSuites ⋒ It's a measure of just how businesslike this particular hotel is that they have a number of units known as "TCB" suites (that's "taking care of business," for you non-Elvis fans out there), but is there one bit of evidence within of the King and the lightning bolt that accompanied his famous motto? No. Waste of an opportunity, if you ask us. All the TCB suites do is add a well considered and accessorized workspace to the already well proportioned but totally bland regular suites. Still, if you are in town for more serious purposes, this hotel offers special rates, a free large buffet breakfast, and a weekly manager's reception with snacks. If you want to cut up your heels more, the Hard Rock is across the street, ready to take care of more frivolous needs.

4520 Paradise Rd., Las Vegas, NV 89109. ℂ 877/774-6467 or 702/369-3366. Fax 702/369-0009. www.amerisuites.com. 202 units. $79 and up double. Rates include breakfast buffet. Children under 18 stay free in parent's room. Crib free; no rollaways. AE, DC, DISC, MC, V. Free self-parking. **Amenities:** Outdoor pool; fitness room; concierge; tour desk; free airport shuttle; laundry service; dry cleaning. *In room:* A/C, TV w/pay movies, dataport, high-speed Internet access (for a fee), kitchenette, hair dryer, iron/ironing board, safe.

Atrium Suites ℛ   The Las Vegas rendition of this business brand name is favored by flight attendants with layovers. Rooms feel cramped, thanks to all the furniture and other amenities (fridge, microwave, coffeemaker) crammed into them. The pool is nothing special (though on summer nights, a calypso band plays by it), but the free and adequate exercise room is open 24 hours. We suggest wandering over to the neighboring Hard Rock and taking advantage of its terrific restaurants and bars; if you make nice with someone, perhaps they will smuggle you into the much better Hard Rock pool area.

4255 Paradise Rd. (north of Harmon Ave.), Las Vegas, NV 89109. ℂ 800/349-1748 or 702/369-4400. Fax 702/369-3770. www.atriumsuiteshotel.com. $125–$185 double. Children 18 and under stay free in parent's room. Crib free; rollaway $10. AE, DC, DISC, MC, V. Free self-parking. Pets under 25 lb. accepted. **Amenities:** Restaurant; outdoor pool; small exercise room; Jacuzzi; sauna; concierge; airport shuttle; business center; limited room service; dry cleaning; executive-level rooms. *In room:* A/C, TV w/pay movies, dataport, fridge, microwave, coffeemaker, hair dryer, iron/ironing board.

Courtyard by Marriott ℛ   Right across the street from the Convention Center, this is precisely the sort of chain hotel that shows you what chain hotels can be: nicely landscaped (yep, arranged around outdoor courtyards), spic-and-span public areas and rooms, a sparkling pool, and just enough style (even if it was ordered up) to make you feel like you are Someplace, rather than Anyplace. Most rooms were designed with the business traveler in mind and have king-size beds; all rooms have balconies or patios.

3275 Paradise Rd. (between Convention Center Dr. and Desert Inn Rd.), Las Vegas, NV 89109. ℂ 800/321-2211 or 702/791-3600. Fax 702/796-7981. www.courtyard.com. 159 units. Sun–Thurs $109 and up double; Fri–Sat $119 and up double; $119 and up

Coming Soon

The latest extravaganza from Steve Wynn, the man who more than anyone else created modern (that would be, the last 15 years) Las Vegas, **Wynn Las Vegas** is set to open April 28, 2005. As it wasn't open at press time, we are left to make predictions on its suitability for the non-gambler, but based on Wynn's previous properties, we can make these guesses: The rooms will be generously sized, in aesthetically pleasing and forgettable good taste; the bathrooms will most likely follow the trend of having a luxurious feel; you will almost certainly have to walk around or through the massive casino to get anywhere; the restaurants will be top notch and priced accordingly; the in-house show will be Tony-award-winning *Avenue Q;* and overall there will be plenty of bells and whistles to attract your attention and keep you occupied, though without a humorous theme to further alleviate the raucous inconvenience of the big casino-hotel experience.

The Wynn Las Vegas is located at 3131 Las Vegas Blvd. South (© **877/770-7077** or 702/770-7800; fax 702/770-1578). For more information, see **www.wynnlasvegas.com**.

suite. No charge for extra person above double occupancy. Crib/rollaway free. AE, DC, DISC, MC, V. Free self-parking at your room door. **Amenities:** Restaurant; outdoor pool; small exercise room; Jacuzzi; business center; limited room service; coin-op washers and dryers; laundry service; dry cleaning; executive-level rooms. *In room:* A/C, TV w/pay movies, dataport, coffeemaker, hair dryer, iron/ironing board.

Hawthorn Suites 🎯🎯 *Kids*   Another of the "all-suite" chain hotels, but one that offers just a little bit more than the others and just the right kinds of "little bit more." The suites (creamy and boring) themselves come not only with full kitchens but also with actual balconies (once you've experienced a stuffy Vegas hotel room with a window that does not open, this becomes a big deal). There is a full, free breakfast buffet and an evening happy hour with snacks. The pool is large, and they've got basketball and volleyball courts. And they take pets! All this, just a block from the corner of the Strip and the Trop! This is really a lifesaver for families looking for a nice place not too far off the beaten path (especially if said family is using Vegas as a stopping point during a family vacation with

Fido)—think of the savings with the free breakfast, the snacks, and that full kitchen for other meals!

5051 Duke Ellington Way, Las Vegas, NV 89119. ℭ **800/527-1133** or 702/739-7000. Fax 702/739-9350. www.hawthorn.com. 280 units. $79–$109 1-bedroom suite (up to 4 people); $109–$169 2-bedroom suite (up to 6 people). Rates include breakfast buffet and evening snacks. Crib free; no rollaways. AE, DC, DISC, MC, V. Free self-parking. Pets accepted. **Amenities:** Large outdoor pool; basketball and volleyball courts; small exercise room; Jacuzzi; coin-op washers; laundry service; dry cleaning. *In room:* A/C, TV w/pay movies, dataport, full kitchen, hair dryer, iron/ironing board.

La Quinta ℛ   La Quinta happens to be on our own private list of "reliable and surprisingly nice" chains, and this branch justifies our expectations. Not that it's anything but pre-fab, but it's that increasingly popular, slightly Spanish, slightly mission-style pre-fab that immediately puts us at our ease. Rooms are decent size (though we would spend the extra few dollars for the Executive Queen for the larger beds, the fridge, and the microwave), and all come with whirlpool tubs. Note that ground-level rooms have patios. Outside, on the oddly relaxing grounds (little pools and benches and whatnot), you can find barbecue grills and picnic tables, which are unusual options in a town that assumes everyone is eating at some cheap buffet. The staff is generally particularly nice. Note also that the hotel takes pets under 25 pounds.

3970 Paradise Rd. (between Twain Ave. and Flamingo Rd.), Las Vegas, NV 89109. ℭ **800/531-5900** or 702/796-9000. Fax 702/796-3537. www.lq.com. 251 units. $79 and up double; $89 and up executive queen; $115 and up suite. Rates include continental breakfast. Children under 18 stay free in parent's room. Crib free; rollaway $10. AE, DC, DISC, MC, V. Free self-parking. Pets under 25 lb. accepted. **Amenities:** Outdoor pool; Jacuzzi; tour desk; car-rental desk; free airport/Strip shuttle; coin-op washers and dryers. *In room:* A/C, TV w/pay movies, dataport, coffeemaker, hair dryer, iron/ironing board.

Las Vegas Marriott Suites ℛ   The price is probably too much for a chain hotel, though this is a nice one. All the rooms are suites (which makes them extra large), are comfortable, and have unexpected touches, such as French doors separating the bedroom from the sitting area, and surprisingly good art on the walls. The on-site coffee shop, Windows, serves quite good Southwestern-style food. Note that it's a bit of a walk from here to the Strip (10 min., which gets longer and longer with every additional 10°).

325 Convention Center Dr., Las Vegas, NV 89109. ℭ **800/228-9290** or 702/650-2000. Fax 702/650-9466. www.marriott.com. 278 units. $159 and up suites (up to 4 people). Children stay free in parent's room. Crib free; no rollaways. AE, DC, DISC, MC, V. Free self-parking. **Amenities:** Restaurant; outdoor pool; small exercise room; Jacuzzi; tour desk; car-rental desk; business center; 24-hr. room service; coin-op washers and dryers available at Residence Inn next door; laundry service; dry cleaning;

executive-level rooms. *In room:* A/C, TV w/pay movies, dataport, high-speed Internet access (for a fee), minifridge, coffeemaker, hair dryer, iron/ironing board, safe.

Residence Inn 🦋🦋   Our favorite among the Marriotts, in part because of the actual accommodations, in part because of the attitude—by and large it is run by people who actually seem involved with the property rather than just earning wages at it. Rooms are like small apartments, each with a separate bedroom, a living room (all with VCRs, some with working fireplaces—the desert gets chilly in the winter), and a kitchen fully loaded with dishes and cookware, which makes the whole thing perfect for extended stays. Rooms are distributed throughout the complex in little condo buildings; each section has its own little garden (the entire facility is set on seven nicely manicured acres), while each room has its own balcony or patio. Guests receive a welcome basket of microwave popcorn and coffee at check-in. There is a generous free breakfast buffet, but the pool is small, and the gym is located next door at another Marriott.

3225 Paradise Rd. (between Desert Inn Rd. and Convention Center Dr.), Las Vegas, NV 89109. ✆ **800/331-3131** or 702/796-9300. www.marriott.com. 192 units. $119 and up studio; $149 and up penthouse. Rates include continental or buffet breakfast. Children stay free in parent's room. Crib free. AE, DC, DISC, MC, V. Free self-parking. Pets accepted. **Amenities:** Outdoor pool; guests have access to small exercise room next door at the Marriott Suites; Jacuzzi; coin-op washers and dryers. *In room:* A/C, TV w/pay movies, dataport, complimentary high-speed Internet access, kitchenette, hair dryer, iron/ironing board.

St. Tropez 🦋   There are several different hotels across the street from the Hard Rock, and each has something to recommend it. While not as glamorous as the name implies (you find that a lot in Vegas), the St. Tropez is still a good choice. Rooms are large, thanks to a loose definition of "all suite"; like at The Venetian, the lowest level of room here is really just one large room with a sitting area. But the nice-size bathrooms are perhaps the best in this group, and some of them have whirlpool tubs. The grounds are attractive, including a grassy pool area, with enough lawn to let children romp. The complimentary continental breakfast is heavy on the donuts, but that works for us. And the off season can bring some great rates, so you might be able to adjust up to a real, two-room suite.

455 E. Harmon Ave. (at Paradise Rd.), Las Vegas, NV 89109. www.sttropezlasvegas. com. ✆ **800/666-5400** or 702/369-5400. Fax 702/369-1150. 149 units. $100 and up suite. Rates include continental breakfast. Children under 12 stay free in parent's room. Crib/rollaway free. AE, MC, V. Free self-parking. **Amenities:** Outdoor pool; fitness room; concierge; tour desk; free airport shuttle; business center. *In room:* A/C, TV w/pay movies, fridge, coffeemaker, hair dryer, iron/ironing board.

Las Vegas Hotel Spas & Gyms

Hotel	Phone	Gym Hours	Gym/Workout Room Fee	Min. Age	Spa Hours	Name	Notes
Aladdin	✆ 702/785-5555	6am–7pm	$25	18	8am–6pm	Elemis Spa	Non-hotel guests $30 per day; multiple-day passes available; can use gym at age 16+, but must have parent present if 16 or 17
Bally's	✆ 702/967-4366	6am–7:30pm	$20	18	6am–6:30pm	The Spa at	Women's spa completely remodeled in 2001; registered hotel guests only
Bellagio	✆ 702/693-7111	6am–8pm	$25	18	6am–8pm	Spa Bellagio	Must be 18 (16+ for workout room with parent); registered hotel guests only
Caesars Palace	✆ 702/731-7110	6am–8pm	$24	18	8am–6pm	The Spa at	Non-hotel guests $30 per day gym fee (waived if spa service is booked); no spa services available for non-hotel guests on weekends

Hotel	Phone	Gym Hours	Gym/Workout Room Fee	Min. Age	Spa Hours	Name	Notes
Flamingo Las Vegas	☎ 702/733-3535	7am–8pm	$20	18	7am–8pm	The Spa at	Non-hotel guests $20 per day
Four Seasons	☎ 702/632-5000	6am–9pm	comp.	18	8am–8pm	The Spa at	Gym is complimentary to hotel guests with spa service appt.; ages 16+ can use workout room with parent present; non-hotel guests can use the gym with spa service appt
Green Valley Resort	☎ 866/782-9487	7am–9pm	comp.	18	7am–9pm	Dolphin Court Grand Spa	Non-hotel guests $25 per day to use gym
Hard Rock	☎ 702/693-5000	6am–10pm	$20	18	8am–8pm	Rock Spa	Non-hotel guests $25 per day
Harrah's	☎ 702/369-5000	6am–8pm	$20	18	8am–8pm	The Spa at	$50 for 3 days; same fees for non-hotel guests; gym usage complimentary with spa service; platinum players card holders get complimentary gym usage

Hotel	Phone	Gym Hours	Gym/Workout Room Fee	Min. Age	Spa Hours	Name	Notes
Las Vegas Hilton	✆ 702/732-5648	6am–8pm	$20	18	8am–6pm	The Spa at	2 days/$36, 3/$51, 4/$64, 5/$75; registered hotel guests only
Luxor	✆ 800/258-9308	24 hr.	$20	18	8am–2am or 6am	Oasis	Non-hotel guests $25 per day
Mandalay Bay	✆ 877/632-7800	5am–10pm	$27	18	6am–10pm	Spa Mandalay	Non-hotel guests $30 per day
MGM Grand	✆ 702/891-7777	6am–7pm	$20	18	6am–7pm	Grand Spa	Gym for hotel guests only, 13+ may use the gym with guardian
The Mirage	✆ 702/791-7111	6am–7pm	$20	18	8am–5:30pm	Spa & Salon	Open to public Mon–Thurs; non-hotel guests $20 per day
Monte Carlo	✆ 702/730-7777	6am–9pm	$17	18	8am–8pm	The Spa at	$22 for gym and spa; open to non-hotel guests Sun–Thu., $24 gym, $25 gym and spa
New York–New York	✆ 702/740-6955	6:30am–7pm	$20	16	8am–6:30pm	Spa	Multiple-day rates available
Palms	✆ 866/942-7777	6am–8pm	$20	18	6am–8pm	Spa & Salon	Non-hotel guests $25 per day

Hotel	Phone	Gym Hours	Gym/Workout Room Fee	Min. Age	Spa Hours	Name	Notes
Paris	☎ 702/946-7000	6am–7 or 9pm	$25	18	6am–7 or 9pm	Spa by Mandara	Non-hotel guests $30 per day; service of $50 or more includes complimentary use of gym
Rio	☎ 702/777-7777	6am–8pm	$20	18	8am–7pm	Spa & Salon	$50 for 3 consecutive days; non-hotel guests same fees
THEhotel	☎ 877/632-9636	5am–10pm	$20 gym only/$30 with spa	18	6am–10pm	Bathhouse	Non-hotel guests $30 per day
Treasure Island	☎ 702/894-7111	7am–7pm	$20	18	8am–5pm	The Spa at	Non-hotel guests $20 per day
The Venetian	☎ 877/283-6423	5:30am–10pm	$30	18	8am–8pm	Canyon Ranch Spa	Non-hotel guests $60 for gym, $30 with spa appt

4 When the Others Are Booked . . .

There are quite a few other hotels in town, of course, but we don't give them full-on listings because they aren't worth your time—unless everything else is booked up, of course. The following are hotels that are perfect for gamblers seeking a cheap bed near the slots, which makes them dandy in many ways—it just probably isn't your way.

THE BEST . . .
MID-STRIP
The Flamingo Las Vegas   Not the home of Bugsy Siegel anymore, just a place that tries hard to keep pace with the bigger boys around it. Still, the pool area is fabulous, a tropical wonderland that ranks with Mandalay Bay's and The Mirage's among the best in the city. It's centrally located, right in the heart of the Strip, so the location is ideal as a jumping-off point for wandering. Otherwise, plan on sticking to the pool because this is another mazelike setup, and getting outside can be tricky.

3555 Las Vegas Blvd. South. (between Sands Ave. and Flamingo Rd.), Las Vegas, NV 89109. ✆ **800/732-2111** or 702/733-3111. Fax 702/733-3353. www.flamingolv.com. 3,999 units. $69–$299 double; $250–$580 suite. Extra person $20. Children under 18 stay free in parent's room. AE, DC, DISC, MC, V. Free self- and valet parking. **Amenities:** Casino; showrooms; 12 restaurants; 5 outdoor pools; 4 night-lit tennis courts; health club; spa; small video arcade; tour desk; car-rental desk; business center; shopping arcade; 24-hr. room service; in-room massage; babysitting; laundry service; dry cleaning; executive-level rooms. *In room:* A/C, TV w/pay movies, dataport, hair dryer, iron/ironing board, safe.

NORTH STRIP
Stratosphere Casino Hotel & Tower   Our other "if all else fails" choice, this is the tallest structure west of the Mississippi, though the rooms themselves are not in the Tower, darn it. The rooms are essentially really, really nice motel rooms, and they can often be had for as little as $29. That, and the genuinely nice staff, are the only reasons for you to stay here; the hotel is located at the far north end of the Strip—much too far to walk anywhere useful. Inside is little of great interest, apart from the revolving Top of the World restaurant and bar, which is located, yes, at the top of the Tower, and the views there are smashing. The roller coaster that goes around the top of the building is one that will test even the sturdiest of stomachs—and don't get us started on the madness that is the rooftop (!) over-the-edge teeter-totter (!!).

2000 Las Vegas Blvd. South (between St. Louis St. and Baltimore Ave.), Las Vegas, NV 89104. ✆ **800/998-6937** or 702/380-7777. Fax 702/383-5334. www.stratosphere hotel.com. 2,500 units. Sun–Thurs $39 and up double; Fri–Sat $59 and up double; $69 and up suite. Extra person $15. Children under 13 stay free in parent's room. AE, DC, DISC, MC, V. Free self- and valet parking. **Amenities:** Casino; showrooms; wedding chapel; 11 restaurants; large pool area w/great views of the Strip; fitness center; spa; children's rides and games located at the base of the Tower; concierge; tour desk; car-rental desk; shopping arcade; salon; 24-hr. room service; laundry service; dry cleaning; executive-level rooms. *In room:* A/C, TV w/pay movies, dataport, hair dryer, iron/ironing board, safe.

Tips Spa Life

Another element of the "Vegas as luxury resort" theme is the addition of particularly nice spas. But it's also another example of Vegas bait-and-switch; the spas are uniformedly expensive—just a pedicure will set you back an absurd $50. And for those of us who want to work off all the nice meals we are eating, that costs even more. On p. 57 is a chart with the daily—yes, daily—fees charged to use the gyms at the major Vegas hotels. (The chain hotels don't charge, but their workout rooms are usually no more than basic.) The fee includes day-long use of equipment, plus saunas, steam rooms, and such. The **Canyon Ranch Spa** at **The Venetian** charges the most, but their workout room is the best, and the fee allows you to take advantage of nearly a dozen daily classes such as yoga, aerobics, and Pilates. Not far behind in the fabulousness and price department is the unfortunately named **Bathhouse** at **THEhotel Mandalay Bay,** a gorgeous, spare-no-cost facility that is nearly alone in charging a lesser (but still up there) price if all you want is to work out and not have spa access. They also have the longest hours. For sheer aesthetics, the nicest spa in town is **Elemis Spa** at the **Aladdin;** the architects were sent to Morocco for design inspiration, and the results are drop-dead gorgeous. Elemis Spa and Canyon Ranch have the widest range of exotic and pampering treatments, but we are highly intrigued by the Passion Dip at the **Dolphin Spa** at **Green Valley,** which leaves a guest smelling like dessert. We've had wonderful facials, waxes, and massages at **Caesars,** but the staff treats you the best at **The Mirage** and **Treasure Island,** keeping you refreshed with iced towels during your workout and smoothies after.

. . . & THE REST
MID-STRIP

Bally's Las Vegas   Adjacent to Paris Las Vegas, and accessible by a tunnel that changes from fairy-tale Parisian cobblestones to, well, we can't remember what, which, by the way, pretty much sums up this entire, forgettable hotel. It did get a kind of nice room makeover, and for the price, we sort of love it. When we can remember it. On the plus side, you can avoid the casino floor if you navigate correctly.

3645 Las Vegas Blvd. South (at Flamingo Rd.), Las Vegas, NV 89109. (✆) **800/634-3434** or 702/739-4111. Fax 702/967-3890. www.ballyslv.com. 2,814 units. $69 and up double; $35–$60 extra for concierge floor (including breakfast); $300 and up suite. Extra person $30. Children under 18 stay free in parent's room. AE, DC, MC, V. Free self- and valet parking. **Amenities:** Casino; showrooms; 14 restaurants; outdoor pool; 8 night-lit tennis courts; health club; spa; video arcade; concierge; tour desk; car-rental desk; business center; shopping arcade; 24-hr. room service; laundry service; dry cleaning; executive-level rooms. *In room:* A/C, TV w/pay movies, dataport, high-speed Internet access (for a fee), iron/ironing board, safe.

Harrah's Las Vegas   Yes, you can get to your room without heading into the casino—if you go through the back door, which should indicate what the hotel thinks of non-gamblers. Actually, the Carnaval Court, the outdoor shopping and dining area, is a lot of fun, thanks to the Ghirardelli Ice Cream Parlor and the regular performing presence of Mr. Cook E. Jarr, the best worst lounge act in Vegas. And Mac King, one of the best bargains in town, plays here in the afternoons.

3475 Las Vegas Blvd. South (between Flamingo and Spring Mountain roads), Las Vegas, NV 89109. (✆) **800/427-7247** or 702/369-5000. Fax 702/369-5283. www.harrahs.com. 2,700 units. $65–$195 "deluxe" double; $85–$250 "superior" double; $195–$1,000 suite. Extra person $20; no discount for children. AE, DC, DISC, MC, V. Free self- and valet parking. **Amenities:** Casino; showrooms; 9 restaurants; outdoor pool; health club; spa; concierge; tour desk; car-rental desk; business center; shopping arcade; 24-hr. room service; laundry service; dry cleaning; executive-level rooms. *In room:* A/C, TV w/pay movies, fax, dataport, minibar, coffeemaker, hair dryer, iron/ironing board, safe.

Rio All-Suite Hotel & Casino   This hotel, located a block off the Strip, is Party Hearty central; come here for the nightlife or if you love large rooms (they do have spacious, if dull, quarters). Definitely leave the kids at home—the fun's aimed at adults only, and the hotel actively discourages parents from bringing kids. If you prefer to make your wagers on the golf course, this one's for you; the 18-hole championship **Rio Secco golf course** was designed by Rees Jones.

3700 W. Flamingo Rd. (at I-15), Las Vegas, NV 89103. © **888/752-9746** or 702/777-7777. Fax 702/777-7611. www.playrio.com. 2,582 units. Sun–Thurs $90 and up suite; Fri–Sat $140 and up suite. Extra person $30; no discount for children. AE, DC, MC, V. Free self- and valet parking. **Amenities:** Casino; showrooms; 14 restaurants; 4 outdoor pools; golf course; health club; spa; Jacuzzi; sauna; video arcade; concierge; car-rental desk; business center; shopping arcade; 24-hr. room service; in-room massage; laundry service; dry cleaning; executive-level rooms. *In room:* A/C, TV w/pay movies, fridge, coffeemaker, hair dryer, iron/ironing board, safe.

NORTH STRIP

Circus Circus *(Kids)*   If you love clowns, you might want to consider this venerable establishment, but if you are a clown-phobe, for the love of everything that is holy, stay far away. But they still do have the circus acts high flyin' over the casino, which is pretty cool, and the theme park is air-conditioned, thanks to the large dome. And, best of all, it is cheap. What with the clown theme, the circus acts, and the pretty good amusement park, this remains a relatively child-friendly place, though lately less by design than by default.

2880 Las Vegas Blvd. South (between Circus Circus Dr. and Convention Center Dr.), Las Vegas, NV 89109. © **800/444-2472,** 800/634-3450, or 702/734-0410. Fax 702/734-5897. www.circuscircus.com. 3,744 units. Sun–Thurs $39 and up double; Fri–Sat $59 and up double. Extra person $12. Children under 17 stay free in parent's room. AE, DC, DISC, MC, V. Free self- and valet parking. **Amenities:** Casino; circus acts; wedding chapel; 8 restaurants; 2 outdoor pools; midway-style carnival games; video arcade; tour desk; car-rental desk; 24-hr. room service; shopping arcade; laundry service; dry cleaning; executive-level rooms. *In room:* A/C, TV w/pay movies, hair dryer, safe.

Where to Dine

You may have heard that a great part of the fun in Vegas these days is the eating. This is true. Where once Vegas was, at best, ignored by anyone with a palate and, at worst, openly mocked, it is now considered one of the best dining towns in the country. All sorts of celebrity chefs have set up shop here, from the ubiquitous Emeril to Julian Serrano. Branches of a number of significant restaurants (**Bouchon, Fleur de Lys, Commander's Palace, Aqua, Aureole, Le Cirque, Lutèce**) can be found here, though of course, rare is the day you are going to find the signature chef in the kitchen. But the city boasts a few Vegas-based master chefs who can compete with any of those dudes on the Food Network.

On the other hand, the town of the great meal deal—the 99¢ shrimp cocktail or $4.99 all-you-can-eat buffet!—has now reversed itself. For the most part, if you want to eat well, you need to be well-heeled. But you, the non-gambler, with all that money you've saved from the clutches of the craps table, may well be able to take full advantage of the haute cuisine currently offered. And while little hole-in-the-wall ethnic places aren't nearly as abundant as we would like, there are a few noteworthy spots—including perhaps the best Thai restaurant on the continent—and we will help you find your way to them. We may make you drive to certain finds, but don't worry; we've included even a few hotel-based midprice restaurants worth your patronage as well, plus we've picked our favorites among the many buffets around—after all, it's not a trip to Vegas unless you've piled your plates with a mound of shrimp and endless helpings of prime rib.

1 South Strip

VERY EXPENSIVE

Aureole *✹✹✹* NOUVELLE AMERICAN   This branch of a New York City fave (it's pronounced are-ree-*all*) run by Charlie Palmer is noted for its glass wine tower. Four stories of carefully chosen bottles (including the largest collection of Austrian wines outside that country—well worth trying) are plucked from their perches by comely, cat-suited lasses who fly up and down via pulleys. It's quite the show, and folks come in just to watch.

Should you come for the food? You bet. The current chef is a wonder, serving a seasonal three-course prix-fixe menu, though flirting with your waiter might earn you luxurious extras like pâté on brioche topped with shaved truffles or an espresso cup of cold yellow pepper soup with crab. Expect other marvels like a tender roasted lamb loin and braised shoulder, or a rack of venison accompanied by sweet potato purée and chestnut crisp. Everything demonstrates the hand of a true chef in the kitchen, someone paying close attention to his work and to his customers. Service is solicitous, and desserts are playful, including a bittersweet chocolate soufflé with blood orange sorbet and a Bartlett pear crisp with toasted cinnamon brioche and lemongrass foam. There is also an excellent cheese plate. Do try the wine list; it comes on a handheld computer, designed not just to guide you through their vast tower but also to recommend pairings with your meal choices.

In Mandalay Bay, 3950 Las Vegas Blvd. South. *©* **877/632-5300.** www.aureole lv.com. Reservations required. Fixed-price dinner $69–$95. AE, DISC, MC, V. Daily 6–11pm.

Charlie Palmer Steak *⭑⭑* STEAKHOUSE
There are many, many steakhouses in Vegas, as if there is some natural law which states that any hotel without one will suffer from entropy and eventually collapse into a black hole. Discerning palates know there can be a significant difference among steakhouses; discerning wallets might not care. If you find yourself among the former, do try Charlie Palmer's, probably the best of the costlier Shrines to Beef. Those with the latter can be reassured that with entrees weighing in at around 22 to 45 ounces *each,* diners can legitimately, and in the name of decency ought to, share portions, which makes this a much more affordable experience than it might appear at first glance. And why not? Those enormous slabs o' meat are as tender as anything because with the big bucks, you do get the best cuts. Charlie Palmer, by the way, is the chef mind behind Aureole on the other side of Mandalay Bay; this makes two for two for this one celeb chef.

In Four Seasons Las Vegas, 3960 Las Vegas Blvd. South. *©* **702/632-5120.** www. charliepalmersteaklv.com. Reservations recommended. Main courses $21–$42. AE, DC, DISC, MC, V. Daily 5–10:30pm.

Commander's Palace *⭑⭑* CREOLE
This is an offshoot of the famous New Orleans restaurant, which is considered the best in that

Dining on the Strip

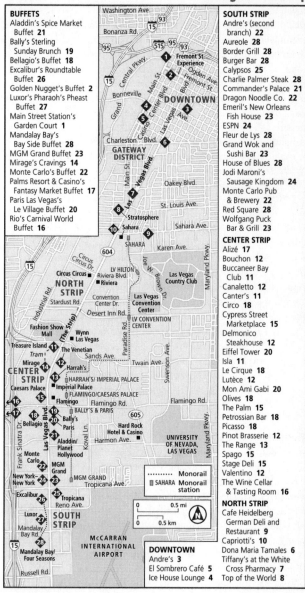

town, and sometimes even the best in the country. Vegas's version isn't nearly all that, but it's one of the better choices in town, with a menu where nary a dish fails. You would be best off getting the $39 three-course Creole favorite, featuring the justly legendary turtle soup with sherry, Louisiana pecan-crusted fish, and signature bread pudding soufflé, three things Commander's does very, very well indeed. Pork chops sound humble, but here they are thick cut and juicy. Try the Chocolate Sheba in addition to the bread pudding for dessert. The menu is shorter at brunch and lunch, but just as delightful. Revel all the while in the fantastic, doting service.

In the Desert Passage in Aladdin Resort & Casino, 3663 Las Vegas Blvd. South. ℭ 702/892-8272. www.commanderspalace.com. Reservations recommended. Main courses $22–$25 at brunch, $16–$28 at lunch, $25–$39 at dinner. AE, DISC, MC, V. Mon–Fri 9am–11am, 11:30am–2pm, and 5:30–10pm; Sat–Sun 10:30am–2pm and 5:30–10pm.

Emeril's New Orleans Fish House ☆ CONTEMPORARY CREOLE

Chef Emeril Lagasse, a ubiquitous presence on cable's Food Network, probably needs to focus on his name restaurants; the original in New Orleans is just as good as ever, but this one has lost some of its punch. How else to explain that the best dish is Creole-spiced rib-eye? And that the duck on the duck salad is better than the salad itself? But the famous savory lobster cheesecake is still a must-try, and we do love his version of barbecue shrimp, slathered in a garlicky herb-Worchester-tinged sauce, paired with a rosemary biscuit. And it all seems worthwhile when you have a slice of the banana cream pie with banana crust and caramel drizzle.

In MGM Grand, 3799 Las Vegas Blvd. South. ℭ 702/891-7374. Reservations required. Main courses $12–$18 at lunch, $18–$38 at dinner (more for lobster). AE, DC, DISC, MC, V. Daily 11am–2:30pm and 5:30–10:30pm.

Fleur de Lys ☆☆☆ FRENCH CONTINENTAL

One of the most sophisticated restaurants in Las Vegas, this is an offshoot of a highly regarded San Francisco establishment run by chef Hubert Keller. Continuing the tradition of visually show-stopping restaurant spaces in Mandalay Bay, most tables are set in the semicircular two-story interior consisting half of '70s-style stone brick walls, half of billowing drapes, behind which are concealed a few dining booths. It's one of the few places in town where you ought to dress up to dine, but in a good way. At this writing, one orders from a three-, four-, or five-course tasting menu (including a well-thought-out vegetarian option), featuring seasonal choices such as an appetizer of delicate seared ahi tuna with a gelee of chili and garlic, a silly appearing but hearty ocean "baeckeoffe" (a collection of seafood options including a sort of seafood burger-style crab cake on a brioche), pan-seared diver scallops with parsnip fires served in a cunning mini flower pot, perfect roasted Maine lobster with an artichoke purée soup, and roasted guinea hen breast and leg confit topped with crispy basil. Our descriptions won't do these playful, sexy dishes justice. It's food as art, certainly, but not so that the point of food—the eating of it, the very taste—is lost. Despite the presence of a perfect white and dark chocolate mousse on the "Chocolate Feast" sampler plate, you owe it to yourself to try the fresh fruit minestrone—basil sorbet, raspberries, mango, and more, all strong fresh fruit flavors that harmonize beautifully—for once, a no-fat dessert worth ordering.

In Mandalay Bay, 3950 Las Vegas Blvd. South. ℂ **877/632-9200.** Reservations recommended. Jacket recommended. 3- to 5-course menu $68–$88. AE, DC, DISC, MC, V. Daily 5:30–10:30pm.

Red Square 🅰🅰 CONTINENTAL/RUSSIAN   It's the restaurant with the giant beheaded statue of Lenin out front and the bar made of ice (all the better to keep your drinks chilled) inside. It's the place for vodka and blow-your-expense-account Beluga (we prefer Osetra, in case you are treating us), along with Roquefort-crusted, tender filet mignon—one of the best filets in a town full of red meat. Silly theme drinks keep up the goofy quotient (the "Cuban Missile Crisis," for example, features rain vodka, dark rum, sugarcane syrup, and lime juice), but do consider trying a vodka flight. Dessert is not so clever but is worth saving room for; we liked the Chocolate Trilogy, a white-chocolate cake tower topped with chocolate mousse and wrapped in chocolate.

In Mandalay Bay, 3950 Las Vegas Blvd. South. ℂ **877/632-5300.** Reservations recommended. Main courses $17–$31. AE, DC, MC, V. Daily 5:30pm–midnight.

EXPENSIVE
Border Grill 🅰🅰🅰 MEXICAN   More entries from Food Network denizens—in this case, the "Two Hot Tamales," Mary Sue Milliken and Susan Feniger. In a riotous-colored venue (the highly popular original is in Los Angeles), you will find truly authentic Mexican home cooking—the Tamales learned their craft from the real McCoy south of the border—but with a nuevo twist. So don't expect precisely the same dishes you'd encounter in your favorite corner joint, but do expect fresh and fabulous food, arranged as brightly on the plates as the decor on the walls. It might be hard to get kids interested in anything other than tacos and enchiladas, but

you should try the *cochinita pibil* (marinated shredded pork) or some of their excellent tamales. Stay away from the occasionally bland fish and head right toward rich and cheesy dishes such as the chiles rellenos (with perfect black beans), or try the mushroom empanadas. Don't miss the dense but fluffy Mexican chocolate cream pie (with a meringue crust).

In Mandalay Bay, 3950 Las Vegas Blvd. South. ✆ **877/632-5300.** Reservations recommended. Main courses $15–$20. AE, DC, DISC, MC, V. Sun–Thurs 11:30am–10:30pm; Fri–Sat 11:30am–11pm.

MODERATE

Burger Bar 👉 DINER What to do, what to do? We get exhausted by the relentless Vegas-high-concept that takes a simple idea like a hamburger and gives it an entire restaurant, an entire menu designed so you can "build" your own burger with dozens of options available—People, cheese! Ketchup! Onions! Why do you need more? Why, why, why?—so that the naïve could suddenly turn their affordable lunch into something approaching $20 a person. Assuming, of course, that you didn't fall for pricey gimmicks like Kobi beef (*Tip:* too soft for a good burger) and foie gras, in which case you would be looking at more like $50 a person. But then again, we love gimmicks. We also see the point of avocado bacon burgers. Plus, they make excellent shakes here, and there is that "sweet burger" (a donut "bun" with a chocolate pâté patty and fruit!), which is so charming we are disarmed. And the burgers are good. So. Order carefully, don't show off, and don't forget about the genuine (and appropriately priced) hamburgers sold at the Tiffany's coffee shop near the Strat.

In Mandalay Place in Mandalay Bay, 3950 Las Vegas Blvd. South. ✆ **702/632-9364.** Burgers $8–$20. AE, DISC, MC, V. Sun–Thurs 10am–11pm; Fri–Sat 10am–1am.

Dragon Noodle Co. 👉👉 ASIAN FUSION A strong choice for a reasonably priced meal, Dragon Noodle is one of the better Chinese restaurants in town. We were glad to see that in addition to the usual suspects, there are some other interesting (if not radically less safe) choices on the menu. Note also the many Asian clients (part of our criteria for the authenticity of a place) and that the restaurant can handle large groups. Food is served family style and prepared in an open kitchen, so you know it's fresh. Be sure to try the very smooth house green tea. You might let your waiter choose your meal for you, but try the crispy Peking pork, the sweet pungent shrimp, the potstickers, and perhaps the generous seafood soup. We were a little disappointed by the popular sizzling black-pepper chicken, but you may not be, so don't let us stop you. And they now have a sushi bar!

In Monte Carlo Resort & Casino, 3770 Las Vegas Blvd. South (between Flamingo Rd. and Tropicana Ave.). ℂ **702/730-7965.** Main courses $5.50–$17 (many under $10). AE, DC, DISC, MC, V. Sun–Thurs 11am–11pm; Fri–Sat 11am–midnight.

Grand Wok and Sushi Bar ⭐⭐ *Value* PAN-ASIAN   A pan-Asian restaurant runs the risk of attempting to be a jack-of-all-trades and master of none, but somehow, this new MGM eatery pulls it off. You can choose among Japanese, Chinese, Korean, Vietnamese, and probably more—we just aren't sure what Laotian food looks like (but would love to learn). Sushi is fresh and lovely, and the Vietnamese soups are enormous, full of noodles and different kinds of meat or fish; four people can easily split an order, so this is a great budget option for lunchtime.

In MGM Grand, 3799 Las Vegas Blvd. South. ℂ **702/891-7777.** Reservations not accepted. Main courses $9–$14; sushi $4.50–$9.50. AE, DC, DISC, MC, V. Restaurant Sun–Thurs 11am–10pm, Fri–Sat 11am–midnight; sushi bar Mon–Thurs 5–10pm, Fri–Sat 11am–midnight, Sun 11am–10pm.

Wolfgang Puck Bar & Grill ⭐⭐ CALIFORNIA   This transformed Puck Café is still a desirable, if slightly less affordable, option in MGM Grand. There is nothing surprising on the menu if you've eaten in any modern cafe in the post-Puck era; it's not his fault his influence has extended so far. There is enough variety that everyone in your party should find something to please them, from crab cakes with basil aioli, to a prime rib sandwich, to homemade veal ravioli, to Puck's pizzas, plus a good wine cellar. The fresh salads (we love the seasonal roasted beet) are better constructed than those at comparable eateries in town while Puck's hand is still on someone's helm; witness the silly potato chips drizzled with truffle oil and melted bleu cheese. It's all set in an almost entirely open space, a minimalist art take on a country kitchen, and it's a bit noisy, thanks to proximity to the casino floor and cheers from the nearby sports book. Expect it to be crowded right before and after *KÀ* but possibly quiet during.

In MGM Grand, 3799 Las Vegas Blvd. South. ℂ **702/895-9653.** Reservations not accepted. Main courses $10–$23. AE, DC, MC, V. Mon–Thurs 11:30am–11pm; Fri 11:30am–11:30pm; Sat 10am–11:30pm; Sun 10am–11pm.

INEXPENSIVE

Calypsos ⭐ *Value* DINER   Here's a solid, reasonably priced place to eat, which is pretty rare on the Strip. Honestly, it's kind of like a Denny's, but its traditional coffee-shop choices (including a "create

You Gotta Have a Theme

It shouldn't be too surprising that a town devoted to themes (what hotel worth its salt doesn't have one, at this point?) has one of virtually every theme restaurant there is. For the most part, these establishments glorify some aspect of pop culture: movies, sports, rock music, and so forth. Almost all have prominent celebrity co-owners and tons of "memorabilia" on the walls, which in virtually every case means throwaway items from blockbuster movies or some article of clothing a celeb wore once (if that) on stage or on the playing field. Almost all have virtually identical menus and have gift shops full of logo items.

This sounds cynical, and it is—but not without reason. Theme restaurants are, for the most part, noisy, cluttered, overpriced tourist traps, and, though some have their devotees, if you eat at one of these places, you've eaten at them all. We don't want to be total killjoys. Fans should have a good time checking out the stuff on the walls of the appropriate restaurant. And while the food won't be the most memorable ever, it probably won't be bad (and all are moderately priced). But that's not really what you go for. In any case, here are our two best bets in the theme department:

The **House of Blues** ★★, in Mandalay Bay, 3950 Las Vegas Blvd. South (☎ 702/632-7607) is, for our money, food and theme-wise, the best of the theme restaurants. The food is really pretty good (if a little more costly than it ought to be), and the mock Delta/New Orleans look works well, even if it

your own burger") are somewhat better than you might expect. There are also some eccentric items, such as a chopped Mediterranean shrimp salad, a smoked salmon plate, a rosemary chicken sandwich on onion focaccia bread, and a strawberry puff swan for dessert. Note also a very good (and low-fat!) Thai shrimp satay, loaded with vegetables, which is listed under "classic American" dishes.

In Tropicana Resort & Casino, 3801 Las Vegas Blvd. South. ☎ 702/739-2222. Reservations not accepted. Main courses $6–$19. AE, MC, V. Daily 24 hr.

Jodi Maroni's Sausage Kingdom ★★★ *Kids* SAUSAGES   There are several worthy fast food stands in the New York–New York food is unavoidably commercial. You can dine here without committing to seeing whatever band is playing since the dining room is separate from the club (note that HOB gets very good bookings from nationally known acts). The gospel brunch might also be worth checking out (the food is good, but there's too much of it), but be warned: It's served inside the actual club, which is miked very loudly, and it can be unbelievably loud, so bring earplugs (we left with splitting headaches). Open daily from 8am until 2am on event nights and midnight on non-event nights.

Presumably filling the hole left by the demise of the All Star Café, so you sports fans won't feel left out in the theme restaurant race, the gigantic **ESPN** ☾, in New York–New York, 3790 Las Vegas Blvd. South (☏ **702/933-3776**), actually has rather wacky and entertaining sports memorabilia (such as Evel Knievel set up as the old Operation game, displaying his many broken bones), plus additions such as a rock-climbing wall/machine. It's pretty fun, actually, and the food, in a couch-potato junk-food-junkie way, is not bad, either, especially when you sit in La-Z-Boy recliners to watch sports and order delights such as three Krispy Kreme donuts topped with ice cream, whipped cream, and syrup. Sadly, we find this entire concept tremendously appealing. It's open Monday through Thursday from 11:30am to 12:30am, Friday from 11:30am to 1am, Saturday from 11am to 1:30am, and Sunday from 11am to 12:30am.

court, but this one deserves an individual mention. What began as a humble stand on the Venice boardwalk in Los Angeles has expanded into a sausage empire, and we are glad. You will be, too, especially if you take a chance on the menu and don't just stick with the basic hot dog (though they do offer three tempting varieties—and kids love 'em) and instead try something a little more adventurous, like the tequila chicken sausage made with jalapenos, corn, and lime. Maybe some chili fries, too. Our first choice for fast food in the immediate area.

In New York–New York Hotel & Casino, 3790 Las Vegas Blvd. South. ☏ **702/740-6969**. Everything under $10. No credit cards. Daily 10am-11pm.

Tips **Quick Bites**

Many Vegas hotels have food courts, but the one in the **New York–New York**, 3790 Las Vegas Blvd. South (© **702/740-6969**), deserves a mention for two reasons: It's the nicest setting for this sort of thing on the Strip, sitting in the Greenwich Village section of New York–New York, and the choices, while not surprising (except at Jodi Maroni's Sausage Kingdom, listed above), are superior. Expect Chinese food and pizza (as befitting an ode to NYC) and excellent, if expensive (for this situation), double-decker burgers, plus **Ben & Jerry's** ice cream.

If you head farther down the Strip, to The Grande Canal Shoppes at **The Venetian**, 3355 Las Vegas Blvd. South (© **702/ 414-1000**), you can find another decent food court, with a Panda Express, a good pizza place (despite the confusing name **LA Pizza Kitchen**), a burrito stand, and a juice joint, and best of all, a **Krispy Kreme**, where they actually make the donuts on the premises. Plus, it's right by the canals of this faux Venice, one of our favorite places in Vegas.

Monte Carlo Pub & Brewery ★★★ *Finds Kids* PUB FARE   Lest you think we are big, fat foodie snobs who can't appreciate a meal unless it comes drenched in truffles and caviar, we hasten to direct you to this lively, working microbrewery (with a sort of rustic factory appearance) and its hearty, not-so-high-falutin' food (pizza, ribs, shrimp salads, chocolate fudge brownies). No fancy French frills and, best of all, no inflated prices. Combine the general high quality with generous portions—a nachos appetizer could probably feed eight (though it was not the best nachos appetizer ever)—and this may be a better deal than most buffets. It's not, however, the place for a quiet rendezvous, with about 40 TVs spread throughout (a sports fan's dream) and music blaring. After 9pm, only pizza is served, and dueling pianos provide dance music and other entertainment.

In Monte Carlo Resort & Casino, 3770 Las Vegas Blvd. South. © **702/730-7777.** Reservations not accepted. Main courses $6–$15 (most under $10). AE, DC, DISC, MC, V. Sun–Thurs 11am–3am; Fri–Sat 11am–4am.

2 Mid-Strip

VERY EXPENSIVE

Alizé ★★★ CONTINENTAL   Situated at the top of the Palms, this restaurant's divine dining room has three sides of full-length windows that allow a panoramic view of the night lights of Vegas; it may also have the best chef in town. It consistently has some of the best chefs in town working in the kitchen. The menu changes seasonally, but anything you order will be heavenly.

On our last visit, we had perhaps 14 different courses, and not a single one disappointed. In the appetizer department, the marinated jumbo lump crabmeat and avocado salad with heirloom tomato consommé and basil oil was a riot of freshness, while the gnocchi with sautéed wild mushrooms, black truffle, and mushroom emulsion was the kind of dish clearly created by someone thoughtful and clever. Fish can be a little dry here, so we suggest either the stunning New York steak with summer truffle jus and potato herb pancakes, or the meltingly tender lamb chops with some shredded lamb shank wrapped in a crispy fried crepe. Desserts are similarly outstanding, and often of great frivolity, such as sorbet in a case of browned marshmallow, floating in raspberry soup. Yeah, we're going over the top on this one, but we bet you won't think we're wrong.

Note: Obviously, window-side tables here are best, but even seats in the center of the room have a good view, so don't despair if you aren't seated right next to the glass. The romance oozes, regardless of where you are seated.

In the Palms, 4321 W. Flamingo Rd. © **702/951-7000.** Fax 702/951-7002. www. alizelv.com. Reservations strongly recommended. Main courses $28–$37. AE, MC, V. Daily 5:30–11pm.

Buccaneer Bay Club ⊛ *Finds* AMERICAN/CONTINENTAL
Here's a solid alternative to some of the higher-priced, higher-profile haute restaurants in town. Serious foodies will know that this is a midlevel restaurant in more than just price, but even they will admit that the food isn't bad. And did we mention the free pirate show outside, easily viewable from the windows? (It's a hoot to see all the nicely dressed diners abandoning their tables and dignity to rush to the windows when the show's on.)

Appetizers come in both hot (shrimp Jamaica and escargot brioche) and cold (shrimp cocktail and Parma prosciutto) varieties; the savory celery-root flan and the quail are the true standouts. (The quail wasn't on the menu on our last visit, so be sure to ask about specials.) Entrees range from poultry to beef to seafood. Consider the Colorado buffalo prime rib, which is roasted and grilled over mesquite wood and served with creamy horseradish potatoes. Desserts include apple beignets, white chocolate cheesecake with raspberry sauce, and the house specialty, apricot or harlequin (Grand Marnier and white and dark chocolate) minisoufflés.

In Treasure Island, 3300 Las Vegas Blvd. South. ℭ **866/286-3809.** Reservations recommended. Main courses $20–$35. AE, DC, DISC, MC, V. Daily 5–11pm.

Delmonico Steakhouse ☆☆ CONTEMPORARY CREOLE/ STEAK   This, the latest of Emeril Lagasse's Vegas variations on his Big Easy brand-name eateries, is a steakhouse version of his hard-core classic Creole restaurant; and this ever-so-slight twist is just enough to make it a superior choice over the more disappointing New Orleans locale. You can try both Emeril concoctions and fabulous cuts of red meat. You can't go wrong with most appetizers, especially the superbly rich smoked mushrooms with homemade tasso over pasta—it's enough for a meal in and of itself—any of the specials, or the gumbo, particularly if it's the hearty, near-homemade country selection. If you want to experiment, definitely do it with the appetizers. You're better off steering clear of complex entrees, no matter how intriguing they sound. The bone-in rib steak is rightly recommended (skip the gummy béarnaise sauce in favor of the fabulous homemade Worcester or the A.O.K. sauce). Too full for dessert? No, you aren't. Have a chocolate soufflé, a bananas Foster cream pie, a chocolate Sheba (a sort of dense chocolate mousse), or the lemon icebox pie, a chunk of curd that blasts tart lemon through your mouth.

In The Venetian, 3355 Las Vegas Blvd. South. ℭ **702/414-3737.** Reservations strongly recommended for dinner. Main courses $10–$36 at lunch, $21–$36 at dinner. AE, DC, DISC, MC, V. Daily 11:30am–2pm; Sun–Thurs 5:30–10:30pm; Fri–Sat 5:30–11pm.

Le Cirque ☆ FRENCH   The influx of haute-cuisine, high-profile restaurants in Vegas means there are ever so many places now where you may feel like you have to take out a bank loan in order to eat there—and you may wonder why you ought to. Although we always feel free to spend your money, we aren't prepared to suggest you should blow it all at Le Cirque. Service is too haughty, the food well prepared, but nothing earthshaking. The menu changes seasonally, but you can expect genuine French cuisine—heavy, with lots of butter, though a recent visit brought a duo of cold cucumber and heirloom tomato soups that were so refreshing, every restaurant in this desert town ought to serve them. The lobster salad is sweet and tender, with a perfect black truffle dressing; risotto is French-style, almost soupy, perfect with fresh morels (in season) and Parmesan. The filet mignon is, oddly, not as good a cut as served elsewhere, but it does come with a generous portion of foie gras. For dessert, we loved the white chocolate cream (solid but not overwhelming), layered with banana and wrapped in phyllo, along with a milk chocolate dome with crème brûlée espresso.

In Bellagio, 3600 Las Vegas Blvd. South. ✆ 877/234-6358. www.lecirque.com. Reservations required. Jacket and tie for gentlemen required. Main courses $29–$39. AE, DC, DISC, MC, V. Daily 5:30–10:30pm.

Lutèce ☆ *Overrated* FRENCH When the beloved NYC original closed, we feared the worst for this, once one of our favorite Vegas restaurants. And while those fears weren't entirely released, certainly the place isn't quite what it once was. Service is haphazard—just a touch chilly and careless, with long, long stretches between attention and, for that matter, courses. Appetizers like a silky foie gras au torchon and a tuna "mille feuille"—layered with granny smith apples—were adequate, and a celery root soup *amuse bouche* was utterly blah. But the roasted wild salmon main course was flawless, with the crispy skin laid separately on top in a geometrically pleasing way, and star anise–crusted scallops perfectly good, and no more. Desserts are unmemorable. Given the prices, it's just too much to pay for what looks very much like indifference.

In The Venetian, 3355 Las Vegas Blvd. South. ✆ 702/414-2220. Reservations strongly recommended. Main courses $26–$38. AE, DC, DISC, MC, V. Daily 5:30–10:30pm.

The Palm ☆☆ STEAK/SEAFOOD A branch of the venerable New York eatery, which has been branching ever further afield, this place attracts a star-studded clientele fond of the reliable and hearty, if not terribly exciting, bill of fare. (The famous may also be hoping to find their faces among the many caricatures that cover the walls.) This is plain but filling food—at manly prices. Red-meat lovers will be happy with the high-quality steaks found here, though those on a budget will shudder in horror. The tendency is to give the meat a good charring, so if you don't like yours blackened, start with it less well done and send it back for more, if necessary. All that money you've saved by not gambling will be well spent on one of the Palm's Buick-size lobsters. They're utterly succulent and outrageously priced, but given their size—they start at 3 pounds—they can easily be shared. Desserts are heavy and unspectacular.

In Caesars Palace Forum Shops, 3570 Las Vegas Blvd. South. ✆ 702/732-7256. Reservations recommended. Main courses $9–$21 at lunch, $18–$38 at dinner. AE, DC, MC, V. Daily 11:30am–11pm.

Picasso ☆☆☆ FRENCH A Spanish chef who cooks French cuisine in an Italian-themed hotel in Vegas? Trust us, it works. This may well be the best restaurant in Vegas, and given the serious competition for such a title, that says a lot. Madrid-born chef Julian Serrano (whose Masa was considered the finest French restaurant in San Francisco) offers an extraordinary dining experience, along with the added thrill of having $30 million worth of Picassos gazing down over your shoulders while you eat.

Needless to say, Serrano's cooking is a work of art that can proudly stand next to the masterpieces. The menu changes nightly and always offers a choice between a four- or five-course fixed-price dinner or tasting menu. The night we ate there, we were bowled over by roasted Maine lobster with a trio of corn—kernels, sauce, and a corn flan that was like slightly solid sunshine. Hudson Valley foie gras was crusted in truffles and went down most smoothly. A filet of roasted sea bass came with a light saffron sauce and dots of cauliflower purée. And finally, hope that they're serving the lamb rôti—it was an outstanding piece of lamb, perfectly done, tender, and crusted with truffles. Portions are dainty but so rich that you'll have plenty to eat without groaning and feeling heavy when you leave. Desserts are powerful yet prettily constructed. Everything is delivered by attentive staff who make you feel quite pampered.

In Bellagio, 3600 Las Vegas Blvd. South. © **877/234-6358**. Reservations recommended. Fixed-price 4-course dinner $90; 5-course dégustation $100. AE, DC, DISC, MC, V. Wed–Mon 6–9:30pm; closed Tues.

Moments **A Dining Room, or Two, with a View**

Both the chic **Eiffel Tower** restaurant, in Paris Las Vegas, 3655 Las Vegas Blvd. South (© **702/948-6937**), located on the 11th floor of said Mid-Strip hotel, and the **Stratosphere's Top of the World,** in the Stratosphere Casino Hotel & Tower, 2000 Las Vegas Blvd. South (© **702/380-7711**), which is almost at the top of the North Strip's Stratosphere Tower, offer fantastic views. The latter revolves 360 degrees, while the former looks down on the Bellagio fountains. Both, however, match sky-high views with sky-high prices and, unfortunately, neither has food worth the price. Go for a special night out, or see if you can get away with just ordering appetizers and dessert (which are both superior to the entrees, anyway). You can also just have a drink at their respective bars, though each is set back far enough from the windows so that drinkers have less choice views than diners.

The Range ⭐ STEAK   This place is worth visiting, if only for the spectacular view of the Strip (few Strip restaurants take advantage of this view, oddly enough) from 40-foot-high wraparound windows. The small menu features the usual steakhouse offerings—various cuts of beef and some chicken dishes, plus a few salads—but at a high-medium price. The quality, however, is better than we've found at the usual Vegas steakhouse suspects. We particularly liked the filet mignon on a Gorgonzola-onion croustade. All entrees come with family-style side dishes (they change nightly but can include such items as marinated mushrooms or horseradish mashed potatoes). Appetizers are also worth noting. The five-onion soup is thick, heavy, creamy, and served in a giant, hollowed-out onion. It's delicious, as was a smoked chicken quesadilla. Don't miss the bread, which comes with a sweet-and-savory apricot-and-basil butter.

In Harrah's, 3475 Las Vegas Blvd. South. ℂ **702/369-5084.** Reservations strongly recommended. Main courses $24–$40. AE, DC, DISC, MC, V. Sun–Thurs 5:30–10:30pm; Fri–Sat 5:30–11:30pm.

Spago ⭐ AMERICAN/ASIAN/CALIFORNIA   With Wolfgang Puck showing up in a different incarnation at every hotel in town these days (or so it seems), his original creation might get lost in the shuffle. Certainly, it's no longer the only foodie game in town—and you get the feeling it was so far ahead of the pack for so long that it has gotten a bit complacent. Which is not to say Spago is not worth the expense—it just means that others have caught up with and, in some cases, surpassed it.

Specialties include Puck's signature Chinois chicken salad and a superb mesquite-fried salmon served with a tangy toss of soba noodles and cashews in a coconut-sesame-chile paste vinaigrette nuanced with lime juice and Szechuan mustard. The main dining room menu changes seasonally, but the signature dish is a Chinese-style duck, moist but with a perfectly crispy skin. It's about as good as duck gets, served with a doughy steamed bun and Chinese vegetables. Lunch in the cafe brings nice enough pastas, salads, and quiches, but you do tend to wonder what the fuss is about.

In Caesars Palace, 3570 Las Vegas Blvd. South. ℂ **702/369-6300.** Reservations recommended for the dining room, not accepted at the cafe. Dining room main courses $14–$43; cafe main courses $9.50–$23. AE, DC, DISC, MC, V. Dining room Sun–Thurs 6–10:30pm; Fri–Sat 5:30–11pm. Cafe Sun–Thurs 11am–11pm; Fri–Sat 11am–midnight.

EXPENSIVE

Bouchon ⭐⭐⭐ BISTRO   Now here is where the whole celebrity chef concept bursts into full glory. Thomas Keller made his name with his Napa Valley restaurant French Laundry, considered by many to be the best restaurant in the United States. (It's temporarily closed while Keller operates his new New York City restaurant, Per Se.) Bouchon is a version of his Napa Valley bistro. We had mixed expectations: On one hand, a certifiably genius chef. On the other hand, he's not going to be in the kitchen, which will be producing bistro (which is to say, not innovative) food and, what's more, is based on the rather lackluster Napa Bouchon.

Our negative expectations were confounded by the right, left, and center of the menu—yeah, we've tried nearly all of it and can report that, humble though these dishes sound, in nearly every case they are gold-standard versions of classics. Someone is certainly keeping a close eye on this kitchen, and that someone has learned their lessons well. Don't miss the bacon and poached egg frisee salad, or the cleanly seared salmon over poached leaks, prepared to such rightness it doesn't need the accompanying sauce. Gnocchi is earthy and assertive, a peasant version of an Italian favorite, while beef bourguignon is exactly as you expect it to be, in the divine perfection sense. Leg of lamb has all chewy bits excised before cooking, leaving it a garlic-permeated bit of tenderness. This is a superlative Vegas restaurant, and while it may be hard to reconcile the prices with the apparent simplicity of the food, recall that it takes serious skill to make even the most humble of dishes correctly, as your palate will reassure you.

In The Venetian, 3355 S. Las Vegas Blvd. South. (C) **702/414-6200.** Reservations strongly recommended. Main courses $17–$30. AE, DC, DISC, MC, V. Daily 5–10:30pm.

Canaletto ⭐⭐ ITALIAN   Come here for solid, true Italian fare—and that means less sauce-intensive than the red-checked-tablecloth establishments of our American youths. Here, the emphasis is on the pasta, not the accompaniments. This place is all the more enjoyable for being perched on the faux St. Mark's Square; in theory, you can pretend you are sitting on the edge of the real thing, a fantasy we don't mind admitting we briefly indulged in. A risotto of porcini, sausage, and white truffle oil was full of strong flavors, while the wood-fired roast chicken was perfectly moist. A properly roasted chicken should be a much-celebrated thing, and that alone may be reason to come here.

In The Venetian Grand Canal Shoppes, 3377 Las Vegas Blvd. South. (C) **702/733-0070.** Reservations recommended for dinner. Main courses $14–$35. AE, DC, MC, V. Sun–Thurs 11:30am–11pm; Fri–Sat 11:30am–midnight.

Circo ★★ ITALIAN   Yes, this is the less expensive offering from the same family who brings you Le Cirque, but going to one does not excuse you from going to the other. (By the way, "less expensive" is a relative term. While dinner prices for entrees other than pasta and pizza fall into our "very expensive" category, lunch prices are less high, and there are, as you will see, ways to make this fall into the "moderate" category. So we decided to split the difference and list this as "expensive." Just thought you'd like to know.)

Order the mista di Campo, a lovely little salad, both visually and in terms of taste; it's a creative construction of vegetables bound with cucumber and topped with a fab balsamic vinaigrette. Or start with the antipasto appetizer sampler of Tuscan sheep's milk cheese, marinated veggies, prosciutto, and Italian pastrami. Follow that with a perfect tagliatelle with rock shrimp—it comes loaded with various crustacean bits in a light sauce. Note that appetizer portions of pastas are plenty filling and cheaper than full-size servings. Nighttime brings more elaborate dishes, such as breast of Moscovy duck with dried organic fruit in port-wine sauce.

In Bellagio, 3600 Las Vegas Blvd. South. ✆ **877/234-6358.** Reservations recommended for dinner. Main courses $17–$24 at lunch (pizza and pasta $12–$19), $20–$32 at dinner (pizza and pasta $12–$22). AE, DC, DISC, MC, V. Daily 11:30am–2:30pm and 5:30–10:30pm.

Pinot Brasserie ★★ BISTRO   Pinot reliably delivers French and American favorites that are thoughtfully conceived and generally delicious. It's an excellent choice if you want a special meal that is neither stratospherically expensive nor too complex. And the space is highly attractive, with various props culled from French auctions and flea markets forming the archetypal, clubby bistro feel. (We particularly like the small room off the bar to the right—just perfect for a tête-à-tête.)

Salads are possibly fresher and more generous than other similar starters in town, and they can come paired with various toppings for crostini (toasted slices of French bread), such as herbed goat cheese. The signature dish, beloved by many, is a roasted chicken accompanied by heaping mounds of garlic fries, but if you wish to get a little more elaborate (and yet rather light), thin slices of smoked salmon with celery rémoulade could be a way to go. Desserts are lovely, and the ice cream is homemade—the chocolate alone should make you wish you'd never eaten at 31 Flavors because those were wasted calories compared to this. *Note:* It's easy to graze through this menu and have a less costly meal here than at most other high-end places, and the long operating hours mean you can also pop in for a nosh at times when other fine-dining options are closed.

In The Venetian, 3355 Las Vegas Blvd. South. ☎ **702/414-8888**. Reservations recommended for dinner. Main courses $12–$18 at lunch, $19–$30 at dinner. AE, DISC, MC, V. Daily 11:30am–3pm and 5:30–10:30pm.

MODERATE

See also the listing for **Spago** (p. 79), an expensive restaurant fronted by a more moderately priced cafe, and **Circo** (p. 81) and **Pinot Brasserie** (p. 81), which are both in the expensive category but provide opportunities for moderately priced dining.

Isla ★★ MEXICAN   Unless you absolutely do not consider Mexican food anything other than a specific form of Southern California burrito, you really should try this new establishment run by Richard Sandoval, who specializes in "modern Mexican cuisine." This means dishes both traditional and with potentially dangerous twists, but since the place starts with handmade tortillas and heads right to guacamole made on demand, it's all trustworthy, even if some of that guac contains lobster and passion fruit (it's a sweet and curious take on tradition). Roast pork *pipian* with tamarind marinade and pumpkin seed sauce is a lovely dish, as are the needlessly fried (though pleasantly crunchy) beef empanadas with dried cherries and chipotle tomato sauce, a satisfying mix of sweet and spice. For the more timid, there is a nice assortment of particularly good tacos and burritos. Isla also has the most charming dessert menu in town, with Mexican themes both culinary and visual, like a desert scape represented by a chocolate cactus stuck into a fudge hill, to complement the caramel cupcakes.

In Treasure Island, 3300 Las Vegas Blvd. South. ☎ **866/286-3809**. Main courses $10–$25. AE, DC, DISC, MC, V. Daily 11am–2am.

Mon Ami Gabi ★★ BISTRO   This charming bistro has it all: a delightful setting, better-than-average food, affordable prices. Sure, it goes overboard in trying to replicate a classic Parisian bistro, but the results are less cheesy than most Vegas attempts at atmosphere, and the patio seating on the Strip (no reservations taken there—first come, first served) actually makes you feel like you're in a real, not a pre-fab, city. You can be budget-conscious and order just the very fine onion soup, or you can eat like a real French person and order classic steak and *pommes frites* (the hanger steak is just a nice, juicy, and sweet cut of meat). There are plenty of cheaper options (which is why we listed this place in the "moderate" category, by the way), especially at lunch. Yes, they have snails, and we loved 'em. Desserts, by the way, are massive and should be shared (another way to save). The baseball-size profiteroles (three or four to an order) filled with fine vanilla ice cream and the football-size bananas foster crepe are particularly good. Ooh, la la!

In Paris Las Vegas, 3655 Las Vegas Blvd. South. ✆ **702/944-GABI (944-4224).** Reservations recommended. Main courses $9–$27. AE, DC, DISC, MC, V. Sun–Thurs 11:30am–11pm; Fri–Sat 11:30am–midnight.

Olives ✿✿ ITALIAN/MEDITERRANEAN   If there were an Olives cafe in our neighborhood, we would eat there regularly. A branch of Todd English's original Boston-based restaurant, Olives is a strong choice for a light lunch that need not be as expensive as you might think. Here's how to enjoy a moderately priced meal here: Don't fill up too much on the focaccia bread and olives they give you at the start (on the other hand, budget-obsessives, go ahead), and skip the small-size and thus costly salads, and instead go right to the flatbreads. Think pizza with an ultrathin crust (like a slightly limp cracker), topped with delicious combinations such as the highly recommended Moroccan spiced lamb, eggplant purée, and feta cheese, or the fig, prosciutto, and Gorgonzola. They are rich and wonderful—split one between two people, along with that salad we just maligned, and you have an affordable and terrific lunch. Or try a pasta; we were steered toward the simple but marvelous spaghettini with roasted tomatoes, garlic, and Parmesan, and were glad. The food gets more complicated and costly at night, adding an array of meats and chickens, plus pastas such as butternut squash with brown butter and sage.

In Bellagio, 3600 Las Vegas Blvd. South. ✆ **877/234-6358.** Reservations recommended. Main courses $15–$19 at lunch, $20–$38 at dinner; flatbreads $10–$15. AE, DC, DISC, MC, V. Daily 11am–10:30pm.

Stage Deli ✿ DELI   New York City's Stage Deli—a legendary hangout for comedians, athletes, and politicians—has been slapping pastrami on rye for more than half a century. Its Las Vegas branch retains the Stage's brightly lit Big Apple essence.

In addition to being handy for those staying at Caesars, it's easy to pop over if you're staying next door at The Mirage, making it a satisfying breakfast alternative to the often overcrowded, overpriced, and not very good hotel breakfast joints in the area. The huge (we mean it) menu means finding something for even the pickiest of eaters. Most of the fare—including fresh-baked pumpernickel and rye, meats, chewy bagels, lox, spicy deli mustard, and pickles—

Value Great Meal Deals

We've already alluded to the rock-bottom budget meals and graveyard specials available at casino hotel restaurants—quality not assured and Pepto-Bismol not provided. Prices and deals can change without notice, though Binion's had a full steak dinner for $14.95, last we checked, and the San Remo was offering a prime rib special for $4.95. Your best bet is to keep your eyes open as you travel through town, as hotels tend to advertise their specials on their marquees.

---

comes in daily from New York. The Stage dishes up authentic 5-inch-high sandwiches stuffed with pastrami, corned beef, brisket, or chopped liver. Maybe "overstuffed" is a better description. Unless you have a hearty appetite, are feeding two, or have a fridge in your room for leftovers, you might want to try a half-sandwich and soup or salad combo. Help yourself to other deli specialties, and wash it all down with a genuine chocolate egg cream.

In Caesars Palace, 3570 Las Vegas Blvd. South. ✆ **702/893-4045.** Reservations accepted for large parties only. Main courses $10–$14; sandwiches $6–$14. AE, DC, DISC, MC, V. Sun–Thurs 8am–10:30pm; Fri–Sat 8am–11:30pm (takeout stays open 30 min. later).

INEXPENSIVE

Canter's 𝕽𝕽 DELI   This is an offshoot of the venerable (1931!) Los Angeles establishment. That one is decidedly genuine old-school, while this one pretends it was built during the Jetson's-Googie age, but it wasn't. You know. Still, that perfect pastrami scent hits you as soon as you walk up, and if the portions aren't as large and the menu is only ⅕ the size of the one in LA, they still have some grand sandwiches (brisket with cole slaw and Russian dressing; we are fools for it). Not to mention black-and-white cookies. And it's open late, like a good deli should be.

In Treasure Island, 3300 Las Vegas Blvd. South. ✆ **866/286-3809.** Everything under $15. AE, DC, DISC, MC, V. Daily 11am–12am.

Cypress Street Marketplace 𝕽𝕽 _(Kids_ FOOD COURT   An interesting middle ground between the food court and the buffet, owing to an original arrangement wherein patrons get a card that gets swiped at whichever food booth is patronized, with the total added up at the end. Given the wide assortment—Vietnamese food, potstickers, very fine burgers and pizza, salads, wraps, and pulled-pork sandwiches, there ought to be something for every single member of even the most finicky of families—the real china and napkins, and the overall quality, we wish other hotel-casinos would put in a version of their own.

In Caesars Palace, 3570 Las Vegas Blvd. South. ✆ 702/731-7110. Everything under $10. AE, MC, V. Mon–Thurs 7am–11pm; Fri–Sat 7am–midnight; closed Sun.

3 North Strip

MODERATE

Cafe Heidelberg German Deli and Restaurant ✦ GERMAN
A once-ponderous and dated German restaurant has been transformed into a German cafe well packed (admittedly, with only six booths, that's not hard to do) with locals. Certainly, it's not a Vegas type of place, and since it's close enough to the Strip, it's a good place for refuge. The food is better than fine, though certainly not "lite" fare, by any means; you will be moaning and holding your stomach in sorrow if you don't share the huge portions. Recommended is the sausage sampler platter so you can finally learn the difference between knockwurst and bratwurst, and the schnitzel sandwich of delicious breaded veal. Wash it down with a vast choice of imported beer. As you nosh, enjoy traditional (or, at times, not so) accordion music and note that the entire staff is German. This is also a full-service deli and German market, so it's a good place to pick up a picnic for sightseeing outside the city.

604 E. Sahara Ave. (at 6th St.). ✆ 702/731-5310. Reservations strongly recommended for Fri–Sat nights. Main courses under $10 at lunch, $15–$20 at dinner. AE, DC, DISC, MC, V. Daily 11am–10pm.

INEXPENSIVE

Capriotti's ✦✦✦ Finds SANDWICHES
It looks like a dump, but Capriotti's is one of the great deals in town, for quality and price. They roast their own beef and turkey on the premises and stuff them (or Italian cold cuts, or whatever) into sandwiches mislabeled "small," "medium," and "large"—the latter clocks in at 20 inches, easily feeding two for under $10 total. And deliciously so. The "Bobby" (turkey, dressing, and cranberry sauce, like Thanksgiving dinner in sandwich form) would be our favorite sandwich in the world had we not tried the "Slaw B Joe": roast beef, cole slaw, and Russian dressing. But other combos, such as the aforementioned Italian cold cuts, have their fans, too, and Capriotti's even has veggie varieties. There are outlets throughout the city, but this one

is not only right off the Strip, but right by the freeway. We never leave town without a stop here, and you shouldn't, either.

324 W. Sahara Ave. (at Las Vegas Blvd. South). © **702/474-0229.** Most sandwiches under $10. No credit cards. Mon–Fri 10am–5pm; Sat 11am–5pm; closed Sun.

Dona Maria Tamales ⋆⋆ MEXICAN   Decorated with Tijuana-style quiltwork and calendars, this is your quintessential Mexican diner, convenient to both the north end of the Strip and Down-town. They use lots of lard, lots of cheese, and lots of sauce. As a result, the food is really good—and really fattening. Yep, the folks who did those health reports showing how bad Mexican food can be for your heart probably did some research here. That just makes it all the better, in our opinion. Locals apparently agree; even at lunchtime the place is crowded. Meals are so large that it shouldn't be a problem getting full just ordering off the sides, which can make this even more of a budget option. Naturally, the specialty is the fantastic tamales, which come in red, green, cheese, or sweet. They also serve up excellent enchiladas, chiles rellenos, burritos, and fajitas. All dinners include rice, beans, tortillas, and soup or salad.

910 Las Vegas Blvd. South (corner of Charleston Blvd.). © **702/382-6538.** Main courses $5.50–$8 at breakfast, $6–$13 at lunch and dinner. AE, MC, V. Daily 8am–10pm.

Tiffany's at the White Cross Pharmacy ⋆⋆ *Value* DINER You can go to any number of retro soda-fountain replicas (such as Johnny Rockets) and theme restaurants that pretend to be cheap diners, but why bother when the real thing is just past the end of the Strip? The decidedly unflashy soda fountain/lunch counter at the White Cross Pharmacy was Las Vegas's first 24-hour restaurant, and it has been going strong for 60 years. Plunk down at the counter and watch the cooks go nuts trying to keep up with the orders. The menu is basic comfort food: standard items such as meatloaf, steaks, and chops; fluffy cream pies; and classic breakfasts served anytime—try the biscuits and cream gravy at 3am. But the best bet is a ⅓-pound burger and "thick creamy shake," both the way they were meant to be and about as good as they get. At around $5, this is half what you would pay for a comparable meal at the Hard Rock Cafe. And as waitress Beverly says, "This is really real." Places like this are a vanishing species—it's worth the short walk from the Stratosphere. Note, however, that the neighborhood remains stubbornly rough in appearance, and that can be a turnoff.

1700 Las Vegas Blvd. South (at East Oakley Blvd.). © **702/383-0196.** Reservations not accepted. Most items under $7. No credit cards. Daily 24 hr.

4 East of the Strip

In this section, we cover restaurants close by the Convention Center, along with those farther south, on Paradise Road, Flamingo Road, and Tropicana Avenue.

VERY EXPENSIVE

Lawry's The Prime Rib ⋔⋔⋔ STEAK/SEAFOOD   If you love prime rib, come here. If you could take or leave prime rib, Lawry's will turn you into a believer. Yes, you can get prime rib all over town for under $5. But, to mix a food metaphor, that's a tuna fish sandwich when you can have caviar at Lawry's.

Eating at Lawry's is a ceremony, with all the parts played the same way for the past 60 years. Waitresses in brown-and-white English maid uniforms, complete with starched white cap, take your order—for side dishes, that is. The real decision, what cut of rib you are going to have, comes later. Actually, that's the only part of the tradition that has changed. Lawry's has added fresh fish (halibut, salmon, or swordfish, depending on the evening) to its menu. Anyway, you tell the waitress what side dishes you might want (sublime creamed spinach, baked potato, and so on) for an extra price. Later, she returns with a spinning salad bowl (think of salad preparation as a Busby Berkeley musical number). The bowl, resting on crushed ice, spins as she pours Lawry's special dressing in a stream from high over her head. Tomatoes garnish. Applause follows.

Eventually, giant metal carving carts come to your table, bearing the meat. You name your cut (the regular Lawry's, the extra-large Diamond Jim Brady for serious carnivores, and the wimpy thin English cut), and specify how you'd like it cooked. Flavorful, tender, perfectly cooked, lightly seasoned, this will be the best prime rib you will ever have. Okay, maybe that's going too far, but the rest is accurate, honest. It just has to be tasted to be believed. You can finish off with a rich dessert (English trifle is highly recommended), but it almost seems pointless.

4043 Howard Hughes Pkwy. (at Flamingo Rd., between Paradise Rd. and Koval Lane). 𝄪 702/893-2223. Reservations recommended. Main courses $22–$35. AE, DC, DISC, MC, V. Sun–Thurs 5–10pm; Fri–Sat 5–11pm.

Pamplemousse ⋔ FRENCH   A little bit off the beaten path, Pamplemousse is a long-established Vegas restaurant that shouldn't be overlooked in the crush of new high-profile eateries. Evoking a cozy French-countryside inn (at least, on the interior), it's a catacomb of low-ceilinged rooms and intimate dining nooks with rough-hewn beams. It's all very charming and un-Vegasy. The restaurant's name, which means grapefruit, was suggested by the late singer Bobby Darin—one of the many celebrity pals of owner Georges La Forge.

Your waiter recites the menu, which changes nightly. Recent menu offerings have included out-of-this-world soups (French onion and cream of asparagus, to name a few) and appetizers such as shrimp in cognac cream sauce and Maryland crab cakes with macadamia nut crust. Recommended entrees include a sterling veal with mushrooms and Dijon sauce, and an even-better rack of lamb with pistachio nut crust and rosemary cream sauce (all sauces, by the way, are made with whatever the chef has on hand that evening in the kitchen). Leave room for the fabulous desserts, such as home-made ice cream in a hard chocolate shell.

400 E. Sahara Ave. (between Santa Paula Dr. and Santa Rita Dr.). ℂ **702/ 733-2066.** Reservations required. Main courses $18–$26. AE, DC, DISC, MC, V. Tues–Sun 5:30–10pm; closed Mon except during major conventions and holidays.

MODERATE

Carluccio's Tivoli Gardens 👤 *Finds* ITALIAN   A bit of a drive, but well worth it for those seeking an authentic—read: older than 10 years—Vegas experience. This otherwise unimposing joint used to be owned by none other than the Rhinestone King Himself, Lib-erace. See, it was formerly Liberace's Tivoli's Gardens, and he designed the interior himself, so you know what that looks like (it was reopened a few years after his death, and they've kept the decor pretty much as is). Expect traditional Italian food (pasta, pasta, and scampi). This kind of history is more and more rare in this town with no memory, plus—no coincidence—it's right next door to the Liberace Museum, so go pay your giggling respects in the late after-noon and then stop in here for dinner.

1775 E. Tropicana Ave. (at Spencer St.). ℂ **702/795-3236.** Reservations rec-ommended. Main courses $10–$25. AE, DC, DISC, MC, V. Tues–Sun 4:30–10pm; closed Mon.

Memphis Championship Barbecue 👤👤 BARBECUE   Okay, we refuse, simply refuse, to get into the debate about Texas vs. Kansas City vs. Mississippi barbecue (and if you've got another state with the best dang barbecue, we really don't want to hear about it). But we can say that if you aren't physically in those places, you gotta take what you can get—and luckily for you, Memphis Champi-onship Barbecue is hardly settling. Their vinegar-based sauce is sweet but has a kick. Food is cooked over mesquite applewood, and the meat falls off the bone just the way you want it to. And they

Accommodations, Dining & Nightlife East of the Strip

ACCOMMODATIONS ■

AmeriSuites **19**
Atrium Suites **17**
Courtyard by Marriott **7**
Green Valley Ranch Resort **25**
Hard Rock Hotel &Casino **18**
Hawthorn Suites **23**
La Quinta **10**
Las Vegas Hilton **3**
Las Vegas Marriott Suites **5**
Residence Inn **6**
St. Tropez **20**
Ritz-Carlton,
  Lake Las Vegas **25**
The Westin Casuarina
  Las Vegas Hotel and Spa **15**

DINING ◆

Bougainvillea **16**
Carluccio's Tivoli
  Gardens **26**
Einstein Bros. Bagels **30**
Lawry's The Prime Rib **13**
Lotus of Siam **2**
Mediterranean Café
  & Market **31**
Memphis Championship
  Barbecue **28**
Pamplemousse **1**
Pink Taco **18**
Shalimar **11**
Toto's **28**
Z Tejas Grill **9**

NIGHTLIFE ●

The Beach **4**
The Buffalo **22**
Champagnes Cafe **8**
The Dispensary **29**
Double Down Saloon **22**
The Eagle **29**
Ellis Island Casino—
  Karaoke **14**
Gipsy **21**
Good Times **27**
Gordon-Biersch
  Brewing Company **12**
Ice **24**
Jazzed Cafe &
  Vinoteca **29**

Las Vegas Is for (Wine) Lovers

The Vegas restaurant boom of the late '90s continues unabated, which is also welcome news for those who worship the grape. If you're one of them, here's a sampling of places to eat *and* drink that we think you'll enjoy. They range from wine bars to haute cuisine, with a few in between:

The Wine Cellar & Tasting Room, in Rio All-Suite Hotel & Casino (② 702/777-7614), offers nearly 100 wines by the glass, ranging from under $10 to over $100. Its more than $10 million worth of inventory includes more than 6,500 labels. Though some may only be gazed upon, not purchased (like the 1890 bottle of Madeira once owned by Thomas Jefferson or the vertical of Chateau d'Yquem going back to 1898), you can indulge yourself with a flight of luxury champagnes. The nonsmoking tasting room is open Monday through Thursday from 3 to 11pm, Friday from 3pm until midnight, and Saturday and Sunday from noon until midnight.

If you agree with Oscar Wilde that "only people with no imagination can't find a good reason to drink champagne," then **Petrossian Bar,** in Bellagio (② 702/693-7111), is the place for you. If you're seeking crumpets with your chardonnay, you'll be glad to know that afternoon tea is served from 2 to 5pm; caviar (Petrossian, of course) is available from noon to midnight. To wash it down, you can select from any of 21 champagnes and sparkling wines (7 of them available by the glass) in addition to non-bubbly whites, reds, and ports. It's open 24 hours.

While you enjoy pizza, pasta, steak, and other expertly prepared traditional Italian dishes at **Valentino,** in The Venetian

have hot links, baked beans, and everything else you would want and hope for. Standouts include a pulled barbecue chicken sandwich, onion straws, and delicious mac and cheese. *Note this special:* A $50 feast includes a rack of baby back ribs, three-fourths of a pork shoulder, ¾-pound of beef brisket, ½-pound of hot links, a whole chicken, baked beans, cole slaw, rolls, creamed corn, and fries. It reportedly feeds four, though even if two of those four are teenage boys, we think you might have leftovers.

(© **702/414-3000**), you can select a wine from the 2,600 bottles on their full list. They also offer 40 different wines (which change regularly) by the glass or in 2-ounce pours. It's open daily from 11:30am to 11:30pm.

Rosemary's Restaurant, 8125 W. Sahara Ave. (between Buffalo Dr. and Cimarron Rd.; © **702/869-2251**), is well off the Strip but equally well worth the trip. In addition to its impressive and well-balanced full-bottle list, Rosemary's offers 30 wines by the glass and three dozen by the half-bottle. For a full review, see p. 95.

Sure, you may want to visit just to see the "wine angels" rappel up and down the four-story glass wine tower at **Aureole,** in Mandalay Bay (© **877/632-5300;** www.ewine tower.com), to fetch your bottle, but the real reason we like this place is its innovative (patent-pending, even) Internet-based wine list. Customers use an "eWine Book" at their table to wirelessly access the restaurant's wine database. Better still, with a few taps of the stylus, you can check out which wine(s) the restaurant recommends to accompany various menu items before discussing your choices with the sommelier. Smoking is permitted in the bar and lounge only.

One of the most intriguing wine cellars is actually a wine loft, perched two-plus stories above the restaurant **Fleur de Lys** (in Mandalay Bay, 3950 Las Vegas Blvd. South; © **877/632-9200**), visible through floor-to-ceiling, candlelight-framed glass. With advance notice, diners can eat here, one of the most stunning, if chilly, tables in town. The "loft" is growing and promises to be most impressive.

2250 E. Warm Springs Rd. (near I-215). © **702/260-6909.** www.memphis-bbq. com. Main courses $8–$17. AE, DC, DISC, MC, V. Sun–Thurs 11am–10pm; Fri–Sat 11am–10:30pm.

Pink Taco ☆ MEXICAN   A megahip Mexican cantina, this folk-art-bedecked spot is a scene just waiting to happen, or rather, it's already happened. There are no surprises in terms of the food—you know the drill: tacos, burritos, quesadillas—but it's all tasty and filling, and some of it comes with some surprising accompaniments, such as tapenade, along with the usual guacamole and sour cream. This is hip Mexican as opposed to a mom-and-pop joint, and it's a good place to eat on this side of town.

In Hard Rock Hotel & Casino, 4455 Paradise Rd. ℂ **702/693-5525.** Reservations not accepted. Main courses $9–$18. AE, DC, DISC, MC, V. Sun–Thurs 11am–10pm; Fri–Sat 11am–midnight.

Shalimar INDIAN   In a town full of buffet deals, it's hard to get excited about another one, but on the other hand, all those other buffet deals offer carbon-copy experiences: carving stations, various cafeteria hot dishes, and so forth. Here at Shalimar, a lunch buffet means about two dozen different North Indian–style dishes, all for about $7.50. It's not as colorful or huge (in fact, it's just a table covered with steam trays) as those buffets up the street, but it is far more interesting. The buffet usually includes *tandoori* (chicken marinated in spiced yogurt cooked in a clay oven), *masala* (tandoori in a curry sauce), *naan* (the flat Indian bread), and various vegetable dishes. (Vegetarians will find plenty to eat here—they offer special veggie dishes daily.) In the evening, a full Indian menu, with *vindaloo* (an especially hot curry where the meat is marinated in vinegar), flavored naans (try the garlic or onion), and other Indian specialties, is offered a la carte. They will spice to order: mild, medium, hot, or very hot. If you make a mistake, you can always order *raita* (yogurt mixed with mild spices and cucumber); it cools your mouth nicely.

In the Citibank Plaza, 3900 Paradise Rd. ℂ **702/796-0302.** Reservations recommended. Lunch buffet $7.50; main courses $11–$16 at dinner. AE, DISC, MC, V. Mon–Fri 11:30am–2:30pm; daily 5:30–10:30pm.

Z Tejas Grill ⭐ TEX-MEX   Because the original chef, a Frenchman, kept referring to it as "Zee" Tejas Grill—we know you were wondering. Enjoy large and excellent margaritas, possibly on the unusual-for-Vegas vine-covered patio, and then hit the "South by Southwestern" menu. The starters are huge, and making a meal of one would be a very cheap meal option. In particular, we like the generously portioned grilled-fish tacos, which come wrapped in fresh tortillas, stuffed with all kinds of veggies and served with a spicy Japanese sauce. Not your usual drippy, fattening tacos. Less of a bargain, but mighty tasty, is the tender and piquant black sesame tuna, with black-peppercorn vinaigrette and soy mustard sauce. A great main course is the spicy-grilled Jamaican-jerk chicken, nuanced with lime and served with peanut sauce and rum-spiked coconut-banana ketchup; it comes with two side dishes—when we were there, garlic mashed potatoes and a corn casserole soufflé.

3824 Paradise Rd. (between Twain Ave. and Corporate Dr.). ℭ **702/732-1660.** Reservations recommended. Main courses $7.25–$12 at lunch, $8.75–$17 at dinner. AE, DC, DISC, MC, V. Mon–Thurs 11am–10pm; Fri–Sat 11am–11pm; Sun 4–10pm.

INEXPENSIVE

Bougainvillea 🍴🍴 *(Value)* COFFEE SHOP   Oh, how we love a Vegas coffee shop. You've got your all-day breakfasts, your graveyard-shift specials (build your own three-egg, three-ingredient omelet for $4.99), your prime rib, and, of course, your full Chinese menu. And it's all hearty and well priced; we're talkin' New York steak and eggs for $5.99 all day long. You can get a full dinner entree or a nice light lunch of a large half a sandwich and soup, also for $4.99 (is that someone's lucky number?). And 24-hour specials, including a slab of meat, potato or rice, veggie, soup or salad, and a 12-ounce draft beer, run between $7.99 and $12.99. Yep. That's the ticket.

In Terrible's Hotel, 4100 Paradise Rd. ℭ **702/733-7000.** Main courses $2–$13. AE, MC, V. Daily 24 hr.

Einstein Bros. Bagels 🍴 BAGELS   You may not like digging into an enormous buffet first thing in the morning, and the continental breakfast in most hotels is a rip-off. A welcome alternative is a fresh-baked bagel, of which there are 15 varieties here—everything from onion to wild blueberry. Cream cheeses also come in many flavors, anything from sun-dried tomato to vegetable and jalapeño. Four special-blend coffees are available each day.

In the University Gardens Shopping Center, 4624 S. Maryland Pkwy. (between Harmon and Tropicana aves.). ℭ **702/795-7800.** All items under $6. MC, V. Mon–Fri 6am–6pm; Sat 6am–5pm; Sun 6:30am–4pm.

Lotus of Siam 🍴🍴🍴 *(Finds)* THAI   So we drag you out to a strip mall in the east end of Nowhere and you wonder why? Because here is what critic Jonathan Gold of *Gourmet* magazine called "no less than the best Thai restaurant in North America."

What makes this place so darn special? First of all, in addition to all the usual beloved Thai and Issan favorites and others, they have a separate menu featuring lesser-known dishes from Northern Thailand—they don't routinely hand this one out (because most of the customers are there for the more pedestrian, if still excellent, $5.99 lunch buffet). Second, the owner drives at least twice a week back to Los Angeles (where his original venue, Renu Na Korn, is still operating under another family member) to pick up the freshest herbs and other ingredients needed for his dishes' authenticity. That's dedication that should be rewarded with superlatives.

You might be best off letting them know you are interested in Northern food (with dried chiles, and more pork, "it's not un-Cajun-like," says the owner) and letting them guide you through, though you must assure them that you aren't of faint heart or palate (some customers complain the heat isn't enough, even with "well-spiced" dishes, though others find even medium spice sufficient). Standouts include the Issan sausage, a grilled sour pork number, the *Nam Kao Tod* (that same sausage, ground up with lime, green onion, fresh chile, and ginger, served with crispy rice), *Nam Sod* (ground pork mixed with ginger, green onion, and lime juice, served with sticky rice), and *Sua Rong Hai* ("weeping tiger"), a dish of soft, sliced, grilled marinated beef. If you insist on more conventional Thai, that's okay, in that it's unlikely that you are going to have better *Tom Kah Kai* (note that this beloved soup can also be served Northern style, if asked, which is without the coconut milk). If in season, finish with mango with sticky rice, or if not, coconut ice cream with sticky rice, something you would find at many a street stall in Thailand.

953 E. Sahara Ave., #A-5 (west of Maryland Pkwy.). © **702/735-3033.** Reservations strongly recommended for dinner. Lunch buffet $5.99; other dishes $4–$14. AE, MC, V. Daily 11:30am–2:30pm and 5–9:30pm.

Mediterranean Café & Market 𝄞 MEDITERRANEAN   It's just so darn nice to find ethnic food in this town, and when it's served in a courtyard with some real, as opposed to ordered-up, character, full of pillows and fabrics and next to an honest-to-goodness hookah lounge, it's even nicer. It's not the best Middle Eastern food we've ever had, but getting away from the Strip makes it taste special. Kabobs take, the menu warns, 25 minutes, so order a maza plate to while away the time. The hummus is too reminiscent of its chickpea origins, but the babaganoush is properly smoky, and the falafel has the right crunch. Gyros may not be the most adventurous thing to order, but who cares about that when you've got a well-stuffed pocket of pita goopy with sweet yogurt sauce? *Fresenjan* is a dish of falling-apart chicken swimming in a tangy pomegranate sauce; ask to ensure that the ratio of sauce to chicken is greater than 10:1.

In the Tiffany Square strip mall, 4147 S. Maryland Pkwy. (at Flamingo Rd.). © **702/731-6030.** Reservations not accepted. Main courses $8–$16 (all sandwiches under $8). AE, DISC, MC, V. Restaurant Mon–Thurs 11am–1am, Fri–Sat 11am–3am, Sun 11am–5pm; lounge Mon–Thurs 5pm–1am, Fri–Sat 5pm–3am, closed Sun.

Toto's ★★ *Value* MEXICAN   A family-style Mexican restaurant favored by locals, with enormous portions and quick service, this is good value for your money. With all that food, you could probably split portions and still be satisfied. There are no surprises on the menu, though there are quite a few seafood dishes. The non-greasy chips come with fresh salsa, and the nachos are terrific. Chicken tamales got a thumbs-up, and non-meat eaters happily dug into the veggie burrito (although it's not especially healthful, all the ingredients were fresh, with huge slices of zucchini and roasted bell peppers). The operative word here is *huge;* the burritos are almost the size of your arm. The generous portions continue with dessert—a piece of flan was practically pie size. The Sunday margarita brunch is quite fun, and the drinks are large (naturally) and yummy.

2055 E. Tropicana Ave. (at Burnham Ave.). *C* **702/895-7923.** Main courses $6.25–$14. AE, DISC, MC, V. Sun–Thurs 9:30am–10pm; Fri–Sat 11am–11pm.

5 West Las Vegas

EXPENSIVE

Austins Steakhouse ★★ *Finds* STEAK/SEAFOOD   Now, understand that we don't send you out to nether regions such as Texas Station lightly. We do so here because, improbably, Austins Steakhouse has gained a reputation for the best steak in town. Really. Even the snooty critics at the *Las Vegas Review-Journal* agree with the hoi polloi. And here's what has everyone, and us, raving: a 24-ounce rib-eye— yes, we know, just split it—aged and marinated, cooked over mesquite applewood, and then rubbed with peppercorns and pan-seared in garlic, butter, and cilantro. A massive chunk of meat with a smoky garlicky flavor like no other steak we can think of. Most of the dishes have a southern twist, such as fried green tomatoes with a remoulade dipping sauce, and for those not watching their cholesterol, shrimp sautéed in garlic butter sauce, dipped in cheese, and wrapped in bacon. The Maui onion soup is also a standout, as is, over in the dessert category, the chocolate decadence cake, which is actually more of a molten-center semisoufflé. Note that a comparable meal on the Strip would cost $10 to $20 more per person—yet another reason to head out to the hinterlands.

In Texas Station, 2101 Texas Star Lane. *C* **702/631-1000.** Reservations recommended. Main courses $17–$35. AE, DC, DISC, MC, V. Sun–Thurs 5–10pm; Fri–Sat 5–11pm.

Rosemary's Restaurant ★★★ *Finds*   You don't have to eat at a name-brand temple of haute cuisine or celebrity chef showcase to

Dining & Nightlife West of the Strip

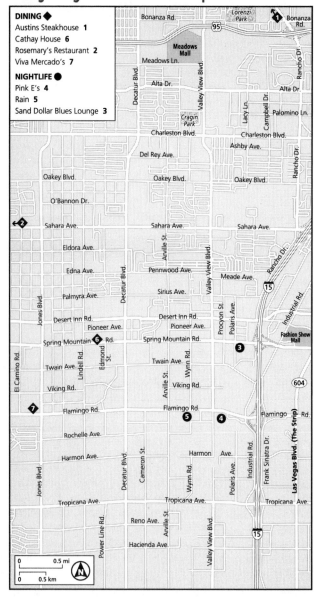

DINING ◆
Austins Steakhouse **1**
Cathay House **6**
Rosemary's Restaurant **2**
Viva Mercado's **7**

NIGHTLIFE ●
Pink E's **4**
Rain **5**
Sand Dollar Blues Lounge **3**

Bonanza Rd.
Lorenzi Park
Bonanza Rd.
95
Meadows Mall
Meadows Ln.
Decatur Blvd.
Alta Dr.
Valley View Blvd.
Rancho Dr.
Alta Dr.
Lacy Ln.
Campbell Dr.
Palomino Ln.
Cragin Park
Charleston Blvd.
Charleston Blvd.
Ashby Ave.
Del Rey Ave.
Rancho Dr.
Oakey Blvd.
Oakey Blvd.
Oakey Blvd.
O'Bannon Dr.
Sahara Ave.
Sahara Ave.
Sahara Ave.
Eldora Ave.
Arville St.
Valley View Blvd.
Rancho Dr.
Edna Ave.
Pennwood Ave.
Meade Ave.
Palmyra Ave.
Sirius Ave.
15
Industrial Rd.
Jones Blvd.
Decatur Blvd.
Desert Inn Rd.
Desert Inn Rd.
Procyon St.
Polaris Ave.
Pioneer Ave.
Pioneer Ave.
Spring Mountain 6 Rd.
Spring Mountain Rd.
Fashion Show Mall
El Camino Rd.
Lindell Rd.
Edmond St.
Twain Ave.
Twain Ave.
Wynn Rd.
604
Viking Rd.
Arville St.
Viking Rd.
Flamingo Rd.
Flamingo Rd.
5
4
Flamingo Rd.
Las Vegas Blvd. (The Strip)
Rochelle Ave.
Harmon Ave.
Cameron St.
Harmon Ave.
Wynn Rd.
Polaris Ave.
Industrial Rd.
Frank Sinatra Dr.
Jones Blvd.
Tropicana Ave.
Decatur Blvd.
Tropicana Ave.
Tropicana Ave.
Power Line Rd.
Reno Ave.
Arville St.
Hacienda Ave.
Valley View Blvd.
15

0   0.5 mi
0   0.5 km
N

have an outstanding meal in Vegas. Chefs Michael and Wendy Jordan cooked at some of the best places in New Orleans, came here to open Emeril's Seafood, but then branched out on their own with two restaurants that showcase their clever twists on American cuisine. This is playful but hearty food; seared foie gras with peach coulis, candied walnuts, and vanilla bean arugula is like a quilt, with distinct flavors that still all hang together nicely. Interesting sides include ultrarich bleu cheese slaw, slightly spicy crispy fried tortilla strips, and perfect cornmeal jalapeño hush puppies, to say nothing of "Grandma's pickled cucumbers." A recent visit found the crispy striped bass fighting it out with the pan-seared honey-glazed salmon for "best fish dish I've ever had." Desserts are similarly southern—lemon icebox pie!—and most pleasant.

There is a nice little wine list with a broad range, especially when it comes to half-price bottles. They also specialize, unusually, in beer suggestions to pair with courses, including some fruity Belgium numbers. This is such a rare treat that if you drink, you must try some of their suggestions.

8125 W. Sahara Ave. (between Buffalo Dr. and Cimarron Rd.). ✆ **702/869-2251.** Reservations strongly recommended. Main courses $12–$16 at lunch; $19–$36 at dinner. AE, MC, V. Mon–Fri 11:30am–2:30pm and 5:30–10:30pm; Sat–Sun 5:30–10:30pm.

MODERATE

Cathay House CHINESE   Las Vegas actually has a Chinatown—a very large strip mall (naturally) on Spring Mountain Road near Wynn. But ask locals who look like they know, and they will send you instead farther up Spring Mountain Road to the Cathay House, which is about a 7-minute drive from Treasure Island.

The standout at the Cathay House is a vegetable *bao* that includes Chinese glass noodles. Lightly browned and not overly doughy like many baos, it is slightly sweet and utterly delicious. The shrimp wrapped in rice noodles are big and plump, and anything fried is so good you should ignore your arteries for a while (we did!). Cathay House (which features quite a good view through the windows on one side) also has a full dinner menu, which includes the strawberry chicken invented by now-defunct local restaurant Chin's.

In Spring Valley, 5300 W. Spring Mountain Rd. ✆ **702/876-3838.** Reservations recommended. Main courses $6.75–$19. AE, DC, DISC, MC, V. Daily 10am-10pm.

Viva Mercado's ✶✶ MEXICAN   Ask any local about Mexican food in Vegas, and almost certainly they will point to Viva Mercado's as the best in town. That recommendation, plus the restaurant's health-conscious attitude, makes this worth the roughly 10-minute drive from the Strip.

Given all those warnings about Mexican food and its heart-attack-inducing properties, the approach at Viva Mercado's is nothing to be sniffed at. No dish is prepared with or cooked in any kind of animal fat. Nope, the lard so dear to Mexican cooking is not found here. The oil used is an artery-friendly canola. This makes the place particularly appealing to vegetarians, who will also be pleased by the regular veggie specials. Everything is quite fresh, and they do particularly amazing things with seafood. Try the Maresco Vallarta, which is orange roughy, shrimp, and scallops cooked in a coconut tomato sauce, with capers and olives. They have all sorts of noteworthy shrimp dishes and 11 different salsas, ranked 1 to 10 for degree of spice (ask for advice).

6182 W. Flamingo Rd. (at Jones Blvd.). ✆ **702/871-8826.** Reservations accepted for large parties only. Main courses $8–$17. AE, DISC, MC, V. Sun–Thurs 11am–9:30pm; Fri–Sat 11am–10:30pm.

6 Downtown

VERY EXPENSIVE

Andre's 🥢🥢 FRENCH Andre's has long been the bastion of gourmet dining in Vegas, but with all the new big boys crowding the Strip, it runs the risk of getting overlooked. It shouldn't. Chef Andre knows his stuff as well as any celeb chef with a Food Network show. Much of the waitstaff is also French, but not the sort who give the French a bad name. They will happily lavish attention on you and guide you through the menu.

The food presentation is exquisite, and choices change seasonally. On a recent visit, an appetizer of Northwest smoked salmon *mille feulle* with cucumber salad and sevruga caviar was especially enjoyed, as was a main course of grilled provini veal tornados with chive sauce accompanied by a mushroom and foie gras crepe. You get the idea. Desserts are similarly lovely, an exotic array of rich delights. An extensive wine list (more than 900 labels) is international in scope and includes many rare vintages; consult the sommelier.

Note: An additional branch of Andre's, just as good as this one, is located in **Monte Carlo Hotel & Casino,** 3775 Las Vegas Blvd. South (✆ **702/798-7151**).

401 S. 6th St. (at Lewis St., 3 blocks south of Fremont St.). ✆ **702/385-5016.** www. andrelv.com. Reservations required. Main courses $25–$41. AE, DC, MC, V. Mon–Sat from 6pm; closing hours vary. Closed most Sun except during major conventions and holidays.

INEXPENSIVE

El Sombrero Cafe 👁️👁️ MEXICAN   This kind of hole-in-the-wall Mexican joint can be found all over California but not always so readily elsewhere. It's also the kind of family-run (since 1950) place increasingly forced out of Vegas by giant hotel conglomerates, making it even more worth your time (it's becoming harder and harder, particularly in Downtown, to find budget options that present you with food that is more than just mere fuel). Mexican food fans, in particular, should seek out this friendly place, though it's not in an attractive part of town. Portions are generous, better than average, and unexpectedly spicy. They also cater to special requests—changing the beef burrito to a chicken one (an option that comes highly recommended), for example, without batting an eyelash. The enchilada and taco combo also won raves.

807 S. Main St. (at Gass Ave.). ✆ **702/382-9234.** All items under $10. AE, MC, V. Mon–Sat 11am–9:30pm; closed Sun.

Ice House Lounge 👁️ DINER   Don't let the dismal surroundings put you off; inside is a lively, popular modern-appearing club, with a menu full of, if not inspired, certainly reliable and well-priced menu options. The late-night hours (at this writing, they say 24 hours, but we are willing to bet that by the time you read this, they will have trimmed that some) also make this a good choice for those located near Downtown. Lunch, in particular, is a bargain, as basketball-circumference-size plates are loaded with towering sandwiches or wide-reaching flatbread-style pizzas, mounds of cole slaw, or piles of crinkly fries. We like the plate of three miniburgers. None of it is thrillingly spiced or especially cleverly crafted, but it's all solidly good and, given the portions, eminently shareable.

650 S. Main St. (corner of Bonneville Ave.). ✆ **702/315-2570.** Everything under $15. AE, MC, V. Daily 24 hr.

7 Buffets & Sunday Brunches

Lavish, low-priced buffets are a Las Vegas tradition, designed to lure you to the gaming tables and to make you feel that you got such a bargain for your meal that you can afford to drop more money. They're a gimmick, and we love them. Something about filling up on too much prime rib and shrimp just says "Vegas" to us. Of course, there is quite a range. Some are just perfunctory steam-table displays and salad bars that are heavy on the iceberg lettuce, while others are unbelievably opulent spreads, with caviar and free-flowing champagne. Some are quite beautifully presented as well. Some of the food is awful, some of it merely works as fuel, and some of it is memorable.

No trip to Las Vegas is complete without trying one or two buffets. Of the dozens, the most noteworthy are described here. Mind you, almost all buffets have some things in common. Unless otherwise noted, every one listed here has at least one carving station, a salad bar (quality differs), and hot main courses and side dishes. We will try to point out only when a buffet has something original or notable.

Note: Buffet meals are extremely popular, and reservations are usually not taken (we've indicated when they are accepted, and in all those cases, they are highly recommended). Arrive early (before opening) or late to avoid a long line, especially on weekends.

SOUTH STRIP
MODERATE

Aladdin's Spice Market Buffet 𝕲 BUFFET   This is a particularly good buffet that's gaining in popularity, though it's not perhaps quite good enough to justify the price. Come for lunch, as a more affordable compromise, and you can take advantage of the better-than-average salads (on our last visit they had one with white balsamic vinegar that was quite good), plus an especially notable Mexican station, Middle Eastern specialties, and other fun goodies. Of course, once the whole Planet Hollywood revamp kicks in, expect this all to change accordingly. Burger bars, anyone?

In the Aladdin, 3667 Las Vegas Blvd. South. 🕐 **702/785-9005.** Breakfast $12.99; lunch $15.99; dinner $22.99; champagne brunch $20.99. AE, DC, DISC, MC, V. Mon–Fri 8am–2:30pm and 4–9:30pm; Sat–Sun 8:30am–2:30pm and 4–9:30pm.

Mandalay Bay's Bay Side Buffet 𝕲 BUFFET   This is a particularly pretty, not overly large buffet. Actual windows—floor to ceiling, no less—overlooking the beach part of the elaborate pool area, make it less stuffy and eliminate that closed-in feeling that so many of the other buffets in town have. The buffet itself is adequately arranged but features nothing particularly special, though there are some nice cold salads, hearty meats, and a larger and better-than-average dessert bar (they make their own desserts, and it shows).

In Mandalay Bay, 3950 Las Vegas Blvd. South. 🕐 **702/632-7402.** Breakfast $12.25; lunch $14.75; dinner $21.75; Sun brunch $21.75. AE, DC, DISC, MC, V. Daily 7am–10pm.

MGM Grand Buffet 𝕲 BUFFET   This rather average buffet does feature a fresh Belgian waffle station at breakfast. Dinner also has all-you-can-eat shrimp and an all-you-can-eat shrimp and prime-rib option. Also available: low-fat, sugar-free desserts! And at all meals, you get a full pot of coffee on your table.

In MGM Grand, 3799 Las Vegas Blvd. South. ✆ **702/891-7777**. Breakfast $11.99; lunch $14.99; Mon–Thurs dinner $21.99; Fri–Sat dinner $24.99; brunch $16.99; reduced prices for children under 10, free for children under 4. AE, DC, DISC, MC, V. Mon–Thurs 7am–10pm; Fri 7am–10:30pm; Sat–Sun 10am–2:30pm and 4:30–10:30pm.

INEXPENSIVE

Excalibur's Roundtable Buffet 🍴 BUFFET   This one strikes the perfect balance of cheap prices, forgettable decor, and adequate food. It's what you want in a cheap Vegas buffet. But they don't always have mashed potatoes or macaroni salad, which are essential for an archetypal buffet. The plates are large, so you don't have to make as many trips to the buffet tables.

In Excalibur, 3850 Las Vegas Blvd. South. ✆ **702/597-7777**. Breakfast $9.99; lunch $10.99; dinner $14.49; Sun champagne brunch $12.99. AE, DC, DISC, MC, V. Sun–Thurs 6:30am–10pm; Fri–Sat 6:30am–11pm.

Luxor's Pharaoh's Pheast Buffet 🍴🍴 BUFFET   Located on the lower level, where the Luxor showroom used to be, this huge buffet looks like it was set in the middle of an archaeological dig, complete with wood braces holding up the ceiling, pot shards, papyrus, and servers dressed in khaki dig outfits. It's a unique and fun decor, but be sure to avoid tripping on the mummies and their sarcophagi sticking half up out of the ground. The food is better than that at most cheap buffets. It features a Mexican station with some genuinely spicy food, a Chinese stir-fry station, and different Italian pastas. Desserts are disappointing, though there are plenty of low-fat and sugar-free options. A beer and wine cart makes the rounds. Word has probably gotten out about this buffet, unfortunately, because the lines are always enormous.

In Luxor, 3900 Las Vegas Blvd. South. ✆ **702/262-4000**. Breakfast $9.99; lunch $10.49; dinner $16.49. AE, DC, DISC, MC, V. Daily 6:30am–11pm.

Monte Carlo's Buffet 🍴 BUFFET   A "courtyard" under a painted sky, the Monte Carlo's buffet room has a Moroccan market theme, with murals of Arab scenes, Moorish archways, Oriental carpets, and walls hung with photographs of and artifacts from Morocco. Dinner includes a rotisserie (for chicken and pork loin, or London broil), a Chinese food station, a taco/fajita bar, a baked potato bar, numerous salads, and more than a dozen desserts, plus frozen yogurt and ice-cream machines. Lunches are similar. At breakfast, the expected fare is supplemented by an omelet station, and choices include crepes, blintzes, and corned beef hash. Fresh-baked New York–style bagels are a plus.

3770 Las Vegas Blvd. South. (𝄐 **702/730-7777.** Breakfast $9.99; lunch $10.49; dinner $14.49; Sun brunch $15.95. AE, DC, DISC, MC, V. Daily 7am–10pm.

MID-STRIP
VERY EXPENSIVE

Bally's Sterling Sunday Brunch 🕸🕸 BUFFET   Now, the admittedly high cost of this brunch seems antithetical to the original purpose of a buffet, which is a lot of food for minimal money. If you're a dedicated buffet fan, however, this is probably a better spree than one of the many new high-priced restaurants. It works out to less money in the long run, and you will get, for your purposes, more bang for your buck. It's a fancy deal—linen- and silver-bedecked tables, waiters to assist you, if you choose—and while the variety of food isn't as massive as at regular buffets, the quality is much higher in terms of both content and execution. We're talking unlimited champagne, broiled lobster, caviar, sushi, and rotating dishes of the day (items such as monkfish with pomegranate essence, tenderloin wrapped in porcini mushroom mousse, and even ostrich). No French toast that's been sitting out for days here! Perfect for a wedding breakfast, business brunch, or just a big treat; stay a long time and eat as much as you can.

In Bally's Las Vegas, 3645 Las Vegas Blvd. South. (𝄐 **702/739-4111.** Reservations recommended. Brunch $58. AE, DC, MC, V. Sun 9:30am–2:30pm.

EXPENSIVE

Bellagio's Buffet 🕸🕸 BUFFET   Pricier than its counterpart over at The Mirage, Bellagio's buffet gets comparably higher marks. The array of foods is fabulous, with one ethnic cuisine after another (Japanese, Chinese that includes unexpected buffet fare like dim sum, build-it-yourself Mexican items, and so on). There are elaborate pastas and semitraditional Italian-style pizza from a wood-fired oven. The cold fish appetizers at each end of the line are not to be missed— scallops, smoked salmon, crab claws, shrimp, oysters, and assorted condiments. Specialties include breast of duck and game hens. There is no carving station, but you can get the meat precarved. The salad bar is more ordinary, though prepared salads have some fine surprises, such as eggplant tofu and an exceptional Chinese chicken salad. Desserts, unfortunately, look better than they actually are.

In Bellagio, 3600 Las Vegas Blvd. South. (𝄐 **888/987-6667.** Breakfast $13; lunch $16; dinner Sun–Thurs $25; dinner Fri–Sat $32; Sat–Sun brunch $22. AE, DC, DISC, MC, V. Sun–Thurs 8am–10pm; Fri–Sat 8am–11pm.

Paris Las Vegas's Le Village Buffet ★★★ BUFFET One of the more ambitious buffets, with a price hike to match—still, you do get, even at the higher-priced dinner, a fine assortment of food, and more value for the dollar than you are likely to find anywhere else (unless it's another buffet).

Plus, the Paris buffet is the most pleasing room of the buffet bunch. It's a Disneyland-esque two-thirds replica of your classic French village clichés; it's either a charming respite from Vegas lights or sickening, depending on your tolerance level for eye candy. Buffet stations are grouped according to French regions, and though in theory entrees change daily, there do seem to be some constants, including most of the following dishes. In Brittany, you find things like made-to-order crepes, surprisingly good roasted duck with green peppercorn and peaches, and steamed mussels with butter and shallots. In Normandy, there's quiche and some dry bay scallops with honey cider. The carving station shows up in Burgundy but distinguishes itself by adding options of chateaubriand sauce and cherry sauce Escoffier. Lamb stew is a possibility for Alsace, while Provence has pasta to order and a solidly good braised beef. The salad station isn't strong on flavors, but the veggies are fresh, and there is even some domestic (darn it) cheese.

You can largely skip the dessert station in favor of heading back to Brittany for some made-to-order crepes, but you might want to try the bananas foster.

In Paris Las Vegas, 3655 Las Vegas Blvd. South. ✆ 888/266-5687. Breakfast $12.95; lunch $17.95; dinner $24.95; Sun brunch $24.95. AE, DC, DISC, MC, V. Sun–Thurs 7am–10pm; Fri–Sat 7am–11pm.

MODERATE

Mirage's Cravings ★ BUFFET Newly remodeled so that it looks like a space-age cafeteria, this is both an ultramodern and a retro buffet, and as such it doesn't quite have any specific personality. You move through a line (you can jump ahead) past various stations—decent Chinese (fine potstickers and barbecue pork), Japanese (tepid), quite good wood-oven pizza, solid barbecue, basic daily hot entrees with extra grease, decent Mexican (including sweet but dry slow-roasted pork), a dessert bar with strawberry soup (or was it sauce? Either way, we liked it), a sandwich stop with salads that is easy to miss (and a made-to-order salad spot that is always backed up), and cookies worth smuggling out in your purse—none of which are as vastly sized as one has come to expect from Vegas buffets over the years. On one hand, this helps reduce the amount of waste these places are prone to; on the other, it feels stingy, not good at these new inflated prices. Seniors may have trouble reading the small signs, and small children are likely to get fretful before they get through. Sure is nifty looking, though.

In The Mirage, 3400 Las Vegas Blvd. South. ☏ 702/791-7111. Breakfast $12.50; lunch $17.50; dinner $22.50; Sun brunch $22.50. Reduced prices for children ages 5–10; free for children under 5. AE, DC, DISC, MC, V. Daily 7am–10pm.

Rio's Carnival World Buffet ⭐⭐ BUFFET This buffet has long been voted by locals as the best in town and just recently reopened after an extensive makeover. It's going to get mixed reactions. Quality-wise, it's probably as good as ever, and maybe even better. Decor-wise, it's better still, since the overhaul was devoted mostly to improving the dining areas. The bad news? It can no longer pretend to be inexpensive—it's right at the top of the "moderate" category. Consider this an upscale food court, with "South American" cooked-to-order stir-fries, Mexican taco fixings and accompaniments, Chinese fare, a Japanese sushi bar and teppanyaki grill, a Brazilian mixed grill, Italian pasta and antipasto, and fish and chips. There's even a diner setup for hot dogs, burgers, fries, and milkshakes. (Make your own milkshakes—is there a happier concept anywhere?) All this is in addition to the usual offerings of most Las Vegas buffets. Best of all, it has a brand new dessert station, featuring at least 70 kinds of pies, cakes, and pastries from an award-winning pastry chef.

In Rio All-Suite Hotel & Casino, 3700 W. Flamingo Rd. ☏ 702/252-7777. Breakfast $12.99; lunch $14.99; dinner $22.99; weekend brunch $22.99. AE, DC, MC, V. Daily 7am–10pm.

INEXPENSIVE

Palms Resort & Casino's Fantasy Market Buffet ⭐⭐ *Finds* BUFFET As a rule, you are better off fulfilling your buffet desires (unless they demand the cheapest of prices) at one of the newer hotels, and the Palms entry in the buffet sweepstakes bears this adage out. Not only does it look rather swell, but since the owners of the hotel are from a Middle Eastern background, that translates into some fresher concepts at the stations—most notably, an emphasis on Middle Eastern fare such as gyros with warm pita bread, hummus, babaganoush, and kabobs of every variety. Plus there's a huge Chinese station, complete with dumplings, a Mongolian barbecue section (where they toss all your chosen ingredients into one stir-fry vat), some Jewish foods (knishes and kugel), an ambitious carving station with ribs and pastrami, and desserts that, as usual, aren't much of anything. And actually, this comes as close as any to classic buffet budget prices while still supplying food that can be described as better than "merely edible."

In Palms Resort & Casino, 4321 W. Flamingo Rd. ℂ **702/942-7777.** Breakfast $5.99; lunch $6.99; dinner $11.99; Sun brunch $12.99. AE, DC, DISC, MC, V. Daily 8am–10pm.

DOWNTOWN
INEXPENSIVE

Golden Nugget's Buffet 🐾🐾 BUFFET   This buffet has often been voted number one in Las Vegas. Much of the seating is in plush booths. The buffet tables are also laden with an extensive salad bar (about 50 items), fresh fruit, and marvelous desserts, including the famous bread pudding made from the secret recipe of Zelma Wynn (Steve's mom). Every night, fresh seafood is featured. Most lavish is the all-day Sunday champagne brunch, which adds such dishes as eggs Benedict, blintzes, pancakes, creamed herring, and smoked fish with bagels and cream cheese.

In Golden Nugget, 129 E. Fremont St. ℂ **702/385-7111.** Breakfast $6.75; lunch $7.75; dinner $11.75; Sun brunch $12.75. AE, DC, DISC, MC, V. Daily 7am–10pm.

Main Street Station's Garden Court 🐾🐾🐾 *Finds* BUFFET   Set in what is truly one of the prettiest buffet spaces in town (and certainly in Downtown), with very high ceilings and tall windows bringing in much-needed natural light, the Main Street Station Garden Court buffet is one of the best in town, let alone Downtown. Featuring nine live-action stations (meaning you can watch your food being prepared), including a wood-fired, brick-oven pizza (delicious), many fresh salsas at the Mexican station, a barbecue rotisserie, fresh sausage at the carving station, Chinese, Hawaiian, and Southern specialties (soul food and the like), and so many more we lost count. On Friday night, they have all this plus nearly infinite varieties of seafood, all the way up to lobster. We ate ourselves into a stupor and didn't regret it.

In Main Street Station, 200 N. Main St. ℂ **702/387-1896.** Breakfast $5; lunch $8; dinner $11–$16; Sat–Sun champagne brunch $10; free for children 3 and under. AE, DC, DISC, MC, V. Daily 7am–10pm.

6

What to See & Do in Las Vegas

Need we tell you the primary activity in Las Vegas? Of course not. By now, you've certainly figured it out—if you were skeptical before you arrived, the slot machines waiting for you when you exited the plane into the airport erased any doubt.

But you won't lack for non-gambling activities in Vegas. The city isn't entirely happy when visitors aren't in the casinos, but it does acknowledge that not everyone (darn it) is going to gamble 24/7. A couple of the hotels have even conceded, for the time being, that some visitors may want a little culture along with their white tigers.

Your first order of business should be strolling the Strip, gaping at those impossible and impossibly large hotels, both during the day (when the hotels are less crowded) and at night (when the Strip is lit up in a garish display like nothing else in the country).

Don't forget to check out the **free hotel attractions,** such as Bellagio's water fountain ballet, The Mirage's volcano and white tiger exhibit, and the masquerade show at Rio.

You could also consider using a spa at a major hotel; they are too pricey (as high as $30 a day) to fill in for your daily gym visit, but spending a couple hours working out, sweating out Vegas toxins in the steam room, and generally pampering yourself will leave you feeling relaxed, refreshed, and ready to go all night again. Really treat yourself and get a massage or a facial.

There are also plenty of out-of-town sightseeing options, like **Hoover Dam** (a major tourist destination), **Red Rock Canyon,** and nexus-of-all-conspiracy-theories Area 51, along with excursions to the Grand Canyon. We've listed the best of these side trips in chapter 9, "Side Trips from Las Vegas."

SUGGESTED ITINERARIES

The itineraries outlined here are for adults. If you're traveling with kids, incorporate some of the suggestions in "Especially for Kids," listed later in this chapter. The activities mentioned briefly here are described more fully later in this chapter and in chapters 8 and 9.

If You Have 1 Day

Spend most of the day **casino-hopping.** These are buildings like no other (thank goodness). Each grandiose interior tops the last. Be sure to see The Venetian, Bellagio, The Mirage (including the white tigers), Treasure Island, Paris Las Vegas, Caesars Palace (including the Forum Shops and the talking statues), New York–New York, MGM Grand, Luxor, and Excalibur. Then at night, take a drive (if you can) down **the Strip** 𝕂𝕂𝕂. As amazing as all this is during the day, you can't believe it at night. Aside from just the Strip itself, there are **Bellagio's water fountains** 𝕂𝕂𝕂, which "perform" to various musical numbers, the **sirens-and-pirates battle at Treasure Island** (stupid and borderline vulgar now that it's turned into more of a showgirl piece than a stunt show), and the **volcano explosion** (no lava, just colored lights and smoke) next door, at The Mirage. Eat at a buffet (details in chapter 5), and have a drink at the top of the Stratosphere, goggling at the view from the tallest building west of the Mississippi.

If You Have 2 Days

Do more of the above since you may well have not covered it all. Then do something really Vegasy and visit the **Liberace Museum.** The **Dolphin Habitat at The Mirage** is also worth a look. At night, take in a show. We think *O* and *Mystère,* the productions from the avant-garde **Cirque du Soleil,** are the finest in Vegas, but there are plenty to choose from. Though buffets are still the most Vegas-appropriate food experience, genuine haute cuisine by celebrity chefs has invaded the town, and you should take advantage of it. **Alizé, Bouchon,** and **Fleur de Lys** are our top choices, but you can't go wrong with **Aureole, Picasso,** or **Andre's,** plus there are branches of Olives, Circo, Pinot Brasserie, and Border Grill. You might also head Downtown to the classic Glitter Gulch and the **Fremont Street Experience** light show.

If You Have 3 Days

By now you've spent 2 days gawking. So take a break and drive out to **Red Rock Canyon.** The panoramic 13-mile Scenic Loop Drive is best seen early in the morning, when there's little traffic. If you're so inclined, spend some time hiking here. If you want to spend the whole day out, have lunch at nearby **Bonnie Springs Ranch.** After lunch, enjoy a guided trail ride into the desert wilderness or enjoy the silliness at **Old Nevada** (see chapter 9 for details).

If You Have 4 Days

Plan a tour to **Hoover Dam.** Leave early in the morning, returning to Las Vegas after lunch via **Valley of Fire State Park,** stopping at the **Lost City Museum** in Overton en route (see chapter 9 for details). Alternatively, you can rest up by spending the day by the hotel pool or going to the hotel spa. At night, presumably refreshed and with toxins purged, eat some more and/or catch another show. If you aren't tired of magic, **Lance Burton** is a wonderful show for a reasonable price, or there is the arty weirdness of the **Blue Man Group** at the Luxor (moving to The Venetian in Oct 2005), or *Jubilee!* if your trip won't be complete without a topless revue. You can also feast at dinner since you certainly haven't tried all there is. If you want a good dinner with a great free show, go to Treasure Island's **Buccaneer Bay Club,** which overlooks the sirens-and-pirates battle.

1 The Top Attractions

See also the listings for theme parks and other fun stuff in "Especially for Kids," later in this chapter.

The Arts Factory ✸✸ *Finds*   Believe it or not, Las Vegas has a burgeoning art scene (what some would consider soul-crushing is what others consider inspirational), and this complex, located in the Gateway District, is the place to find proof. It features a few galleries and a number of workspaces for local artists. Several of the spaces are closed to the public.

101–109 E. Charleston Blvd. ✆ 702/676-1111. www.theartsfactory.com. Free admission. Mon–Tues and Thurs–Fri noon–5pm and by appointment.

The Auto Collections at the Imperial Palace ✸✸   Even if you're not a car person, don't assume you won't be interested in this premier collection of antique, classic, and special-interest vehicles. There's more here than just cars and trucks. Check out the graceful lines and handsome sculpture of one of the largest collections of Duesenbergs in the world. The craftsmanship and attention to detail make these cars, and others here, true works of art.

The vehicles on display change regularly, and some are occasionally sold, so there's no telling what you may see when you visit. Highlights include a 1964 Chaika that belonged to Soviet leader Nikita Krushchev, FDR's unrestored 1936 V-16 Cadillac, an ultrarare 1934 Ford Coupe, and a 1965 Rolls-Royce Silver Cloud III once owned—at different times—by both Debbie Reynolds and Lucille Ball.

In the Imperial Palace Hotel, 3535 Las Vegas Blvd. South. ✆ **702/794-3174.** www.autocollections.com. Admission $7 adults, $3 seniors and children under 12,

Las Vegas Attractions

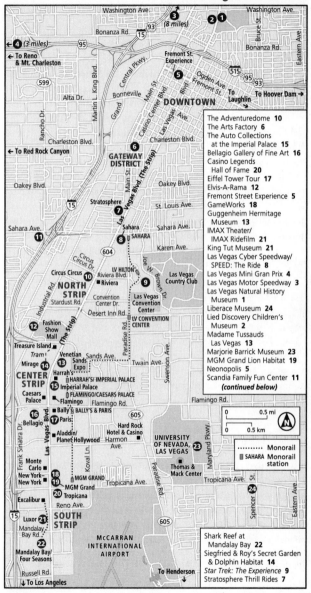

The Adventuredome **10**
The Arts Factory **6**
The Auto Collections
  at the Imperial Palace **15**
Bellagio Gallery of Fine Art **16**
Casino Legends
  Hall of Fame **20**
Eiffel Tower Tour **17**
Elvis-A-Rama **12**
Fremont Street Experience **5**
GameWorks **18**
Guggenheim Hermitage
  Museum **13**
IMAX Theater/
  IMAX Ridefilm **21**
King Tut Museum **21**
Las Vegas Cyber Speedway/
  SPEED: The Ride **8**
Las Vegas Mini Gran Prix **4**
Las Vegas Motor Speedway **3**
Las Vegas Natural History
  Museum **1**
Liberace Museum **24**
Lied Discovery Children's
  Museum **2**
Madame Tussauds
  Las Vegas **13**
Marjorie Barrick Museum **23**
MGM Grand Lion Habitat **19**
Neonopolis **5**
Scandia Family Fun Center **11**
(continued below)

·········· Monorail
▌ SAHARA Monorail
  station

Shark Reef at
  Mandalay Bay **22**
Siegfried & Roy's Secret Garden
  & Dolphin Habitat **14**
Star Trek: The Experience **9**
Stratosphere Thrill Rides **7**

free for children under 4 and AAA members. Daily 9:30am–9:30pm. Check website for free admission coupon.

Bellagio Gallery of Fine Art 𝕲

No one was more surprised than we were when then-Bellagio owner Steve Wynn opened up an art gallery—and people came to see the art. We were surprised again after Wynn's departure when not only did the gallery stay open, with traveling exhibits in place of Wynn's own collection, but that the popularity stayed high. Indeed, when the gallery hosted a show by Steve Martin (yes, that one), a long-time modern art collector, the show was reviewed in none other than *Time* magazine. In other words, this is serious, and for real.

Now, will there be as interesting a show up when you go? Beats us. Then there's that ticket price: Let us point out that the Louvre and the Vatican art collections, both of which are, needless to say, quite a bit larger and both of which, one can safely say, have some notable works, cost around $9.

In Bellagio, 3600 Las Vegas Blvd. South. ✆ **702/693-7871.** Reservations recommended, but walk-ins taken every 15 min. Admission $15 adults, $12 seniors over 65, students with ID, and Nevada residents. Daily 9am–9pm.

Casino Legends Hall of Fame 𝕲 *(Finds)*

Yeah, yeah, you aren't here to gamble, but nonetheless, with more than 150,000 items (the largest collection of its kind in the world) of not just gaming memorabilia but also bits and bobs of genuine Las Vegas history (including old photos that show just how extraordinary the town's explosion has been), it's well worth the time and small admissions charge (though you can sometimes avoid even that, courtesy of the hotel's free slot pull area, and local magazines, both of which often offer free passes).

In the Tropicana, 3801 Las Vegas Blvd. South. ✆ **702/739-5444.** Admission $7 adults, $6 seniors; must be 18 to enter. Daily 9am–9pm.

Eiffel Tower Tour *(Overrated)*

It's a view. From the top (more or less) of a half-size replica of the Pride of Paris. With an elevator operator giving you facts about the structure (a half-size replica, did we mention that?) during the few seconds it takes to ride to the top. If you like views, it might be worth the money.

In Paris Las Vegas, 3655 Las Vegas Blvd. South. ✆ **702/946-7000.** Admission $9 for adults Mon–Thurs, $12 Fri–Sun; $7 for seniors over 65 and children 6–12 Mon–Thurs, $10 Fri–Sun; free for children under 5. Daily 10am–1am, weather permitting.

Elvis-A-Rama 𝕲

Now, we wish we could say this rivals the Liberace Museum, and certainly, it oughta—it's *Elvis,* for pity's sake—

but it doesn't. Sure, the amount of Elvis-bilia is impressive, if largely litter (his Social Security card, his little black book, a love letter to his hometown girlfriend, even his Army uniform), all displayed about the same way holy relics are in European churches, which is to say, reverently and with insufficient information. King fans can't miss it; the rest of you might be able to.

3401 Industrial Rd. ✆ **702/309-7200.** www.elvisarama.com. Admission $10 adults; $8 seniors, students with ID, and Nevada residents; free for children under 12. Daily 10am–6pm. Call for free shuttle bus.

Fremont Street Experience ✿✿ It's so good that the city spent the money to turn the dying Downtown area into essentially a pedestrian mall, covered for 5 blocks by a light canopy (that presents, four times nightly, the **Sky Parade,** a light show complete with music). There still isn't much to do down here after you've stopped looking up overhead other than gamble. Still, the light thing is just cool, especially now that it's gotten an expensive, state-of-the-art LED makeover, and when watchers break out into dance beneath it. Not only does the canopy provide shade, it cools the area through a misting system in summer and warms you with radiant heaters in winter. The neighborhood is pretty safe, friendlier than the Strip, and certainly less crowded. And if you need something else to do, **Neonopolis,** an open-air mall and movie theater complex, has opened at the corner of Fremont and the Strip (see listing later in this chapter).

And in a further effort to retain as much of classic Las Vegas as possible, the **Neon Museum** is installing vintage hotel and casino signs along the promenade. The first installation is the horse and rider from the old Hacienda, which presently rides the sky over the intersection of Fremont and Las Vegas Boulevard. Eventually, the Neon Museum hopes to have an indoor installation, a couple blocks from the Fremont Street Experience, to showcase some of the smaller signs it has collected. It's uncertain when it will open, but in the meantime, the Neon Graveyard is there, and it's amusing to see the (unlit, of course) old signs languishing away until they once again get lit up in their glittery glory.

Fremont St. (between Main St. and Las Vegas Blvd.), Downtown. www.vegas experience.com. Free admission. Shows nightly.

⎛*Tips* **Insider Info**

A good place to view the Sky Parade light show is from the balcony at Fitzgeralds Casino/Hotel.

GameWorks ★★ *Kids* Though it shows a need for some mainte-
nance here and there, this is the place for fun-loving families of teens
to come because it has such a range of activities, from rock climbing to
the most high tech of virtual reality games (what you would expect
when Steven Spielberg and Dreamworks get into the video game
arcade business?). Hunt dinosaurs in the *Jurassic Park* game, take
swings in a virtual reality batting cage, or just play classics ranging from
pool to Pac-Man. There is something for everyone, pretty much,
though none of it comes cheap. There are two routes to pricing. First
is the standard version, where $15 gets you $15 in game play, $20 gets
you $25, or $25 gets you $35. Alternately, you can purchase a block of
time ($20 for 1 hr., $25 for 2 hr., $27 for 3 hr., or if you get there at
opening or closing you get 2 hr. for $20), which goes on a debit card
that you then insert into the various machines to activate them. As it's
geared for people college age and up, children should probably be at
least 10 years old, unless part of their fun is playing with their folks.

In the Showcase Mall, 3785 Las Vegas Blvd. South. ☏ **702/432-4263.** www.
gameworks.com. Sun–Thurs 10am–midnight; Fri–Sat 10am–1am. Hours may vary.

Guggenheim Hermitage Museum ★★ We weren't kidding
about that whole art and culture thing being an unexpected smash in
Vegas. Or is it? The Guggenheim Hermitage Museum, along with
the now-defunct Guggenheim Las Vegas, attracted considerable press
and fanfare when they opened, but the Guggenheim Las Vegas went
bust in January 2003, and its sister is teetering on the brink as well.
If it's still around when you get to Las Vegas, the Guggenheim Hermitage does have something special to offer and is well worth your
attention. The museum shows off collections from the Guggenheim
New York and the State Hermitage Museum in St. Petersburg, Rus-
sia, and given that the latter rarely lets any of its collection leave the
country, this provides a rare opportunity to see some extraordinary
works. The exhibit here at press time is called "The Pursuit of Pleasure" (*so* Vegas), featuring works from Picasso, Rubens, Chagall,
Degas, Kandinsky, Klee, and many more high-powered names.

   Note: The cynic in us would like to think greed and not a cultural
backlash caused the Guggenheim Las Vegas's demise—tickets to
that museum cost more than those to the Louvre. Management
doesn't seem to agree with us: The Hermitage museum is still charging premium prices to view the collection.

In The Venetian, 3355 Las Vegas Blvd. South. ☏ **866/484-4849.** www.guggenheim
lasvegas.org. Admission $15 adults, $12 seniors and Nevada residents, $11 stu-
dents with ID, $7 children 6–12, free for children under 6. Daily 9:30am–8:30pm.

IMAX Theater/IMAX Ridefilm 🎯 *Kids*   Luxor has a state-of-the-art IMAX theater that projects films on a seven-story screen. There are two different films running: one in standard two dimensions, the other 3-D. The glasses for the latter are really cool headsets (though they are a little heavy) that include built-in speakers, bringing certain sounds right into your head. The movies change periodically but always include some extraordinary special effects. If you have a fear of heights, make sure to ask for a seat on one of the lower levels.

In Search of the Obelisk is one of three IMAX Ridefilms; it is a motion-simulator ride in which technology is used to create an action adventure involving a chase sequence inside a pyramid. In a thrill ride through the temple's maze, you'll experience an explosive battle with evil forces, rescue Carina from the clutches of Dr. Osiris, and narrowly escape death before returning to the surface. You have an option to take a different route if you have motion sickness, which means you won't get the best special effects. Otherwise, it's a standard thrill ride with interesting touches.

In Luxor Las Vegas, 3900 Las Vegas Blvd. South. 📞 **702/262-4629.** Admission $9 for IMAX 2-D, $10 for 3-D, $7.50 for IMAX Ridefilms. Prices may vary, depending on the movie. Can be purchased as part of an all-attractions package for $25. Daily 9am–11pm. IMAX show times vary, depending on the length of the film.

King Tut Museum 🎯   After making such a fuss over the presence of real live art in town, we feel a tad embarrassed endorsing a mere replica—but can we say it's a really good copy? A full-scale simulation of King Tutankhamen's tomb, all the rooms, all the "things, marvelous things" discovered by archaeologists Howard Carter and Lord Carnarvon in the Valley of Kings at Luxor in 1922. The reproductions were all handcrafted in Egypt by artisans using historically correct gold leaf and linens, pigments, tools, and ancient methods, and all items have been meticulously positioned according to Carter's records. It's hardly like seeing the real thing, but if you aren't going to Egypt any time soon, perhaps checking out a meticulously detailed mock-up isn't a bad idea—and for a Vegas fake, it's surprisingly enjoyable. A 4-minute introductory film precedes a 15-minute self-guided audio tour (available in English, French, Spanish, and Japanese).

In Luxor Las Vegas, 3900 Las Vegas Blvd. South. 📞 **702/262-4000.** Admission $5. Daily 9am–11pm.

Las Vegas Cyber Speedway/SPEED: The Ride 🎯🎯   Auto racing is the fastest-growing spectator sport in America, so this is a popular stop. The first part of this attraction is an 8-minute virtual-reality ride, Cyber Speedway, featuring a three-quarter-size replica of a NASCAR race car. Hop aboard for an animated, simulated ride—either at the Las Vegas Motor Speedway or a race around the streets of Las Vegas (starting with the Strip, with all the hotels flashing by, and then going through the Forum Shops—whoops! there goes Versace!—and so forth). Press the gas, and you lean back and feel the rush of speed; hit a bump, and you go flying. Should your car get in a crash, off you go to a pit stop. At the end, a computer-generated report tells you your average speed, how many laps you made, how you did racing against the others next to you, and so forth. It's a pretty remarkable experience.

In a separate 3-D motion theater, you'll don goggles to view a film that puts you right inside another race car for yet another stomach-churning ride (even more dizzying than the virtual-reality portion). SPEED: The Ride is a roller coaster that blasts riders out through a hole in the wall by the new NASCAR Cafe, then through a loop, under the sidewalk, through the hotel's marquee, and finally straight up a 250-foot tower. At the peak, you feel a moment of weightlessness, and then you do the whole thing backward! Not for the faint of heart.

In Sahara Hotel & Casino, 2535 Las Vegas Blvd. South. ✆ **702/737-2111.** Cyber Speedway $10 (you must be at least 48 in. tall to ride), 3-D simulator $5, SPEED: The Ride (roller coaster) $10. Multiple-ride, all-day, and combination packages also available. Daily 10am–10pm (but closing hour may vary).

Las Vegas Mini Gran Prix ✵✵✵ (Kids)   Here's an absolute gem of a family fun center, featuring a good-size and well-stocked arcade (both current video and classic arcade games), a mini-roller coaster, a giant slide, and, best of all, four go-cart tracks. The latter features not just basic whizzing around a circle, but a track where drivers can time themselves through a twisting course that, in your head, takes on whatever race fantasy you have—Formula One or chasin' after bad guys in the General Lee, whatever. The facility is well maintained by the family owners/operators, and it features a genuinely good snack stand, including pizzas bigger and better than what you will find in your hotel, which just adds to the pleasures of this as an outing. It's also affordable, assuming that you have your own car, because otherwise it's a costly cab ride from the Strip.

1401 N. Rainbow Blvd. (just off U.S. 95 N.). ✆ **702/259-7000.** www.lvmgp.com. Tickets $5.50, 5 for $25 (each attraction costs either 1 or ½ ticket). Hours seasonal, call ahead.

Las Vegas Motor Speedway ✵✵   This 107,000-seat facility was the first new super-speedway to be built in the Southwest in over 2 decades. A $100-million state-of-the-art motor-sports enter-tainment complex, it includes a 1½-mile super-speedway, a 2½-mile FIA-approved road course, paved and dirt short-track ovals, and a 4,000-foot drag strip. Also on the property are facilities for Go-Kart, Legends Car, Sand Drag, and Motocross competitions. The speed-way is accessible via shuttle buses to and from the Imperial Palace, and some of the other major hotels have their own shuttles as well.

7000 Las Vegas Blvd. North, directly across from Nellis Air Force Base (take I-15 north to exit 54). ✆ **800/644-4444** or 702/644-4443. www.lvms.com. Tickets $10–$75 (higher prices for major events).

Liberace Museum ✿✿✿ *Moments*   Culture, schmulture. You can keep your Louvres and Vaticans and Smithsonians; *this* is a museum. Housed, like everything else in Vegas, in a strip mall, this is a shrine to the glory and excess that was the art project known as Liberace. You've got your costumes (bejeweled), your many cars (bejeweled), your many pianos (bejeweled), and many jewels (also bejeweled). It's a testament to what can be bought with lots of money and no taste.

This is a one-of-a-kind place. Unless you have a severely under-developed appreciation for camp or take your museum-going very seriously, you shouldn't miss it. And you probably won't, given a renovation that added an entrance shaped like a giant rhinestone topped with a giant pink piano. The museum is 2½ miles east of the Strip, on your right.

1775 E. Tropicana Ave. (at Spencer St.). ✆ **702/798-5595.** www.liberace.org. Admission $12 adults, $8 seniors over 65 and students ages 6 and up, free for chil-dren under 6. Mon–Sat 10am–5pm; Sun 12–4pm. Call ✆ **702/335-3530** for free shuttle bus.

Madame Tussauds Las Vegas ✿ *Kids*   Madame Tussauds wax-works exhibition has been the top London attraction for nearly 2 centuries, so even if you aren't a fan of wax museums, this, its sole branch west of the Mississippi, may be worth a stop—if you can stomach the price. We, frankly, cannot. Figures here are state-of-the-art, painstakingly constructed to perfectly match the original person. (Truth be told, though some are nearly identical to their living counterparts—Brad Pitt gave us a start—others look about as much like the celebrity in question as a department store mannequin.) There's no Chamber of Horrors here, but the exhibit makes up for it since all the waxworks are free-standing, allowing, and indeed encouraging, guests to get up close and personal.

In The Venetian, 3355 Las Vegas Blvd. South. ✆ **702/862-7800.** www.madame tussaudslv.com. Admission $21 adults; $15 seniors, students with ID, and Nevada

When Temptation Strikes

You are not a gambler. You are not interested in wagering or betting of any sort. We can respect that. We can also respect the effects the bells and whistles of the ubiquitous slot machines (they'll greet you at the airport, for heaven's sake!) and the cries of victory from the casino floor may have on even the most rabid non-gamblers. After all, we watched just such a person transform before our very eyes this summer when she discovered craps on her first trip to Vegas. By the end of her vacation, she was tossing the dice with the best of them.

So, should the siren song of the casinos lure you to take part in the primary sin of Sin City, we offer the following advice to help you avoid losing your halo, wings, and—most important—your wallet:

1. **Go back to school.** Many of the casino hotels offer free gambling lessons (ask a dealer to find out if lessons are offered in a particular casino) to those interested in the major table games. If you're merely curious instead of highly interested, these will more than satisfy your casino cravings. Not only won't you lose money, but you'll probably have some fun, too. And if the lesson proves instructive, some casinos offer low-stakes games following their gambling lessons, so your indulgence won't prove as costly. Note that most lessons are given on weekdays, so if you're in town for the weekend, you'll be out of luck.

residents; $10 children 6–12; free for children under 6; $55 for a family. Daily 10am–10pm.

Marjorie Barrick Museum ✪   Formerly known as the Natural History Museum (as opposed to the Las Vegas Natural History Museum, which still exists—and now you can see why they changed the name), this is a cool place to beat the heat and noise of Vegas while examining some attractive, if not overly imaginative, displays on Native American craftwork and Las Vegas history. Crafts include 19th-century Mexican religious folk art, a variety of colorful dance masks from Mexico, and Native American pottery. The first part of the hall is often the highlight, with impressive traveling art exhibits.

2. **Daylight is your friend.** Unless you decide to try your luck at the slot machines, stick to playing during mornings and afternoons, when table limits (the minimum bet you must make) will be lower than they are at night. The excitement level may not be as high, but neither will the risk. The same advice holds for weekdays—Las Vegas is busiest on weekends, and the price of playing rises accordingly.

3. **Find a friendly table.** Gambling is supposed to be fun. If you're not having any (and not just because you're losing—that's just plain old probability in action) then you're in the wrong place. If a dealer is being surly, a casino is too smoky or too crowded, or the players at your table rub you the wrong way, go someplace else or go back to your non-gambling ways.

4. **Gamble by proxy.** If your personal risk quotient is zero, there is perhaps no bigger thrill in Vegas than to watch others gamble their own fortunes. Watching the games on the floor costs nothing and is a lot more entertaining than you might think. We've seen people risk hundreds of thousands of dollars on a single role of the dice and guarantee you that gambling is a lot more fun when it's somebody else's bank account on the line. And watching them lose it all will have you congratulating yourself that you resisted the temptation to toy with Lady Luck.

Children won't find much that's entertaining, other than some glass cases containing examples of local, usually poisonous, reptiles (who, if you are lucky—or unlucky, depending on your view—will be dining on mice when you drop by).

On the UNLV campus, 4505 Maryland Pkwy. © **702/895-3381.** http://hrcweb. nevada.edu/Museum. Free admission. Mon–Fri 8am–4:45pm; Sat 10am–2pm.

MGM Grand Lion Habitat 🐾🐾 (Kids) Hit this attraction at the right time, and it's one of the best freebies in town. It's a large, multilevel glass enclosure, in which various lions frolic during various times of day. In addition to regular viewing spots, you can walk through a glass tunnel and get a worm's-eye view of the underside of a lion. Multiple lions share show duties (about 6 hr. on and then 2 days off at a ranch for some free-range activity, so they're never cooped up here for long). So you could see any combo from one giant male to a pack of five females who have grown from cub to near adult size during their MGM time.

In MGM Grand, 3799 Las Vegas Blvd. South. *©* **702/891-7777.** Free admission. Daily 11am–10pm.

Neonopolis 🍅 Yet another earnest attempt to revitalize the Downtown area, this one is aimed squarely at locals. But you should join them, especially if your party includes teens, or if your own evening plans don't immediately include more adult pursuits. Which is not to say that this is kiddieland—it's a large mall complex, the center of which is an entertainment facility anchored by Jillian's, the force behind similar setups in parts of the country ranging from Raleigh to San Francisco. In addition to a large game room (everything from motion ride simulators to Skee Ball), there is a terrific retro bowling alley, a pool hall, a surprisingly good and varied cafe for the nachos and sports on TV crowd, and a 14-screen movie theater.

450 Fremont St. *©* **702/759-0450.** www.neonopolis.com. Sun–Thurs 11am–9am; Fri–Sat 11am–10pm.

Shark Reef at Mandalay Bay *Overrated* It's just a big aquarium, and mind you, we love big aquariums, so our only beef (or is that fish?) against this exhibit is the price. (Though standing in the all-glass tunnel, surrounded by sharks and finny friends, is kinda cool.) Note also that it is waaay off in a remote part of Mandalay Bay, which might be a hassle for those with mobility problems.

In Mandalay Bay, 3950 Las Vegas Blvd. South. *©* **702/632-4555.** Admission $16 adults, $10 children 5–12, free for children under 5. Daily 10am–11pm.

Siegfried & Roy's Secret Garden & Dolphin Habitat *Kids* Not to be confused with the free white tiger exhibit (which is small and usually features only one tiger at a time), the **Secret Garden** 🍅🍅 is a larger (though not zoo-size) display of several of S&R's feline friends, plus an elephant or two. It's surprisingly charming, full of foliage and close-up views of some very large cats. Zoo purists shouldn't fret; these are just the daytime digs for these animals, who spend their nights in great, and often entirely unfettered, luxury, over at their owners' home. It's a little weird of a vibe, given the abrupt end to the animals'—to say nothing of their owners'—performing careers, but it's still a pleasant diversion.

The **Dolphin Habitat** ☆☆☆ is even more satisfying than the Secret Garden—maybe the most fun thing to do in all of Vegas. It was designed to provide a healthy and nurturing environment and to educate the public about marine mammals and their role in the ecosystem. Specialists worldwide were consulted in creating the habitat, which was designed to serve as a model of a quality, secured environment. It must be working because the adult dolphins here are breeding regularly. The Mirage displays only dolphins already in captivity—no dolphins are taken from the wild. You can watch the dolphins frolic both above and below ground through viewing windows, in three different pools. (There is nothing quite like the kick you get from seeing a baby dolphin play.) The knowledgeable staff, who surely have the best jobs in Vegas, will answer questions and frequently play with the dolphins to help stimulate them. If you are lucky, you can toss a ball to a dolphin, who will knock it back to you with its snout, and if you do anything cooler than that during your trip, we'd like to hear about it. There is also a video of a resident dolphin (Duchess) giving birth (to Squirt) underwater. You can stay as long as you like, which might just be hours.

In The Mirage, 3400 Las Vegas Blvd. South. ✆ 702/791-7111. Admission $12, free for children under 10 if accompanied by an adult, $6 Wed (when only the Dolphin Habitat is open). Secret Garden Mon–Tues and Thurs–Fri 11am–5pm; Sat–Sun 10am–5pm. Dolphin Habitat Mon–Fri 11am–7pm; Sat–Sun 10am–7pm. Hours subject to change and vary by season.

Star Trek: The Experience ☆ This is the best motion-simulator ride in Vegas. It goes without saying that hardcore Trekkers (note use of correct term) will be delighted. On the other hand, normal, sensible fans and those who couldn't care less about *Star Trek* may find themselves saying, "I spent $35 for this?"

There is a story line, but we won't spoil it for you. Suffice to say that it involves time travel and evil doings by the Borg, and if all doesn't work out, the very history of *Star Trek* could be affected. And there is an additional *Borg: 4-D Adventure*. If the words "Picard" and "Borg" don't mean anything to you, neither will this attraction. Do expect to be beamed aboard the *Enterprise* (that's really kind of cool), and know that if you have a sensitive stomach, you can skip the actual motion-simulator part, a wild and sometimes headache-inducing chase through space. The ridiculously high-priced pass is good for all-day rerides. The quality of your experience can vary depending on the quality of those Trek-garbed actors, whose line delivery can be awfully stilted. On the way out, through the shops selling everything Trek- and space-related, don't miss the TV showing a "news report" about some of the very things you just experienced.

In Las Vegas Hilton, 3000 Paradise Rd. © **888/GO-BOLDLY.** www.startrekexp.com. Admission $35 adults, $32 children under 12 and seniors, includes unlimited all-day access to museum and both "experiences." Sun–Thurs 11am–10pm; Fri–Sat 11am–11pm.

Stratosphere Thrill Rides *Kids* You won't get this kind of a thrill-ride experience anywhere else. You also will never, ever see us on any of it. Atop the 1,149-foot Stratosphere Tower, the **Let It Ride High Roller** (the world's highest roller coaster) has been revamped to go at even faster speeds, as it zooms around a hilly track that is seemingly suspended in midair. Even more "fun" is the **Big Shot,** a breathtaking free-fall ride that thrusts you 160 feet in the air along a 228-foot spire at the top of the Tower, then plummets back down again. Sitting in an open car, you seem to be dangling in space over Las Vegas. We have one relative, a thrill-ride enthusiast, who said he never felt more scared than when he rode the Big Shot. And then there is the **X-Scream,** a giant teeter-totter, that plunges one end over the edge of the Strat—you know, so you feel like you are plunging to the Strip, 1,149 feet below. There are so many languages we can say "no" in, and when we aren't using them on that ride, we will be saving them for 2005's upcoming **Insanity: The Ride,** which will dangle hapless victims—er, riders—from a giant arm, out over the edge of the Strat, spinning them around in a whirlygig contraption. *Nein, nyet, non!* But don't let our scaredy-cat attitude stop you. *Note:* The rides are shut down during inclement weather and high winds.

Atop Stratosphere Casino Hotel & Tower, 2000 Las Vegas Blvd. South. © **702/ 380-7777.** Tower admission $9; $6 for Nevada residents, seniors, Stratosphere hotel guests, and children 4–12; free for children under 4. X-Scream $8, Big Shot $8, High Roller $4. Multiride packages also available for varying costs. Minimum height requirement for both rides is 48 in. Sun–Thurs 10am–midnight; Fri–Sat 10am–1am. Hours vary seasonally.

2 Getting Married

Getting married is one of the most popular things to do in Las Vegas. Why? It's very easy to get married here. Too easy. See that total stranger standing next to you? Grab him or her, and head down to the **Clark Country Marriage License Bureau,** 200 S. 3rd St., at Briger Avenue (© **702/455-3156;** open Mon–Sun 8am–midnight, 24 hr. legal holidays), to get your license. Find a wedding chapel (not hard, as there are about 50 of them in town; they line the north end of the Strip, and most hotels have them), and tie the knot. Just like that. No blood test, no waiting period—heck, not even an awkward dating period. Ah, c'mon. If we've learned anything from the impetuous actions of Britney Spears and Nicki Hilton, it's that annulments are almost as easy as weddings!

But even if you have actually known your intended for some time, Las Vegas is a great place to get married. The ease is the primary attraction, but there are a number of other appealing reasons. You can have any kind of wedding you want, from a big, traditional production number to a small, intimate affair; from a spur-of-the-moment "just-the-happy-couple-in-blue-jeans" kind of thing to an Elvis-in-a-pink-Cadillac-at-a-drive-through-window kind of thing. (Oh, yes. More on that later.) The wedding chapels take care of everything; usually they'll even provide a limo to take you to the license bureau and back. Most offer all the accessories, from rings to flowers, to a videotaped memory of the event.

We personally know several very happy couples who opted for the Vegas route. Motivations differed, with the ease factor heading the list (though the Vegasness of the whole thing came in a close second), but one and all reported having great fun. Really, is there a more romantic way to start off your life together than in gales of laughter?

In any event, the more than 100,000 couples who yearly take advantage of all this can't be wrong. If you want to follow in the footsteps of Elvis and Priscilla (at the original Aladdin hotel), Michael Jordan, Joan Collins, Bruce Willis and Demi Moore, and, of course, Dennis Rodman and Carmen Electra, you'll want to peruse the following list of the most notable wedding chapels on or near the Strip. There are many more in town, and almost all the major hotels offer chapels as well; though the latter are cleaner and less tacky than some of the Strip chapels, they do tend to be without any personality at all. (Two exceptions might be the chapel at the Excalibur Hotel, where you can dress in medieval costumes, and the lovely chapel at the Bellagio, which has personal wedding coordinators and a high level of customer service, holding only 8–10 weddings a day—seems like a lot, but it's nothing compared to the volume on the Strip.)

With regard to decor, there isn't a radical difference between the major places (hence, no star ratings here), though some are decidedly spiffier and less sad than others. Attitude certainly makes a difference with several and varies radically, depending on who's working at any given time. Given how important your wedding is—or should be—

we encourage you to give yourself time to comparison-shop, and spurn anyone who doesn't seem eager enough for your business.

You can also call **Las Vegas Weddings and Rooms** (© **800/488-MATE**), which offers one-stop-shopping for wedding services. They'll find a chapel or an outdoor garden that suits your taste (not to mention such only-in-Vegas venues as the former mansions of Elvis Presley and Liberace); book you into a hotel for the honeymoon; arrange the ceremony; and provide flowers, a photographer (or videographer), wedding cake, limo, car rental, music, champagne, balloons, and garter for the bride. Basically, they can arrange anything you like.

Weddings can be very cheap in Vegas: A license is about $55, and a basic service not much more. Even a full-blown shebang package—photos, music, some flowers, video, cake, and other doodads—will run only about $500 total. We haven't quoted any prices here, since the ultimate cost depends entirely on how much you want to spend. Go cheap, and the whole thing will put you back maybe $100, including the license (maybe even somewhat less); go elaborate, and the price is still reasonable by today's wedding price standards. Be sure to remember that there are often hidden charges, such as expected gratuities for the minister (about $25 would do; no real need to tip anyone else), and so forth. If you're penny-pinching, you'll want to keep those in mind.

Be aware that Valentine's Day is a very popular day to get married in Vegas. Some of the chapels perform as many as 80 services on February 14.

But remember, you also don't have to plan ahead. Just show up, get your paperwork, close your eyes, and pick a chapel. And above all, have fun. Good luck and best wishes to you both.

Chapel of the Bells   Sporting perhaps the largest and gaudiest sign on the Strip, this chapel also shares a parking lot with the bright pink Fun City Motel. We won't make any jokes. Kitschy on the outside, but nice kitsch on the inside. The chapel has white drapes behind the podium, a white piano, wood paneling, and icky green carpeting. It seats only about 25. They prefer advance booking but can do same-day ceremonies if called to.

2233 Las Vegas Blvd. South (at Sahara Ave.). © **800/233-2391** or 702/735-6803. www.vegas.com/weddings/chapelofthebells. Mon–Thurs 9am–9pm; Fri–Sat 9am–midnight. Open as late as needed on holidays.

Chapel of Love   This is a friendly place largely run by women (men take the photos and are the limo drivers), featuring four different chapels. The Divine Madness fantasy chapel has moved all its costumes (and quite a range it's got), and much of its gestalt, over here. Currently in place is the multitasking Gothic/Renaissance or (depending on how you tilt your head) Egyptian-themed chapel, with plans for a gangster-era room, and another with a jungle-heavy (think lots of plastic plants) room for Tarzan-themed ceremonies. The packages are quite reasonable, and all the "hidden" charges (such as suggested gratuities for the minister and so forth) are listed right in the brochure, so there are no surprises.

1431 Las Vegas Blvd. South (between E. Oakey and E. Charleston boulevards). © 800/922-5683 or 702/387-0155. www.chapelsoflove.com. Mon–Thurs 8am–10pm; Fri–Sat 8am–midnight; Sun 9am–9pm.

Cupid's Wedding Chapel   "The little chapel with the big heart." Well, it just might be. The manager explains that, unlike other chapels on the Strip, this one schedules weddings an hour apart to provide time for the full production number. The folks at Cupid's pride themselves on offering "a traditional church wedding at a chapel price." The chapel is pleasantly low-frills and down to earth, with white walls and pews, and modern stained glass with doves and roses. (Kitsch-phobes will be pleased to know the cupids are only in the lobby.) It seats 60 to 70. They have added two good-size reception rooms, one rather banquet-hall in style, the other more '50s diner in feel. And, yes, if they don't have something already scheduled, they will take walk-ups.

827 Las Vegas Blvd. South (between Gass and Hoover aves.). © 800/543-2933 or 702/598-4444. www.cupidswedding.com. Sun–Thurs 10am–10pm; Fri–Sat 10am–1am.

Graceland Wedding Chapel   Housed in a landmark building that's one of the oldest wedding chapels in Vegas, the Graceland bills itself as "the proverbial mom-and-pop outfit. We offer friendly, courteous service, and are willing to go that extra step." No, there's no Elvis connection (one of the owners was friends with Elvis and asked his permission to use the name). This is a tiny New England church building with a small bridge and white picket fence out front. Inside is a 33-seat chapel; the walls are burgundy and white, with a large, modern stained-glass window of doves and roses behind the pulpit. The pews are dark blond wood. It's not the nicest of the chapels, but Catherine Oxenberg and Caspar Van Diem got married here. Jon Bon Jovi and Lorenzo Lamas did also, though not to each other.

Note: If the King is important to you, you should know that there is an Elvis impersonator on-site who will do your ceremony—for the right price.

619 Las Vegas Blvd. South (at E. Bonneville Ave.). © **800/824-5732** or 702/382-0091. www.gracelandchapel.com. Sun–Thurs 9am–9pm; Fri–Sat 9am–midnight.

Little Chapel of the Flowers   This chapel's claim to fame is that Dennis Rodman and Carmen Electra exchanged their deathless vows here. Don't hold it against the place; this is the slickest operation on the Strip, a big complex that offers your best shot at a traditional wedding. The Heritage Chapel fits 65 and has a cutesy church feel, with wood pews and a ghastly brass chandelier. The Victorian chapel, which holds only 30, has white walls and dark-wood pews and doesn't look very Victorian at all—but as the plainest, it's also the nicest. The smallest is the Magnolia Chapel, full of artificial flowers and a freestanding archway. If you want an outdoor vow exchange, you might choose the gazebo by a running stream and waterfall that nearly drowns out Strip noise. The Heritage Chapel holds 70 and adds rose-colored drapes and electric candle chandeliers. There's also a medium-size reception room and live organ music upon request. It's a pretty, friendly place that seems to keep an eye on its bustling business. It does not allow rice or confetti throwing.

1717 Las Vegas Blvd. South (at E. Oakey Blvd.). © **800/843-2410** or 702/ 735-4331. www.littlechapel.com. Mon–Thurs 9am–10pm; Fri–Sat 9am–11pm.

Little White Chapel   This is arguably the most famous of the chapels on the Strip, maybe because blue-jean-clad Brit strolled down this aisle with What's His Name, maybe because it has the big sign saying Michael Jordan and Joan Collins were married there (again, not to each other), maybe because it was the first to do the drive-up window. It is indeed little and white. There is a factory-line atmosphere, however, as the place processes wedding after wedding after wedding, 24 hours a day. Move 'em in, and move 'em out. (No wonder they put in that drive-up window!) The staff are brusque, hasty, and can have a bit of an attitude (though we know one couple who got married here and had no complaints). Little White Chapel does offer full wedding ceremonies, complete with candle-light service and traditional music. There are two chapels, the larger of which—decorated with tulle and white fake flowers—is the nicest. There is also a gazebo for outdoor services, but since it's right on the Strip, it's not as nice as it sounds. If you want something special, there are probably better choices, but for a true Vegas wedding experience, this is Kitsch Wedding Central.

1301 Las Vegas Blvd. South (between E. Oakey and Charleston boulevards). © **800/ 545-8111** or 702/382-5943. www.alittlewhitechapel.com. Daily 24 hr.

San Francisco Sally's Victorian Chapel (Finds) This is an extremely tiny wedding chapel, bursting at the seams with Victorian frills (fringed lamps, swags of lace curtains). It basically offers "an Olde Tyme Parlor Wedding." This is perfect if you want a very intimate wedding—like you, your intended, and someone to officiate. It literally can't hold more than six people. (And the space at the back of the room opens for an even tinier reception area—it can barely fit the cake!) But if you love Victoriana, or you want to play dress-up at your wedding, this is the place. The shop rents out

---

(Tips) **Photo Ops**

In a town full of nothing but Artificial Wonders of the World, camera shutters will be kept busy clicking. For those looking for Christmas card possibilities, gather your brood around the famous vintage **"Welcome to Las Vegas"** sign on the outskirts of town (or call up Jesse Garon, an Elvis impersonator, at ℂ **877/ELVIS-35**—or visit his website, at **www.elvis-vegas.com**—and see if you can pay him to pose in his pink Caddie along with you).

From there, you can choose among posing with the replica of Michelangelo's David or the talking animatronic statues at **The Forum Shops at Caesars Palace,** the talking animatronic camels at the Luxor, or the non-talking lions at the **MGM Grand Lion Habitat** (glass safely between you and Kitty, of course—you'll need a polarizing filter on your camera to capture them properly). More kitty critters can be found at The Mirage—again behind glass—at the **white tiger exhibit,** or behind bars at **Siegfried & Roy's Secret Garden.** Ask nicely, and maybe a trainer at the **Dolphin Habitat** will get a finny friend to leap behind you at just the right moment.

If beasties aren't your thing, you can stand with a gladiator back at **Caesars** or with one of the roaming Italian Renaissance dressed figures (Casanova, perhaps) at **The Venetian.** Confuse the folks at home and pose by the **Statue of Liberty** outside New York–New York (while the tug boats shoot water into the air), or really confuse them with shots of you amid the gorgeously arranged seasonal flora in **The Conservatory** at Bellagio.

dresses and costumes, so you can wear a Scarlett O'Hara antebellum outfit or some other period number for your big day. (It's all fantasy anyway, so why not go whole hog?) They specialize in extras without extra charges, such as altering and whatnot. The women who run it refer to themselves as "a bunch of mother hens"; they're delightful and will pamper you to within an inch of your life.

1304 Las Vegas Blvd. South (between E. Oakey and Charleston boulevards). ✆ **800/ 658-8677** or 702/385-7777. Mon–Thurs 10am–6pm; Fri–Sat 10am–8pm; Sun 10am–4pm.

Wee Kirk O' the Heather This is the oldest wedding chapel in Las Vegas (it's been here since 1940) and the one at the very end of the Strip, right before Downtown (and thus really close to the license bureau). It would be declared a historic landmark except that some renovations in the past moved just enough interior walls to alter it sufficiently to keep it from being official. A recent renovation has gussied it up nicely.

231 Las Vegas Blvd. South (between Bridger and Carson aves.). ✆ **800/843-5266** or 702/382-9830. www.weekirk.com. Daily 10am–midnight.

3 Especially for Kids

Like much of the rest of the world, you may be under the impression that Las Vegas has evolved from an adults-only fantasyland into a vacation destination suitable for the entire family. The only explanation for this myth is that Las Vegas was referred to as "Disneyland for adults" by so many and for so long that the town became momentarily confused and decided it actually *was* Disneyland. Some of the gargantuan hotels then spent small fortunes on redecorating in an attempt to lure families with vast quantities of junk food and a lot of hype. They now vehemently deny that any such notion ever crossed their collective minds, and, no, they don't know how that roller coaster got into the parking lot.

To put things simply, Las Vegas makes money—lots and lots of money—by promoting gambling, drinking, and sex. These are all fine pursuits if you happen to be an adult, but if you haven't reached the magical age of 21, you really don't count in this town. In any case, the casinos and even the Strip itself are simply too stimulating, noisy, and smoky for young kids.

Older progeny may have a tolerance for crowds and the incessant pinging of the slot machines, but they will be thoroughly annoyed with you when casino security chastises them if they so much as stop to tie their shoe laces anywhere near the gaming tables. Since you can't get from your hotel room to the parking lot without ambling through a casino, you can't reasonably expect a teenager to be in a good mood once you stagger outside. And those amusement parks and video halls that haven't yet been purged are expensive places to park your kids for an afternoon or evening, assuming that they are old enough to be left unsupervised. And it can be tough just going about your business on the Strip, what with the two-story-tall, thong-clad showgirl rear ends advertising *Jubilee!* and *Folies Bergere,* on the sides of Bally's and the Tropicana, respectively, to say nothing of the bare-breasted giantess on the prow of the pirate boat at the Strip entrance to TI. Or the guys handing out flyers for "escort" services and porn phone lines. Really, if you don't want to engage in any biology discussions with your progeny, you might want to keep them at home.

Nevertheless, you may have a perfectly legitimate reason for bringing your children to Las Vegas (like Grandma was busy, or you were just stopping off on your way from somewhere else), so here are some places to take the children both on and off the Strip.

Circus Circus (p. 64) has ongoing circus acts throughout the day, a vast video-game and pinball arcade, and dozens of carnival games on its mezzanine level. Behind the hotel is **The Adventuredome,** detailed below.

Excalibur (p. 41) also offers video and carnival games, plus thrill cinemas and free shows (jugglers, puppets, and so on).

At **Caesars Palace** (p. 45), animated talking statues in the **Forum Shops** are a kick, while kids should also be wowed by clamoring around inside the giant moving Trojan horse outside FAO Schwarz, exploring the shops, and marveling at the Atlantis fountain show.

Star Trek: The Experience (p. 119) deserves to draw families to the **Las Vegas Hilton,** but it may be a bit much for younger children.

The **battle** in front of **Treasure Island** (p. 107) is no longer G-rated, thanks to the addition of nekkid girls, so stick with the erupting volcano and **Siegfried & Roy's Secret Garden** and **Dolphin Habitat** at **The Mirage** (p. 46) and **Shark Reef at Mandalay Bay** (p. 36). Ditto the various attractions at **Luxor Las Vegas** (the IMAX Theater and IMAX Ridefilm, p. 113, and King Tut's Tomb) and **Las Vegas Cyber Speedway** (p. 113) at the **Sahara.**

Children 10 and up will love the many options for play (from high tech to low tech, from video wonders to actual physical activity) offered at **GameWorks** (p. 112), as will their parents.

Appropriate shows for kids include *Tournament of Kings* at Excalibur, *Lance Burton* at the Monte Carlo, and Cirque du Soleil's *Mystère* at Treasure Island. As a general rule, early shows are less racy than late-night shows. All these productions are reviewed in detail in chapter 8.

Beyond the city limits (see chapter 9 for details on all these) is **Bonnie Springs Ranch/Old Nevada,** with trail and stagecoach rides, a petting zoo, old-fashioned melodramas, stunt shootouts, a Nevada-themed wax museum, crafts demonstrations, and more. **Lake Mead** has great recreational facilities for family vacations. Finally, organized tours (see "Organized Tours," later in this chapter) to the Grand Canyon and other interesting sights in southern Nevada and neighboring states can be fun family activities. Check with your hotel's sightseeing desk. Kids would also be entertained by the personalized tours offered by **Creative Adventures** (✆ 702/361-5565); see p. 131.

Specifically kid-pleasing attractions are described below.

The Adventuredome ᏗᏗ *(Kids)*   This isn't a half-bad place to spend a hot afternoon, especially since Circus Circus, the casino

---

(Kids) Hotel Arcades

Virtually every hotel has some kind of video arcade—all the better to prep the under-21s for their upcoming gambling days, we say, because we are cynical (and also probably right). These vary considerably in size and quality. The top dog in town is the **Coney Island Emporium** (✆ 702/740-6969) at New York–New York, where video machines are joined by carney style, and kids can redeem tickets earned from wins for various cheap trinkets and stuffed animals. Both **Games of the Gods** at Luxor (✆ 702/262-4000) and the **Wizard's Arcade** at Excalibur (✆ 702/597-7700) have motion-simulator rides in or next to their arcades. And the Sahara's **Pit Pass Arcade** (✆ 702/734-7223) has additional racing-themed games, as the arcade is part of the NASCAR Cafe.

Note: Several arcades restrict the times those under 18 can play while unaccompanied by an adult. Call or stop in to check on policies if you plan to leave your kids in the arcade for a while.

hotel that built this indoor amusement park, is still more child-friendly than not. The glass dome that towers overhead lets in natural light, a solace to those of us who look peaked under the glow of the artificial kind. A double-loop roller coaster careens around the simulated Grand Canyon, and there's the requisite water flume, a laser tag area, and a modest number of other rides for kids of all ages. Video games and an arcade are separate from the attractions, cutting down just a tad on the noise level. Our only caveat is not to leave kids here alone; they could easily get lost.

2880 Las Vegas Blvd. South. (behind Circus Circus). ✆ 702/794-3939. www. adventuredome.com. Free admission; pay per ride $4–$6 or daily pass for $22 adults, $14 children 33–47 in. tall. AE, DC, DISC, MC, V. Park hours vary seasonally but usually Mon–Thurs 10am–6pm; Fri–Sat 10am–midnight; Sun 10am–8pm.

Las Vegas Natural History Museum ⋒ *Kids*   Conveniently located across the street from the Lied Discovery Children's Museum (described below), this humble temple of taxidermy harkens back to elementary school field trips around 1965, when stuffed elk and brown bears forever protecting their kill were as close as most of us got to exotic animals. Worn around the edges but very sweet and relaxed, the museum is enlivened by a hands-on activity room and two life-size dinosaurs that roar at one another intermittently. A small boy was observed leaping toward his dad upon watching this display, so you might want to warn any sensitive little ones that the big tyrannosaurs aren't going anywhere. Surprisingly, the gift shop here is particularly well stocked with neat items you won't too terribly mind buying for the kids.

900 Las Vegas Blvd. North (at Washington). ✆ 702/384-3466. www.lvnhm.org. Admission $6 adults; $5 seniors, students, and military personnel; $3 children 3–11; free for children under 3. Daily 9am–4pm.

Lied Discovery Children's Museum ⋒⋒ *Finds* *Kids*   A hands-on science museum designed for curious kids, the bright, airy, two-story Lied makes an ideal outing for toddlers and young children. Lots of interactive exhibits to examine; they change periodically, but past exhibits have included a miniature grocery store, a tube for encasing oneself inside a soap bubble, a radio station, and music and drawing areas. Clever, thought-inducing exhibits are everywhere. Learn how it feels to have a disability by playing basketball from a wheelchair. Feed a wooden "sandwich" to a cutout of a snake and to a human cutout, and see how much nutrition each receives. See how much sunscreen the giant stuffed mascot needs to keep from burning. On weekend afternoons from 1 to 3pm, free drop-in art classes

are offered, giving adults a bit of time to ramble around the gift store or read the fine print on the exhibit placards. The Lied also shares space with a city library branch, so after the kids run around, you can calm them back down with a story or two.

833 Las Vegas Blvd. North (½ block south of Washington, across the street from Cashman Field). ✆ **702/382-5437.** www.ldcm.org. Admission $7 adults; $6 seniors, military personnel, and children 1–17; free for under 1 year. Tues–Sun 10am–5pm.

Scandia Family Fun Center 🐱🐱 *Kids*   This family-amusement center, located just a few blocks off the Strip, is still the most viable alternative for those who need to amuse children not quite old enough for GameWorks or for those on a tighter budget. Certainly, it's where local families come for outings, and they keep the batting cages hopping ($1.25 for 25 pitches). The arcade is a bit warm and stinky, and other offerings (including miniature car racing and bumper boats, $4 per ride; small children ride free with an adult) are a bit worn, but the miniature golf course (three 18-hole courses, $5.50 per game, free for children under 6) is quite cute. Still, we do have to wonder about those 'round-the-clock weekend hours; we certainly hope those playing miniature golf at 4am are not parents accompanied by children.

2900 Sirius Ave. (at Rancho Dr. just south of Sahara Ave.). ✆ **702/364-0070.** Free admission, but there's a fee for each game or activity. Super Saver Pass $13 (includes 1 round of miniature golf, 2 rides, and 5 game tokens); Unlimited Wristband Package $18 (includes unlimited bumper boat and car rides, unlimited miniature golf, and 10 tokens for batting cages or arcade games). Mar–Oct daily 24 hr.; Nov–Feb Sun–Thurs 10am–11pm, Fri–Sat 10am–midnight.

4 Organized Tours

Just about every hotel in town has a sightseeing desk offering a seemingly infinite number of tours in and around Las Vegas. You're sure to find a tour company that will take you where you want to go.

Coach USA (✆ **800/828-6699;** www.coachusa.us) offers a rather comprehensive roster, including:

- Several 3½-hour **city tours,** with various itineraries, including visits to Ethel M Chocolates, The Liberace Museum, Tropicana Legends Museum, and the Fremont Street Experience.
- Half-day excursions to **Hoover Dam, Mt. Charleston,** and **Red Rock Canyon** (see chapter 9 for details).
- A 6-hour tour to the **Valley of Fire** and **Lake Mead.**
- A 13-hour **Grand Canyon excursion.**

Call for details or inquire at your hotel sightseeing desk, where you'll also find free magazines with coupons for discounts on these tours.

GRAND CANYON TOURS

Generally, tourists visiting Las Vegas don't drive 300 miles to Arizona to see the Grand Canyon, but dozens of sightseeing tours depart from the city daily. In addition to the Coach USA tours described above, the major operator, **Scenic Airlines** (© **800/634-6801** or 702/638-3200; www.scenic.com), runs deluxe, full-day guided air–ground tours starting at $219 per person ($189 for children 2–11); the price includes a bus excursion through the national park, a flight over the canyon, and lunch. All scenic tours include flightseeing. The company also offers both full-day and overnight tours with hiking.

UNIQUE DESERT TOURS BY CREATIVE ADVENTURES 🐾🐾🐾

A totally different type of tour is offered by Char Cruze of **Creative Adventures** (© **702/361-5565;** www.pcap.com/creativeadventures). Char, a charming fourth-generation Las Vegan (she was at the opening of the Flamingo), spent her childhood riding horseback through the mesquite and cottonwoods of the Mojave Desert, discovering magical places you'd never find on your own or on a commercial tour. A lecturer and storyteller as well as a tour guide, Char has extensively studied southern Nevada's geology and desert wildlife, its regional history, and its Native American cultures. Her personalized tours, enhanced by fascinating stories about everything from miners to mobsters, visit haunted mines, sacred Paiute grounds, ghost towns, canyons, and ancient petroglyphs. She also has many things to entertain and educate children, and she carries a tote bag full of visual aids, like a board covered in labeled rocks to better illustrate a lecture on local geology. Char has certain structured tours, but she loves to do individual tours tailored to a group. This is absolutely worth the money—you are definitely going to get something different than you would on a conventional tour, while Char herself is most accommodating, thoughtful, knowledgeable, and prompt. Char rents transport according to the size of the group and can handle clients with disabilities.

Depending on your itinerary, the cost is about $100 a day if you use your own car (more, depending on the number of people, if rental transportation is required; however, it's even more of a bargain with a larger group). It's a good idea to make arrangements with Char prior to leaving home.

5 Fore! Great Desert Golf

In addition to the listings below, there are dozens of local courses, including some very challenging ones that have hosted PGA tournaments. *Note:* Greens fees vary radically depending on time of day and year.

If you're a serious golfer, you may want to contact **American Golf** (© **800/468-7918**), a nationwide reservations service that's based in Arizona. They can help you arrange golf packages and book hard-to-get tee times.

Note also that the **Rio All-Suite Hotel & Casino** has a golf course; see p. 62.

Angel Park Golf Club 👿👿   This 36-hole par-70/71 public course is a local favorite. Arnold Palmer originally designed the Mountain and Palm courses (the Palm Course was redesigned several years later by Bob Cupp). Players call this a great escape from the casinos, claiming that no matter how many times they play it, they never get tired of it. The Palm Course has gently rolling fairways that offer golfers of all abilities a challenging yet forgiving layout. The Mountain Course has rolling natural terrain and gorgeous panoramic views. In addition to these two challenging 18-hole courses, Angel Park offers a night-lit Cloud 9 Course (12 holes for daylight play, 9 at night), where each hole is patterned after a famous par-3. You can reserve tee times up to 60 days in advance with a credit card guarantee.

Yardage: Palm Course 6,525 championship and 5,438 resort; Mountain Course 6,722 championship and 5,164 resort.

Facilities: Pro shop, night-lit driving range, 18-hole putting course, restaurant, snack bar, cocktail bar, and beverage cart.

100 S. Rampart Blvd. (between Summerlin Pkwy. and Alta St.; 20 min. northwest of the Strip). © **888/446-5358** or 702/254-4653. www.angelpark.com. Greens fees $95–$145. Discounted twilight rates available.

Bali Hai Golf Club 👿👿👿   One of the newest and most exclusive golf addresses belongs to this multimillion-dollar course built in 2000 on the strip just south of Mandalay Bay. Done in a wild South Seas theme, the par-72 course features over 7 acres of water features, including an island green, palm trees, and tropical foliage everywhere you look. Not impressed yet? How about the fact that all of their golf carts are equipped with global positioning systems (GPSs)? Or that celeb chef Wolfgang Puck chose to open his newest Vegas eatery here? Okay, if that doesn't convince you of the upscale

Going Vegas

If you're looking for a quintessential Las Vegas experience, try these suggestions from James P. Reza, Geoff Carter, and the editors of *Las Vegas Weekly:*

- **Peppermill's Fireside Lounge** (p. 170). This lounge is so evocative of the Me Decade, it's impossible not to love it. Dark, cozy, sexy, and somewhat kitschy, it's a great place for romantic encounters. Try to sit by the year-round fire pit, if you can stand the heat.

- **GameWorks** (p. 112). This multilevel entertainment center gives visitors a chance to wreak digitized havoc on the latest video-game creations. A few brave souls try the 75-foot climbing wall; most just hang in the lounge and shoot pool.

- **Cheetah's** (p. 178). How could you possibly visit Sin City and not sample the ubiquitous lap dance? Couples are welcome at Cheetah's, the site of Paul Verhoven's laughably overdone film *Showgirls.* More quality, less silicone, and a VIP lounge that has hosted lap dances for the likes of Sting and Drew Barrymore.

- **The Forum Shops at Caesars Palace** (p. 143). The most unique shopping experience in the world. Take Rodeo Drive, marry it to Rome, douse the whole thing in Spielberg, and you're still nowhere near this elegant retail space.

- **Sky Lounge at the Polo Towers** (p. 171). Hidden on the 19th floor of a timeshare condominium complex, this lounge offers a far more engaging view than the Stratosphere Tower, absolutely free of charge. Watch out for kamikaze tour groups.

- **Hard Rock Hotel & Casino** (p. 50). Everything about this hotel/casino—the bars, The Joint showroom, Mr. Lucky's 24/7—manages to evoke classic Vegas, a city that was built for young hipsters, not fanny-pack-wielding families.

- **Red Rock Canyon** (p. 193). Providing needed respite from the neon jungle, Red Rock is as beautiful as the desert gets. This haven for hikers and rock climbers gets a bit overrun at times, but it is still worth the trip. *Note:* Don't feed the wild burros. Unlike the entertainers at Cheetah's, they bite.

nature of the joint, check out the greens fees. Even at those prices, tee times are often booked 6 months in advance.

Yardage: 7,002 championship.

Facilities: Pro shop, putting green, gourmet restaurant, grill, and lounge.

5150 Las Vegas Blvd. South (at W. Russell Rd.). ℂ **888/397-2499**. www.walters golf.com. Greens fees $175–$245.

Black Mountain Golf & Country Club 🏌🏌   Two new greens have recently been added to this 18-hole, par-72 semiprivate course, which requires reservations 4 days in advance. It's considered a great old course, with lots of wildlife, including roadrunners. Unpredictable winds, however, may blow during your game.

Yardage: 6,550 championship, 6,223 regular, and 5,518 ladies'.

Facilities: Pro shop, putting green, driving range, restaurant, snack bar, and cocktail lounge.

500 Greenway Rd., Henderson, NV. ℂ **702/565-7933**. www.golfblackmountain.com. Greens fees $50–$145.

Desert Rose Golf Club 🏌 *Value*   This is an 18-hole, par-71 public course built in 1963 and designed by Dick Wilson/Joe Lee. Narrow fairways feature Bermuda turf. You can reserve tee times up to 7 days in advance.

Yardage: 6,511 championship, 6,135 regular, and 5,458 ladies'.

Facilities: Driving range, putting and chipping greens, PGA teaching pro, pro shop, restaurant, and cocktail lounge.

5483 Clubhouse Dr. (3 blocks west of Nellis Blvd., off Sahara Ave.). ℂ **702/431-4653**. www.desert-rose-golf-course.com. Greens fees $33–$79; some packages include cart rental.

Las Vegas National Golf Club 🏌   This is an 18-hole (about 8 with water on them), par-72 public course, and a classic layout (not the desert layout you'd expect). If you play from the back tees, it can really be a challenge. The 1996 Las Vegas Invitational, won by Tiger Woods, was held here. Discounted tee times are often available. Reservations are taken up to 60 days in advance; a $5 to $7 fee applies.

Yardage: 6,815 championship, 6,418 regular, and 5,741 ladies'.

Facilities: Pro shop, golf school, driving range, restaurant, and cocktail lounge.

1911 Desert Inn Rd. (between Maryland Pkwy. and Eastern Ave.). ℂ **702/734-1796**. www.lasvegasnational.com. Greens fees $35–$150, some including cart rental.

Royal Links Golf Club 🏌🏌🏌 *Finds*   More than just greens and water traps, Royal Links was designed to simulate play on some of

the greatest courses on the British Open rotation. St. Andrews Road Hole, the Postage Stamp at the Royal Troon in Scotland, and a dozen others are all faithfully re-created here for a unique game and an interesting history lesson.

Also fun is the clubhouse, designed (of course) to resemble a medieval castle, complete with an English pub inside.

Yardage: 7,029 championship, 6,602 regular, and 5,864 ladies'.

Facilities: Pro shop, golf school, driving range, restaurant, and cocktail lounge.

5995 East Vegas Valley (east of Boulder Hwy., between Flamingo Rd. and Sahara Ave.). ✆ **702/450-8000.** www.waltersgolf.com. Greens fees $135–$275.

6 Staying Active

For our tastes, it's way too hot (or, alternatively, too cold) to do much outside—that's why they invented indoor climate control. But if you are more active than we, first of all, we are impressed, and second, here are some ways to get physical in and around Vegas.

BOWLING   Gold Coast Hotel, 4000 W. Flamingo Rd. (at Valley View; ✆ **702/367-7111**), has a 72-lane bowling center open 24 hours a day.

The **Orleans,** 4500 W. Tropicana (✆ **702/365-7111**), has 70 lanes, a pro shop, lockers, meeting rooms, and more. Open 24 hours.

Out on the east side of town, you'll find 56 lanes at **Sam's Town,** 5111 Boulder Hwy. (✆ **702/456-7777**), plus a snack shop, cocktail lounge, video arcade, day-care center, pro shop, and more. Open daily 24 hours.

Suncoast, 9090 Alta Dr., in Summerlin (✆ **702/636-7111**), offers one of the newer facilities in town, with 64 lanes divided by a unique center aisle. The high-tech center with touch-screen scoring has become a regular stop on the Pro Bowlers tours. Open daily 24 hours.

BUNGEE JUMPING   If you want to take a *real* gamble, **A. J. Hackett Bungy,** 810 Circus Circus Dr., between Las Vegas Blvd. South and Industrial Road (✆ **702/385-4321;** www.aj-hackett. com), is the place to do it—the odds are stacked in your favor, but the thrill is nearly immeasurable. A. J. Hackett Bungy is a worldwide chain; they've done more than 1 million jumps, and they haven't lost anyone yet. The instructors are enthusiastic and do much to make you feel comfortable. Expect about an hour wait (there is a bar with a TV and pool table to keep you occupied), but given how meticulous and careful they are with each jumper, you'll be glad they aren't rushing people through.

An elevator in the shape of a rocket takes you to the top of a 175-foot tower, the base for an exhilarating plunge toward a large swimming pool below. During the ride up, you will receive your instructions (which basically amount to "stick your toes over the edge, arms out in front, and dive"). Our guinea pig needed a gentle shove. The whole jump lasts perhaps 3 minutes, but you will have enough adrenaline pumping through your veins to keep you up all night. (Which may tempt even the most steadfast of you to go gamble!) Dive at night, and you sail right into the lights of Vegas. The price is $59 for your first jump; an extra $5 will get you a T-shirt, and an extra $15 will snare you a video of yourself. Each subsequent jump is $25. Students and military personnel with ID should inquire about discounts. If you're under 18, you must be accompanied by a parent. Call for hours.

HORSEBACK RIDING Cowboy Trail Rides 🐴 (📞 702/387-2457; www.cowboytrailrides.com) offers a variety of rides and trails in Red Rock Canyon and on Mt. Charleston (at the 12-mile marker), ranging in price from $89 to $139. The high end is for a Red Rock Canyon sunset trail ride; it's about 2 hours, with the canyon providing a glorious backdrop for the end of the day. Riders then return to camp for a barbecue dinner (including a 16-oz. T-bone steak), joined by the cowboys for singalongs and marshmallow roasting. The company also offers hourly rates of $25, and buses from the MGM Grand. Riding stables at **Bonnie Springs Ranch** (📞 702/875-4191; www.bonnie springs.com/ranch.html) also offer guided trail rides daily. Rates are $25 per person for a 1-hour ride and go up to $135 for dinner rides.

ROCK CLIMBING Red Rock Canyon 🐴🐴🐴, just 19 miles west of Las Vegas, is one of the world's most popular rock-climbing areas. In addition to awe-inspiring natural beauty, it offers everything from boulders to big walls. If you'd like to join the bighorn sheep, Red Rock has more than 1,000 routes to inaugurate beginners and challenge accomplished climbers. Experienced climbers can contact the **visitor center** (📞 702/515-5350; www.redrockcanyon.blm.gov) for information.

If you're interested in learning or improving your skills, check out the excellent rock-climbing school and guide service **Sky's the Limit** (📞 800/733-7597 or 702/363-4533; www.skysthelimit.com), which offers programs for beginning, intermediate, and advanced climbers.

Tips **Desert Hiking Advice**

Except in summer, when temperatures can reach 120°F (49°C) in the shade, the Las Vegas area is great for hiking. The best hiking season is November to March. Great locales include the incredibly scenic Red Rock Canyon and Valley of Fire State Park (see chapter 9 for details on both).

Hiking in the desert is exceptionally rewarding, but it can be dangerous. Here are some safety tips:

1. Don't hike alone.
2. Carry plenty of water and drink it often. Don't assume that spring water is safe to drink. A gallon of water per person per day is recommended for hikers.
3. Be alert for signs of heat exhaustion (headache; nausea; dizziness; fatigue; and cool, damp, pale, or red skin).
4. Gauge your fitness accurately. Desert hiking may involve rough or steep terrain. Don't take on more than you can handle.
5. Check weather forecasts before starting out. Thunderstorms can turn into raging flash floods, which are extremely hazardous to hikers.
6. Dress properly. Wear sturdy walking shoes for rock scrambling, long pants (to protect yourself from rocks and cacti), a hat, sunscreen, and sunglasses.
7. Carry a small first-aid kit.
8. Be careful when climbing on sandstone, which can be surprisingly soft and crumbly.
9. Don't feed or play with animals, such as the wild burros in Red Rock Canyon. (It's actually illegal to approach them.)
10. Be alert for snakes and insects. Though they're rarely encountered, you'll want to look into a crevice before putting your hand into it.
11. Visit park or other information offices before you start out and acquaint yourself with rules and regulations and any possible hazards. It's also a good idea to tell the staff where you're going, when you'll return, how many are in your party, and so on. Some park offices offer hiker registration programs.
12. Follow the hiker's rule of thumb: Take only photographs and leave only footprints.

No experience is needed. The school is accredited by the American Mountain Guides Association.

TENNIS   Tennis buffs should choose one of the many hotels in town that have tennis courts.

Bally's ★★ (© **702/739-4111**) has eight night-lit hard courts. Fees per hour start at $10 for guests and $15 for non-guests. Facilities include a pro shop. Hours vary seasonally. Reservations are advised.

The Flamingo Las Vegas ★★ (© **702/733-3444**) has four outdoor hard courts (all lit for night play) and a pro shop. It's open to the public daily from 7am to 7pm. Rates are $12 per hour for guests, $20 for non-guests. Lessons are available. Reservations are required.

Monte Carlo Resort & Casino ★ (© **702/730-7777**) has three night-lit courts available to the public for $15 per hour.

In addition to hotels, the **University of Nevada–Las Vegas (UNLV)** ★★, Harmon Avenue just east of Swenson Street (© **702/895-0844**), has a dozen courts (all lit for night play) that are open weekdays from 6am to 9:45pm, weekends 8am to 9pm. Rates are $5 per person per day. You should call before going to find out if a court is available.

7

Shopping

Where you rank shopping in Vegas will depend on your own personal philosophy toward shopping. If shopping is its own excuse for being, then you ought to find this a sublime experience. In addition to four major malls, plus three outlet centers, every hotel has its own shopping arcade, including three (Desert Passage at Aladdin, The Forum Shops at Caesars, and the Grand Canal Shoppes at The Venetian) that are possibly things of great beauty and certainly joys forever, provided that you don't want much in the way of quaint, original stores.

Because, dropping the Keats references for the moment, while Vegas has at least one representative of every major name-brand store you can think of (don't just start and stop with Gap and Victoria's Secret; go to Sur La Table and Tiffany & Co.), what it does not have is much of anything that would distinguish shopping here from shopping in, say, Miami, or even Duluth. Sure, everything you could want, from Chanel to Cost Plus, is somewhere within a 5-mile radius, so if all you want to do is drop some change, or kill some time in between conferences or while other members of your family are whooping it up in a casino, you're in luck. But there is probably nothing here you can't get at home, with perhaps the exception of the high-end stores found in some of the hotel arcades.

You might consider driving **Maryland Parkway,** which runs parallel to the Strip on the east and has just about one of everything: Target, Toys "R" Us, several major department stores, Tower Records, major drugstores, some alternative-culture stores (tattoo parlors and hip clothing stores), and so forth. It goes on for blocks.

1 The Malls

You aren't going to find any surprises in any of the following malls—name brands and chain stores rule the day—but some are better in terms of ambience and location.

The Boulevard ☆   This is the second-largest mall in Las Vegas— Fashion Show on the Strip has it beat. Its 144-plus stores and restaurants are arranged in arcade fashion on a single floor—read, strictly formula mall layout—occupying 1.2 million square feet. Geared to the average consumer, it has anchors like Sears, JCPenney, Macy's, Dillard's, and Marshalls. In short, you can find just about anything you need here. There's free valet parking. The mall is open Monday through Saturday from 10am to 9pm and Sunday from 11am to 6pm. 3528 S. Maryland Pkwy. (between Twain Ave. and Desert Inn Rd.). ℂ 702/732-8949. www.blvdmall.com.

Fashion Show 👜👜   This luxurious and centrally located mall, the city's largest, is bigger than ever, thanks to a $100-million expansion that added the city's first Nordstrom and a Bloomingdale's, in addition to Neiman Marcus, Sak's Fifth Avenue, and Macy's. It also added a weird spaceship-shaped doohickey on top, and a block-long LED screen, neither of which adds to our shopping experience, but even a mall in Vegas has a have a visual and electronic gimmick, apparently. It's well located for visitors since it's the only real mall on the Strip, and it's a nicely posh-feeling one. Valet parking is available, and you can even arrange to have your car hand-washed while you shop. Fashion Show is open Monday through Friday from 10am to 9pm, Saturday from 10am to 7pm, and Sunday from noon until 6pm. 3200 Las Vegas Blvd. South (at the corner of Spring Mountain Rd.). ℂ 702/369-0704. www.thefashionshow.com.

Galleria at Sunset 👜   This is the farthest-away mall of the bunch (9 miles southeast of Downtown Las Vegas, in Henderson) but the most aesthetically pleasing, a 1-million-square-foot Southwestern-themed shopping center, with topiary animals adding a sweet touch to the food court. Anchored by Dillard's, Galyan's, JCPenney, Mervyn's, and Robinsons-May, the Galleria's 110 emporia include branches of The Disney Store, Gap/Gap Kids/Baby Gap, Limited Too, Eddie Bauer, Ann Taylor, bebe, Caché, Lane Bryant, Victoria's Secret, The Body Shop, B. Dalton, and Sam Goody. Open Monday through Saturday from 10am to 9pm and Sunday from 11am to 6pm. In nearby Henderson, 1300 W. Sunset Rd. (at Stephanie St., just off I-515). ℂ 702/434-0202. www.galleriaatsunset.com.

Meadows Mall 👜   Another immense mall, this one has more than 144 shops, services, and eateries, anchored by four department stores: Macy's, Dillard's, Sears, and JCPenney. Fountains and trees enhance Meadows Mall's ultramodern, high-ceilinged interior, and there are a few comfortable conversation/seating areas for resting your feet a moment. Meadows Mall is open Monday through Saturday from

10am to 9pm and Sunday from 10am to 6pm. 4300 Meadows Lane (at the intersection of Valley View and U.S. 95). ℂ 702/878-4849. www.themeadows mall.com.

2 Outlet Centers

To reach the Las Vegas Outlet Center, if you don't have a car, you can take a no. 301 CAT bus from anywhere on the Strip and change to a no. 303.

Fashion Outlets Las Vegas 𝒜𝒜𝒜   Dedicated bargain hunters may want to make the roughly 40-minute drive along I-15 (there's also a $13 shuttle from New York–New York or MGM Grand) to this big outlet complex, right on the border of California and Nevada. On your left is a large factory outlet with some designer names prominent enough to make that drive well worthwhile— Kenneth Cole, Donna Karan, Gap, Banana Republic, Old Navy, even a rare Williams-Sonoma, among several others. Why so far out of town? Our guess is because all these designers have full-price boutiques in various hotels, and they don't want you ignoring those in favor of discounted items. Open Monday through Saturday from 10am to 9pm, Sunday from 10am to 8pm. 32100 Las Vegas Blvd. South. ℂ 888/424-6898. www.fashionoutletlasvegas.com.

Las Vegas Outlet Center 𝒜   Formerly Belz Outlet Center, this massive complex houses more than 150 air-conditioned outlets, including a few dozen clothing stores and shoe stores. It offers a range of merchandise, but even given our understanding of the hit-and-miss nature of outlets, we've never bought a thing here and feel nothing but apathy for the center. Among other stores (which you will perhaps find less disappointing than we have), you'll find Casual Corner, Liz Claiborne, Perry Ellis, Calvin Klein, Levi's, Nike, Dress Barn, Oshkosh B'Gosh, Leggs/Hanes/Bali, Esprit, Carter's, Reebok, Spiegel, Jockey, Oneida, Springmaid, Bose, Danskin, Van Heusen, Tommy Hilfiger, Royal Doulton, Waterford, Black & Decker, and Geoffrey Beene. There is also a carousel and a food court. Open Monday through Saturday from 10am to 9pm, Sunday from 10am to 6pm. 7400 Las Vegas Blvd. South (at Warm Springs Rd.). ℂ 702/896-5599. www.premiumoutlets.com.

Las Vegas Premium Outlets   We had such high hopes for this, the most conveniently located, and largest, outlet mall in Vegas. We can say that it looks nice, in that pretty outdoor mall kind of way. But the key here is "outdoor." It's fine on a regular day, but on a hot

Vegas day—and there are plenty of those—this is an open oven of misery. They should put a roof over the thing or at least install a whole bunch of misters. You'll roast away while shopping among disappointingly dull stores, some of which are "outlets" only because they aren't in regular malls. Maybe we are just feeling bitter about that pair of Bass shoes that were half a size too small. Or that we can't quite fit into the Dolce & Gabbana sample sizes. Still, bring a lot of water if you go during the summer. Stores include Armani, Bernini, Brooks Brothers, Calvin Klein, Coach, Crabtree & Evelyn, Kenneth Cole, Lacoste, Nike, Perry Ellis, Ralph Lauren, Quicksilver, Samsonite, Timberland, Tommy Hilfiger, Wilson's Leather, and Zales. Open Monday through Saturday from 10am to 10pm, Sunday from 10am to 9pm. 875 S. Grand Central Pkwy. (at I-15). © 702/474-7500. www. premiumoutlets.com. From I-15 North, take exit 41B, Charleston Blvd. West From I-15 South, take the exit for Charleston Blvd. onto Martin Luther King Blvd., turn left on Charleston Blvd., and then left on Grand Central Pkwy.

3 Hotel Shopping Arcades

Just about every Las Vegas hotel offers some shopping opportunities. The following have the most extensive arcades. The physical spaces of these shopping arcades are always open, but individual stores keep unpredictable hours.

Note: The Forum Shops at Caesars, The Grand Canal Shoppes at The Venetian, and Desert Passage at Aladdin—as much sightseeing attractions as shopping arcades—are in the must-see category.

ALADDIN ✪✪✪   A particularly fine example of Vegas "shopping as amusement park" experience (the others being at Caesars and The Venetian), **Desert Passage** uses the "come with me to the Casbah" architectural appeal (or re-creations thereof) of northern Africa (Egypt, Morocco, Turkey) as its theme. It's visually most delightful— even the ceiling overhead is painted to replicate sultry days and nights, including the occasional thunderstorm. There is a lot to look at beyond the shops, and even more, since, at this writing, they have frequent live entertainers—acrobats, jugglers, belly dancers—to add to the visuals. And it's not just visual but odiferous; they pipe in spices and other evocative scents appropriate to those regions. The whole thing allows you to have that northern Africa souk-shopping experience without all the pesky touts trying to drag you into their stall for hours of haggling. You can even take a pedicab (a bicycle-powered vehicle pedaled by some comely worker) for a tour of Morocco, kinda. The stores are the assortment of mid- and high-end name brands one would expect (so the gouging happens in a different way than in the souks!). It's one of our favorite shopping areas in Vegas. But its days may be numbered, depending on what happens with redesigns once Planet Hollywood moves in properly. For information, see **www.desertpassage.com**.

The shops are open Sunday to Thursday 10am to 11pm, Friday and Saturday 10am to midnight.

BALLY'S   Bally's **Avenue Shoppes** number around 20 emporia offering, you know, stuff. In addition, there are several gift shops, art galleries, and a pool-wear shop. A recent addition of a walkway to neighbor Paris Las Vegas features more stores and restaurants.

BELLAGIO 🏺🏺   **Via Bellagio** is where the high rollers go to spend their winnings or, at least, send their bored partners to amuse themselves during marathon gambling sessions. It's a veritable roll call of glossy magazine ads: Armani, Prada, Chanel, Tiffany, Hermès, Fred Leighton, Gucci, Dior, and Yves Saint Laurent. That's about it. You need anything else? Well, yes—money. We can't even afford the oxygen in these places. (Actually, we've discovered affordable, good-taste items in every store here, from a Tiffany's $30 silver key chain to a $100 Prada business card holder.) A nice touch is a parking lot by the far entrance to Via Bellagio, so you need not navigate the great distance from Bellagio's main parking structure, but can simply pop in and pick yourself up a little something.

CAESARS PALACE 🏺🏺🏺   Until they got competition from The Venetian and Aladdin, **The Forum Shops** were the pinnacle of silly shopping in Vegas, a 375,000-square-foot Rodeo-Drive-meets-the-Roman-Empire affair complete with a 3-story courtyard entryway with its own circular escalator (has to be seen to be believed). Its architecture and sculpture span a period from 300 B.C. to A.D. 1700, so you get all your Italian ancient cityscape clichés. Then there is the Festival Fountain, where a scary-looking, tipsy Bacchus and some toga-clad Roman god and goddess pals come to animatronic life for 7 minutes once an hour, not that you can understand a word they

---

Impressions

Tip Number 3: Win a bunch of money. I can't recommend this too highly. If it hasn't occurred to you, win $1,200 and see for yourself. It's very energizing and really adds to your Vegas fun.

—Merrill Markoe, *Viva Las Wine Goddesses!*

say apart from vague urgings toward "revel." Which is just a fancy Roman god way of saying "spend," and you can do that nicely, thanks to more than 70 prestigious emporia here, including Louis Vuitton, Bernini, Christian Dior, A/X Armani Exchange, bebe, Gucci, Ann Taylor, and Gianni Versace, along with many other clothing, shoe, and jewelry stores.

In case that's not enough, there's the Roman Hall extension, which has for a centerpiece a 50,000-gallon circular aquarium and another fountain that also comes to life with a show of fire (don't stand too close—it gets really hot), dancing waters, and animatronic figures as the mythical continent of Atlantis rises and falls every hour. The production values are much higher than those of the Bacchus extravaganza, but it takes itself more seriously, so the giggle factor remains. In this shopping area, you'll find a number of significant stores, including a DKNY, Emporio Armani, Niketown, Fendi, Polo, Guess, and Virgin Megastore. Also in the shops are Wolfgang Puck's Chinois and a Cheesecake Factory.

It's in the brand-new multistoried extension, one that tries to move past "kitsch" and into "classy rich person's shopping experience"— though any sort of movement, literal or metaphoric, is tricky, what with all the giant marbled pillars, statues, and fountains, plus an atrium that actually admits sunlight. There are fab new stores, the kind we can really get excited about because of their otherwise limited availability: MAC, Kiehl's cosmetics, Agent Provocateur lingerie, Vosges Haut-Chocolat, and more, plus other dining options, like a Joe's Stone Crab.

The shops are open Sunday to Thursday 10am to 11pm, Friday and Saturday 10am to midnight.

CIRCUS CIRCUS   The shopping promenade here is adjacent to Adventuredome, so if you've left your kids (assuming they are old enough to be left) in the theme park, you can browse through about 20 shops, offering a selection of gifts and sundries, plus a newer shopping arcade themed as a European village, with cobblestone walkways and fake woods and so forth, decorated with replicas of vintage circus posters. It's much nicer than what the tacky Circus Circus has had before.

EXCALIBUR   The shops of **The Realm** for the most part reflect the hotel's medieval theme. Dragon's Lair, for example, features items ranging from pewter swords and shields to full suits of armor, and Merlin's Mystic Shop carries crystals, luck charms, and gargoyles. Other shops carry more conventional wares—gifts, candy, jewelry, women's clothing, and Excalibur logo items. At Fantasy Faire, you can have your photo taken in Renaissance attire. And most important, there is a branch of that royal staple—Krispy Kreme!

HARRAH'S Harrah's **Carnivale Court** 𝒜 shopping center is the only outdoor shopping mall on the Strip, and it's a surprisingly pleasant place to browse through. Among the store highlights is a Ghirardelli Chocolate store, a branch of the famous San Francisco–based chocolate company. This store is remarkably like a smaller version of the one in SF (alas, without the vats of liquid chocolate being mixed up), and in addition to candy, you can get a variety of delicious sundaes and other ice-cream treats.

LUXOR **Giza Galleria** is a 20,000-square-foot shopping arcade with eight full shops. Most of the stores emphasize clothing, and one sells Egyptian reproductions and artifacts. Adjacent is the Cairo Bazaar, a trinket shop.

MONTE CARLO A cobblestone arcade of retail shops, the **Street of Dreams,** includes several upscale clothing, timepiece, eyewear, and gift boutiques, plus a Lance Burton magic shop.

RIO The 60,000-square-foot **Masquerade Village** is a nicely executed shopping arcade at Rio. It's done as a European village and is two stories, featuring a wide variety of shops.

THE VENETIAN 𝒜𝒜 After you've shopped Ancient Rome at Caesars, come to **The Grand Canal Shoppes** and see if shopping in Renaissance- (more or less) era Venice is any different. Certainly the production values stay high; this is a re-created Italian village, complete with a painted, cloud-studded blue sky overhead, and a canal right down the center on which gondoliers float and sing. Pay them ($12), and you can take a lazy float down and back, serenaded by your boatsman (actors hired especially for this purpose and with accents perfect enough to fool Roberto Benigni). As you pass by, under and over bridges, flower girls will serenade you and courtesans will flirt with you, and you may have an encounter with a famous Venetian or two, as Marco Polo discusses his travels and Casanova exerts his famous charm. The stroll (or float) ends at a miniature (though not by all that much) version of St. Mark's Square, the central landmark of Venice. Here, you'll find opera singers, strolling musicians, glass blowers, and other bustling marketplace activity. It's all most ambitious and beats the heck out of animatronic statues.

The Shoppes are accessible directly from outside (so you don't have to navigate miles of casino and other clutter), via a grand staircase whose ceiling features more of those impressive hand-painted art reproductions. It's quite smashing.

Oh, the shops themselves? The usual high- and medium-end brand names: Jimmy Choo, Mikimoto, Movado, Davidoff, Kenneth Cole, Ann Taylor, BCBG, bebe, and more, plus Venetian glass and paper shops. Madame Tussauds waxworks (p. 115) is also located here, and so is the Canyon Ranch SpaClub. The shops are open Sunday to Thursday 10am to 11pm, Friday and Saturday 10am to midnight.

4 Vintage Clothing

The Attic 𝒜 The Attic shares a large space with Cafe Neon, a coffeehouse that also serves Greek-influenced cafe food (so you can raise your blood sugar again after a long stretch of shopping), and a comedy club stage; it's also upstairs from an attempt at a weekly club (as of this writing, the Sat-night Underworld). The store itself, former star of a Visa commercial, offers plenty of clothing choices on many racks. During a recent visit, a man came in asking for a poodle skirt for his 8-year-old. They had one. Open Monday through Thursday from 10am until 5pm, Friday from 10am until 6pm, Saturday from 11am until 6pm, and closed Sunday. 1018 S. Main St. ℭ **702/388-4088.** www.theatticlasvegas.com.

Buffalo Exchange 𝒜 This is actually a branch of a chain of stores spread out across the western United States. Don't let the chain part worry you—this merchandise doesn't feel processed. Staffed by plenty of incredibly hip alt-culture kids (ask them what's happening in town during your visit), it is stuffed with dresses, shirts, pants, and so forth. As with any vintage shop, the contents are hit or miss. You can easily go in one day and come out with 12 fabulous new outfits, and go in another and come up dry. But it's still probably the most reliable of the local vintage shops. The store is open Monday through Saturday from 10am to 8pm and Sunday from 11am until 7pm. 4110 S. Maryland Pkwy. (at Flamingo). ℭ **702/791-3960.** www.buffaloexchange.com.

5 Souvenirs

Now, you'd think Vegas would be *the* place for kitschy souvenirs—the town itself is such a bastion of good taste, after all. But alas, even by generous standards, most of the crap sold is, well, crap. But there are a few places for some of your snow globe and fuzzy dice needs.

The **Arts Factory Complex** 𝒜𝒜𝒜, 103 E. Charleston Blvd. (ℭ **702/382-3886**), has a gift shop full of pink flamingos and

Vegas-specific items. There should be something here for every camp fancy.

If you prefer your souvenirs to be less deliberately iconic, head over to the **Bonanza Gift and Souvenir Shop** 🎯🎯, 2460 Las Vegas Blvd. South (© **702/384-0005**). We looked, and we felt the tackiest item available was the pair of earrings made out of poker chips. Though we really liked the bracelets made out of dice.

For reverent camp, encrusted with sequins, do take a peek at the **Liberace Museum gift store** 🎯🎯, 1775 E. Tropicana Ave. (© **702/ 798-5595**). Encourage them to get even more out there (don't you think they should add Liberace mouse pads and screensavers?).

If you like your souvenirs with more style (spoilsports), **Cirque de Soleil's O** has a gift shop in the Bellagio, 3600 Las Vegas Blvd. South (© **702/693-7444**), with Cirque-specific articles, but also fanciful pottery, masks, and other curiosities.

6 Candy

M&M World 🎯🎯 *(Kids)* Everybody needs one vice, and for us, it's chocolate, by gosh. Its lure is so powerful, it overwhelms our usual snooty stance against anything even remotely resembling a tourist trap and leads us right to M&M World. What can one do when faced with a wall of M&M's in colors never before seen by man (silver! hot pink! turquoise!)? Overpriced? Hell, yeah! Who cares? There are doodads galore, replete with the M&M logo, and a surprisingly enjoyable short film and comedy routine, ostensibly about the "history" of the candy but really just a cute little adventure with a decent budget behind it. Open Sunday through Thursday from 9am until midnight, Friday and Saturday from 9am until 1am. In the Showcase Mall, 3785 Las Vegas Blvd. South (just north of the MGM Grand). © **702/736-7611.**

7 Antiques

Curiously, the one area where Vegas breaks out of the chain store minimall mode is with antiques shops. There are quite a few—two dozen—of consistent quality and price, nearly all located within a few blocks of each other. We have one friend, someone who takes interior design very seriously, who comes straight to Vegas for most of her best finds (you should see her antique chandelier collection!). And we treasure our Charles and Diana wedding tea cup and saucer set, purchased for next to nothing along this very street.

To get there, start in the middle of the **1600 block of East Charleston Boulevard** and keep driving east. The little stores, nearly all in old houses dating from the '30s, line each side of the street. Or you can stop in at **Silver Horse Antiques,** 1651 E. Charleston Blvd. (© **702/385-2700**), and pick up a map to almost all the locations, with phone numbers and hours of operation.

Antique Sampler Shoppes ✰ Head here for everything under one roof. More than 200 small antiques shops sell their wares in this mall, which offers a diversity of antiques ranging from exquisite Indian bird cages to *Star Wars* memorabilia (let's not call those sorts of items "antiques" but rather "nostalgia"). Changing selections, of course, mean you can never guarantee what will be available, but you can probably count on antique clothing and shoes, lamps, silver, decorative plates and china, old sewing machines, antique furniture, and '50s prom dresses. The displays are well labeled and well laid out, making it easy to take in all the antiques. The oldest antiques are from the mid-1800s and range in price from $100 to $4,000. Open Monday through Saturday from 10am until 7pm, Sunday from noon until 7pm. 6115 W. Tropicana Ave. © 702/368-1170. www.antiquesampler.com.

Antique Square ✰ A cruddy-looking collection of stores in several remodeled houses arranged in a square. But every good antiques shopper knows that these kinds of crammed junk stores are the place to find real treasures and to do real antiques hunting (because once they've been really picked through and prettily displayed by pros, you can kiss bargains and real finds goodbye). Individual store hours vary, but most are closed on Sunday and Monday. 2014–2034 E. Charleston Blvd. (at Eastern Ave.). © 702/471-6500.

8 Wigs

Serge's Showgirl Wigs ✰ Oh, you probably thought all those showgirls just naturally had bountiful thick manes. Sorry to burst your bubble. If you have a desire to look like a showgirl yourself (and why not?), come to Serge's, which for 23 years has been supplying Vegas's wiggy needs, with more than 2,000 wigs to choose from. Wigs range in price from $130 to over $1,500, depending on quality and realness, and you can pick from Dolly Parton's wig line or get something custom-made. They also make hairpieces and toupees, and carry hair-care products. Open Monday through Saturday from 10am until 5:30pm.

And, if the prices at Serge's are too rich to bring your fantasy alive, right across the way is **Serge's Showgirl Wigs outlet,** with prices running from a more reasonable $60 to $70. 953 E. Sahara Ave., no. A-2. © 702/732-1015. www.showgirlwigs.com.

8

Las Vegas After Dark

If there is anything Vegas has as much of as gambling, it's nightlife. You wouldn't be the first to make your visit entirely nocturnal. Every hotel has several bars and several free lounges with live music, plus a club or two. Elsewhere in the city are more bars, more clubs, plus strip joints, coffeehouses, and more. On top of that, Vegas is booming once again as a legitimate stop for concert acts and also has its own showy spectaculars and special theater productions.

Naturally, much of this will cost you, and naturally, we have ways of getting around that. While the production shows are comped freely to the high-rollers who court Lady Luck at the slots and tables, you'll need to look instead at those free magazines (*What's On* and *Show Biz*) in your hotel room for discount coupons. Note that there are a few afternoon shows that are considerably cheaper than the nighttime events. Hotel bars can be more expensive than independent operators, but you can drink for free if you stand at a slot machine or sit in the keno lounge, pretending to play, until a cocktail waitress comes around, as drinks are free for gamblers. (Waitresses ought to make sure you are gambling before offering, but they almost never do.) Club admission tends to be free for Nevada residents, so try talking up people standing in lines with you, and see if they are from the state, and if so, if they are willing to pretend you are with them.

Several things to keep in mind: While Vegas is fairly casual, many of the dance clubs have dress codes, which basically means no jeans or sneakers or anything that makes you look like a gangster. Bar and club life doesn't kick in until quite late, when all the local restaurant staff and showgirls get off work. (Seriously, places can be dead at 10:30pm and unbelievably crowded at midnight—and stay that way until the wee, wee hours, thanks to the backward work schedules of a large portion of Young Vegas.)

To find out who'll be performing during your stay and for up-to-date listings of shows (prices change, shows close), you can call the various hotels, using their toll-free numbers. Or call the **Las Vegas Convention and Visitors Authority** (© 877/VISITLV) and ask them to send you free copies of *Showguide* or *What's On in Las Vegas* (one or both of which will probably be in your hotel room). You can also check out what's playing at **www.vegasfreedom.com**. It's best to plan well ahead if you have your heart set on seeing one of the most popular shows or catching a major headliner.

The hotel entertainment options described in this chapter include information on ticket prices, what's included in that price (drinks, dinner, taxes, and/or gratuities), showroom policies, and reservations. Whenever possible, reserve in advance, especially for shows on weekends and holidays. If the showroom has **maitre d' seating** (as opposed to preassigned seats), you may want to tip him to upgrade your seat. A tip of $15 to $20 per couple will usually do the trick at a major show, less at a small showroom. An alternative to tipping the maitre d' is to wait until the captain shows you to your seat. Perhaps it will be adequate, in which case you've saved some money. If not, you can offer the captain a tip for a better seat. If you do plan to tip, have the money ready; maitres d' and captains tend to get annoyed if you fumble around for it. You can also tip with casino chips (from the hotel casino where the show is taking place only) in lieu of cash. Whatever you tip, the proper etiquette is to do it rather subtly—a kind of palm-to-palm action. There's really no reason for this since everyone knows what's going on, but being blatant is in poor taste. Arrive early at maitre d' shows to get the best choice of seats.

If you buy tickets for an assigned-seat show in person, you can look over a seating chart. Avoid sitting right up by the stage if possible, especially for big production shows. Dance numbers are better viewed from the middle of the theater. With headliners, you might like to sit up close.

Note: All these caveats and instructions aside, most showrooms offer good visibility from just about every seat in the house.

If you prefer rock or alternative music, your choices used to be limited, but that's changing. More of these bands are coming to town, attracted to the House of Blues and the Hard Rock Hotel's The Joint, which means you can actually see the likes of Marilyn Manson and Beck in Vegas. Check out the listings in this chapter for bars and coffeehouses, several of which offer live alternative or blues music. If you want to know what's playing during your stay, consult *Las Vegas Weekly,* formerly *Scope* magazine (biweekly, with great club and bar descriptions in its listings). You can pick it up at restaurants, bars, music stores, and hip retail stores. If you're looking for good alt-culture tips, try asking the cool staff at the **Buffalo**

Exchange vintage clothing store (© **702/791-3960**); they have their fingers right on the pulse of the underground.

In addition to the listings below, consider the **Fremont Street Experience,** described on p. 111.

1 The Major Production Shows

The shows in Vegas are as glitzy and over the top as ever, but with a few exceptions, they aren't worth the ever-climbing ticket prices. We aren't talking Broadway caliber here, but there are some exceptions. Most of the Cirque du Soleil acts and the Blue Man Group can hold their own with the best. And then there is Celine Dion and her still rather puzzling success (look, Girlfriend can sing, but have you seen those ticket prices?), which has inspired Elton John to take up his own, equally costly and sadly not as frequent (his show is better than Celine's, whose space he uses when she's not in the house) residency, and now word comes that Barry Manilow will be doing the same at the Las Vegas Hilton, starting in February 2005.

But for the most part, your money is better spent elsewhere, perhaps on a name act in town for a brief stand, than on a major production show. Otherwise, the hotel shows are just heavily sequined versions of the classic vaudeville revue: a little song (lip-synched), a little dance (not going to knock your socks off), a little seltzer down the pants, if the pants are even there to being with. Plus some magic acts.

Note: Although every effort has been made to keep up with the volatile Las Vegas show scene, keep in mind that the following reviews may not be indicative of the actual show you'll see, but the basic concept and idea will be the same. What's more, the show itself may have closed, so it's a good idea to call the venue and check.

American Superstars *Kids* One of a number of celebrity impersonator shows (well, it's cheaper than getting the real headliners), *American Superstars* is one of the few where said impersonators actually sing live. Five performers do their thing; the celebs impersonated vary, depending on the evening.

A typical Friday night featured Gloria Estefan, Charlie Daniels, Madonna, Michael Jackson, and Diana Ross and the Supremes. The performers won't be putting the originals out of work any time soon, but they aren't bad. Actually, they were closer in voice than in looks to the celebs in question (half the black performers were played by white actors), which is an unusual switch for Vegas impersonators. In the Stratosphere Casino Hotel & Tower, 2000 Las Vegas Blvd. South. © **800/99-TOWER** or 702/380-7711. Tickets $39 adults, $28 children 5–12 (including tax and handling

Tips **Our Favorites**

Our vote for **best show?** It's a toss-up between *O* at Bellagio and *Mystère* at Treasure Island, both by Cirque du Soleil. Either must be seen to be believed—and even then you may not believe it, but you won't be forgetting the experience any time soon. The **smartest show in town** is Penn & Teller at the Rio. The only reason we don't call it the **best magic show** is so that we can acknowledge the delightful Lance Burton at Monte Carlo. **Best classic Vegas topless revue** is *Jubilee!* at Bally's. **Best we aren't sure what the heck to call it** is Blue Man Group at Luxor (it will be moving to The Venetian in October 2005). **Best for the whole family** is the musical *Mamma Mia!* (at Mandalay Bay), based on the hits of Abba.

---

fee); dinner and show packages available. Wed and Fri–Sat 6:30 and 8:30pm; Sun–Tues 7pm.

Blue Man Group: Live at Luxor ₳₳₳   Are they blue? Indeed they are—three hairless, non-speaking men dipped in azure paint, doing decidedly odd stunts with marshmallows, art supplies, audience members, tons of paper, and an amazing array of percussion instruments fashioned fancifully from PVC pipe. If that doesn't sound very Vegas, well, it's not. It's the latest franchise of a New York–originated performance-art troupe that seems to have slipped into town through a side door opened by Cirque du Soleil's groundbreaking successes. Don't get the wrong idea; this is no Cirque clone. There's no acrobatics or flowing choreography, no attempt to create an alternate universe, just a series of unconnected bits. But even if the whole is no greater than the sum of the parts, the parts are pretty great themselves. It's funny in the weirdest and most unexpected ways, and the crowd is usually roaring by the end. Fans of typical Vegas shows may leave scratching their heads, but we are glad there is another color in the Vegas entertainment spectrum. ***Note:*** This production is moving to The Venetian in October 2005. In the Luxor Las Vegas, 3900 Las Vegas Blvd. South. ✆ **702/262-4000.** Tickets $83 (including tax). Tues 7pm; Sun–Mon and Wed–Fri 7 and 10pm; Sat 4, 7, and 10pm.

Celine Dion ₳   A fancy plush theater built just for her. A production spectacular inspired by the acrobatic antics of Cirque du Soleil. The world's biggest LED screen. A special germ-free elevator just for her vocal chords. All this so that the angular diva can display her talents a few nights a week just for you. Provided that you can pay the price. Oh, and that you care about Celine Dion. Because while this is a visual spectacle, and there is some value in that, and the girl can sing (or, at times, most likely, lip sync), and there is value in that, it may not add up to the value of the costly tickets. Because when all is said and done, this is a Celine Dion concert. If you weren't planning on going to one before, there is no particular reason to go to one now. In Caesars Palace, 3570 Las Vegas Blvd. South. 📞 877/CELINE-4. Tickets $88–$225. Wed–Sun 8:30pm.

Crazy Girls *Crazy Girls*, presented in an intimate theater, is probably the raciest revue on the Strip. It features sexy showgirls with perfect bodies in erotic song-and-dance numbers enhanced by innovative lighting effects. Think of *Penthouse* poses coming to life. Perhaps one older man from Kentucky best summed it up: "It's okay if you like boobs and butt. But most of the girls can't even dance." In Riviera Hotel & Casino, 2901 Las Vegas Blvd. South. 📞 800/634-6753 or 702/794-9433. Tickets $35; dinner and show packages available. Ages 18 and over only. Wed–Mon 9:30pm.

Kids Family-Friendly Shows

Given the increasingly high cost of show tickets in Vegas, a family of four may have to think twice about taking the kids out for the night. And it doesn't help that Vegas is showing its preference for legal adults, with productions that are showing more and more bare skin. Even **Lance Burton** (p. 156), whose show is otherwise entirely suitable for kids, has showgirls with outfits that are rather skimpy in the back. Other than Burton, you are best off taking kids to impersonator show *American Superstars* (p. 151), which offers a children's price ticket, and the afternoon magic show **Mac King** (p. 159). The other main afternoon show, *Viva Las Vegas* (p. 160), can feature comic patter too raunchy for immature ears. Artistic kids will love either *KÀ* (p. 155), *Mystère* (p. 158), or *O* (p. 158), but wait until they are at least 8 years old because of the pacing and surreal imagery. And while grown-ups may roll their eyes, kids do adore the clash and clang of the knightly battles waged at the **Tournament of Kings** (p. 160); teens may like it, too, but be way too cool to admit it.

Clint Holmes ✎ Who? "My name is Mickey, I've got a nickel." Oh, right. So why should you go? Because you miss, or simply still long for, the days of pure Vegas *entertainers*—you know, guys who sang (competently), told jokes and self-deprecating stories (competently), and dared the audience to love them with great confidence and, well, competence. You will hear some originals, some covers ("Banana Boat Song," "What Kind of Fool Am I?"), in addition to stories of how Holmes was influenced by Sammy Davis, Jr., which explains a lot, and we mean that in a positive way. He's good, but you need to want to see this kind of retro entertainment, and we mean that in a positive way as well. In Harrah's, 3475 Las Vegas Blvd. South. ✆ **800/392-9002**, ext. 5222. Tickets $60; dinner and show packages available. Mon–Sat 7:30pm.

Danny Gans: The Man of Many Voices ✎ In a town where the consistent sellouts are costly, elaborate extravaganzas, it's a tribute to Danny Gans's charisma and appeal that his one-man variety act can draw the same crowds with nothing more than a back-up band and a few props. Gans is "the man of many voices"—more than 400 of them—and his show features impressions of 80 different celebrities, usually a different mix each night.

The emphasis is on musical impressions (everyone from Sinatra to Springsteen), with some movie scenes thrown in. Gans's vocal flexibility is impressive, though his impersonations are hit or miss (his Springsteen needs work). That said, when we last saw him, he did a dead-on impression of comedian Jeff Foxworthy that had the crowd rolling, a hilarious bit involving George Burns imitating MC Hammer, and a somewhat freaky but totally on-target impression of Macy Gray. He's a consistent crowd-pleaser, and the lack of bombast can be a refreshing change of pace. In The Mirage, 3400 Las Vegas Blvd. South. ✆ **800/963-9634** or 702/792-7777. Tickets $100 (including tax). Tues–Thurs and Sat–Sun 8pm.

An Evening at La Cage No, it wasn't inspired by the French movie or the recent American remake, or even the Broadway musical. Actually, it's more like the stage show from *Priscilla, Queen of the Desert*. Female impersonators dress up as various entertainers (with varying degrees of success) to lip-synch to said performers' greatest hits (with varying degrees of success). The celebs lampooned can include Cher, Bette Midler, Judy Garland, Whitney Houston, Dionne Warwick, and, intriguingly, Michael Jackson. A Joan Rivers impersonator, looking not unlike the original but sounding not at all like her (even with the aid of an odd constant echo), is the hostess, delivering scatological phrases and stale jokes. They do make the most of a tiny stage with some pretty stunning lighting, though the choreography is bland. Still, it's a crowd-pleaser—one couple was back for their fourth visit (all comped, but still . . .). In Riviera Hotel & Casino, 2901 Las Vegas Blvd. South. ☎ 877/892-7469 or 702/794-9433. Ages 12 and over only. Tickets $55; dinner and show packages available. Wed–Mon 7:30pm.

Folies Bergère ⟨⟨ The longest-running production show in town constantly claims to have had a "sexier than ever" face-lift, but the result is more tamed-down burlesque, as done by a college drama department. Bare breasts pop up (sorry) at odd moments (late shows only), not during the can-can line, but rather during a fashion show and an en-pointe ballet sequence. The effect is neither erotic nor titillating, suggesting only that absent-minded dancers simply forgot to put their shirts on. The dance sequences (more acrobatics than true dance) range from the aforementioned ballet and can-can to jazz and hoedown, and are only occasionally well costumed. A coyly cute '50s striptease number on a *Hollywood Squares*–type set is more successful, as is a clever and funny juggling act (don't miss the finale with the vest and hat). In Tropicana Resort & Casino, 3801 Las Vegas Blvd. South. ☎ 800/829-9034 or 702/739-2411. Tickets $45–$55. Mon, Wed, Thurs, and Sat 7:30 and 10pm; Tues and Fri 8:30pm.

Jubilee! ⟨⟨ A classic Vegas spectacular, crammed with singing, dancing, magic, acrobats, elaborate costumes and sets, and, of course bare breasts. It's a basic revue, with production numbers featuring homogenized versions of standards (Gershwin, Cole Porter, some Fred Astaire numbers) sometimes sung live, sometimes lip-synched, and always accompanied by lavishly costumed and frequently topless showgirls. Humorous set pieces about Samson and Delilah and the sinking of the *Titanic* (!) show off some pretty awesome sets. (They were doing the *Titanic* long before a certain movie, and recent attendees claimed the ship-sinking effect on stage here was a better production than the one in the movie.) The finale features aerodynamically impossible feathered and bejeweled costumes and headpieces designed by Bob Mackie. In Bally's Las Vegas, 3645 Las Vegas Blvd. South. ☎ 800/237-7469 or 702/739-4567. Ages 18 and over only. Tickets $60–$74. Sat–Thurs 7:30 and 10:30pm.

KÀ ⟨⟨⟨ *Kids* The fourth Cirque du Soleil show on the Strip is an Asian-themed affair (though its name is actually Egyptian and means "dual spirit," but we're not going to be picky about that) with an actual storyline (the plot about separated twins searching for each

---

Phantom Is Coming

An abbreviated version of *Phantom of the Opera*—only 90 minutes, so figure the highlights ("Music of the Night," crashing chandelier, and so on)—directed by Tony Award–winning Harold Prince, will, around Spring 2006, take up residency in a superexpensive (like Vegas does anything else *but* these days) theater in The Venetian.

---

other is a little vague but easy enough to follow), making it perfect for those who like their entertainment a little less Dadaist and a tad more literal. That's not to say that *KÀ* doesn't have the look and feel of a Cirque production. The divine artistry, technical wizardry, fabulous costumes, fast pacing, and acrobatics that are the hallmarks of Cirque du Soleil are still very much present and accounted for. But if its brethren lean more toward Fellini and Dali, then *KÀ* is more Kabuki and kung fu. The opening two scenes, with their *Crouching Tiger, Hidden Dragon* choreography, are alone worth the steep price of admission. This show's probably the most accessible of the Cirque productions for the young set. In MGM Grand, 3799 Las Vegas Blvd. South. ☎ **800/929-1111** or 702/891-7777. www.ka.com. Ages 5 and over only. Tickets $99–$150. Fri–Tues 7:30 and 10:30pm.

La Femme ☆ Further proof that Vegas is trying to distance itself from the "Vegas is for families" debacle, "classy adult entertainment" is the new watchword, with *La Femme* leading the pack. Allegedly the same show that has been running for years in a famous racy French nightclub, *La Femme* is just a bunch of girls taking their clothes off. Except that the girls are smashingly pretty, with the kind of bodies just not found on real live human beings, and they take their clothes off in curious and, yes, artistic ways: gyrating on pointe shoes while holding onto ropes or hoops, and falling over sofas while lip-synching to French torch songs. In short, it's what striptease ought to be, and by gosh, if strip clubs were this well staged, we'd go to them all the time. But at $60 a ticket, it's a great deal to pay for arty nudie fun. In MGM Grand, 3799 Las Vegas Blvd. South. ☎ **800/929-1111** or 702/891-7777. Ages 18 and over only. Tickets $59. Wed–Mon 8:30 and 10:30pm.

Lance Burton: Master Magician ☆☆☆ (Kids) Magic acts are a dime a dozen in Vegas of late. So when someone pops up who is original—not to mention charming and, yes, actually good at his job—it comes as a relief. Handsome and folksy, Burton is talented and engaging, for the most part shunning the big-ticket special effects that seem to have swamped most other shows in town. Instead, he offers an extremely appealing production that starts small, with "close-up" magic. These rather lovely tricks, he tells us, are what won him a number of prestigious magic competitions. They are truly extraordinary. (We swear that he tossed a bird up in the air, and the darned thing turned into confetti in front of our eyes. Really.) His dry, laconic, low-key delivery is plenty amusing and contrasts nicely to other performers in town, who seem as if they have been spending way too much time at Starbucks. He is joined by standout comic-juggler Michael Goudreau; the man juggles a chainsaw, a bowling ball, and a flaming torch *all at once.* In Monte Carlo Resort & Casino, 3770 Las Vegas Blvd. South. ✆ **800/311-8999** or 702/730-7000. Tickets $60–$65. Tues and Sat 7 and 10pm; Wed–Fri 7pm.

Legends in Concert   This crowd pleaser has been running since May 1983. Arguably the best of the Vegas impersonator shows (though it's hard to quantify such things), *Legends* does feature performers singing live rather than lip-synching. And the performers look remarkably like the originals; free use of video cutting between action on stage and the real performer generally shows what a good simulation the former is. Acts vary from night to night: When we went, the performers included a carbon copy (at least in looks) of the early Little Richard, a crowd-pleasing Shania Twain, an energetic Prince, an appropriately flamboyant Liberace, a striking Bette Midler, and one helluva Elvis impersonator. In Imperial Palace, 3535 Las Vegas Blvd. South. ✆ **888/777-7664.** Tickets $40–$60 adults (includes 1 drink, tax, and gratuity), $25-$45 children 2–12. Mon–Sat 7 and 10pm.

Mamma Mia! 👀   This charming show is well suited for Vegas audiences since it's all-ages and promotes much clapping and dancing. There is little of substance in the story, a loose narrative created solely for the purposes of bringing the many, many hit songs of the Swedish '70s wonder group ABBA to the stage. Don't get us wrong; it's quite cute. A young woman on the eve of her wedding, longing for the father she never knew to be a part of her present happiness, brings the three men who are the most likely biological daddy to her Greek island home, forcing her long-independent mother to face up to her past and make choices for the future. Some of the songs fit better than others, but all are sung with the appropriate breezy joy—and after 30 years, whatever we thought of them back in the day, we have to admit said songs are infectious. In Mandalay Bay, 3950 Las Vegas Blvd. South. ✆ 877/632-7400. Tickets $45–$100. Mon–Thurs 7pm; Sat–Sun 5 and 9pm.

Mystère ★★★ *Kids*   The in-house ads for Cirque du Soleil's *Mystère* (say miss-*tair*) say "Words don't do it justice," and for once, that's not just hype. The show is so visual that trying to describe it is a losing proposition. And simply calling it a circus is like calling the Hope Diamond a gem or the Taj Mahal a building: It's accurate but doesn't begin to do it justice. The show features one simply unbelievable act after another (seemingly boneless contortionists and acrobats, breathtakingly beautiful aerial maneuvers), interspersed with Dadaist/commedia dell'arte clowns, and everyone clad in costumes like nothing you've ever seen before.

The show is dreamlike, suspenseful, funny, erotic, mesmerizing, and just lovely. At times, you might find yourself moved to tears. For some children, however, it might be a bit too sophisticated and arty. Even if you've seen Cirque before, it's worth coming to check out, thanks to the large production values. It's a world-class show, no matter where it's playing; that this is playing in Vegas is astonishing. In Treasure Island, 3300 Las Vegas Blvd. South. ✆ **800/288-7206** or 702/894-7722. www.cirquedusoleil.com. Tickets $60–$95 (including tax). Wed–Sat 7:30 and 10:30pm; Sun 4:30 and 7:30pm.

O ★★★ *Finds* *Kids*   How to describe the seemingly indescribable wonder and artistry of Cirque du Soleil's most dazzling display? An Esther Williams–Busby Berkeley spectacular on peyote? A Salvador Dalí painting come to life? A stage show by Fellini? The French troupe has topped itself with this production—and not simply because its breathtaking acrobatics are situated in, on, around, and above a 1½-million-gallon pool (*eau*—pronounced O—is French for water). Even without those impossible feats, this might be worth the price just to see the presentation, a constantly shifting dreamscape tableau that's a marvel of imagination and staging. If you've never seen a Cirque show, prepare to have your brain turned inside out. We know—those ticket prices—*ouch*. We want to say that we can guarantee it's worth it, but that's a decision only you can make. But we can say this: Watch this show, and you'll know where a good chunk of your money is going (in other words, they spend a bundle nightly to mount this thing). Note that no tank tops, shorts, or sneakers are allowed. In Bellagio, 3600 Las Vegas Blvd. South. ✆ **888/488-7111** or 702/693-7722. Tickets $99–$150 (including tax). Wed–Sun 7:30 and 10:30pm.

Penn & Teller ★★★ *Moments*   The most intelligent show in Vegas, as these two—magicians? illusionists? truth-tellers? BS artists? geniuses?—put on 90 minutes of, yes, magic and juggling, but also acerbic comedy, mean stunts, and great quiet beauty. Looking like two characters out of Dr. Seuss, big loud Penn and smaller quiet Teller (to reduce them to their basic characteristics) perform magic, reveal the secrets behind a few major magic tricks, discuss why magic is nothing but a bunch of lies, and then turn around and show why magic is as lovely an art form as any other. In Rio All-Suite Hotel & Casino, 3700 W. Flamingo Rd. ✆ 888/746-7784. Tickets $75. Wed–Mon 9pm.

The Second City ★★ *Value*   Second City is the Chicago-based comedy group that spawned not only *SCTV* but also some of the best modern-day comics (Gilda Radner, John Belushi, Martin Short, Mike Myers). This is an improv and sketch comedy show, with cast members performing stunts similar to those you might have seen on *Whose Line Is It Anyway?*—you know, taking suggestions from the audience and creating bizarre little skits and such out of them, all of it done at lightening speed with wit and a wink. Some of it can turn R-rated, so be careful bringing the kids, but do not hesitate to see it yourself. And join in—any improv group is only as good as the material fed it (so remember, there's only so much a group can do with jokes about sex and vomiting, especially if every single audience thinks that would be funny material with which to work). One of the best values and highest-quality shows in Vegas. In Flamingo Las Vegas, 3555 Las Vegas Blvd. South. ✆ 800/732-2111. www.secondcity.com. Tickets $30. Daily 8 and 10:30pm.

Splash   They took out the mermaids and water tank that gave this show its name, froze the water, and added ice skaters and some increased production values. If this show is now the one in town that most closely resembles the guffaw-inducing extravaganza in *Showgirls,* it's nonetheless a considerable improvement over its previous incarnations. That may be because we are partial to ice skaters in any form, even if they are performing to the music from *Titanic*

Value **Seeing the King . . . No, Not That One**

One of the best bargains in Las Vegas is an afternoon show at Harrah's. **Mac King** offers deliberately less-than-slick and charming, likable comedy as well as entertaining magic (Harrah's, 3475 Las Vegas Blvd. South; ✆ 800/427-7247 or 702/369-5222; Tues–Sat 1 and 3pm; $17). *Tip:* You can make this an even bigger bargain if you sign up for Harrah's slot club. The club usually offers two free show tickets (you still have to pay the one-drink minimum) to new enrollees, and you won't have to gamble a cent.

while topless dancers preen on a small version of the deck of same. Expect up-close looks at bare breasts as the flashy and not-terribly-competent dancers parade through the crowd (sometimes in see-through filmy net catsuits that show less and are thus considerably more sexy—more topless shows should go this teasing route). Some "comedy gauchos" crack whips and insensitive jokes, and there's a truly talented trio of juggling brothers. Pass the time wondering if it's uncomfortable skating in a thong. ***Seating warning:*** Seats on the sides are so bad that fully three-quarters of the stage might be obscured. In Riviera Hotel & Casino, 2901 Las Vegas Blvd. South. (✆ 877/892-7469 or 702/734-9301. Ages 18 and over only. Tickets $65–$80; dinner and show packages available. Tues-Sat 7 and 9:30pm.

Tournament of Kings ⊛⊛ (Kids) This one's for lovers of medieval yore or families looking for wholesome entertainment. For a fixed price, you get a dinner that's better than you might expect (Cornish game hen, very fine baked potato, and more), which you eat with your hands (in keeping with the theme), while Merlin (or someone like him) spends too much time trying to work up the crowd with a singalong. This gives way to a competition between the kings of various medieval countries, competing for titles in knightly contests (jousting, horse races, and such) that are every bit as unrehearsed and spontaneous as a professional wrestling match. Eventually, good triumphs over evil and all that.

Each section of the arena is given a king to be the subject of and to root for, and the audience is encouraged to hoot, holler, and pound on the tables, which kids love, but teens will be too jaded for (though we know some from whom a spontaneous "way cool" slipped out a few times unchecked). Many adults might find it tiresome. Acrobatics are terrific, and certain buff performers make for a different sort of enjoyment. In Excalibur, 3850 Las Vegas Blvd. South. (✆ 800/933-1334 or 702/597-7600. Tickets $48 (includes dinner). Daily 6 and 8:30pm.

Viva Las Vegas (Kids) An everything-but-the-kitchen-sink Vegas variety show, *Viva* is good only if you really need an hour's respite from the afternoon heat. A lead singer and a small troupe of dancers perform numbers, including the now-ubiquitous "My Heart Will Go On." A comedian delivers some very adult humor (fat jokes, gay jokes, breast jokes, and so on) given the time of day and the number of kids in the audience. Another comedian does a manly-man routine ripped off from Tim Allen. One bright point is when the white female dancers don Jackson Five outfits and lip-synch "ABC," fully aware of the giggles this sight engenders (unlike, unfortunately, the Elvis impersonator who closes the show).

Note: Discount coupons are often found in those free magazines in your hotel room. Sometimes the discount gets you in free, with just the price of a drink. In Stratosphere Casino Hotel & Tower, 2000 Las Vegas Blvd. South. ☎ 800/99-TOWER or 702/380-7777. Tickets $17 (including tax and handling fee). Mon–Sat 2 and 4pm.

We Will Rock You ☆

This show is inevitably compared to *Mamma Mia!* in that the hits of a beloved group of the '70s (this time, Queen) have been gathered around a loose plot line and are presented on stage as a conventional musical. The narrative here is even thinner than MM's: Some time in the future, evil corporations control everything and have banned rock music because it's rebellious and independent and can't be corporately marketed as tidily as prefab boy and girl pop bands. It's up to a ragtag bunch of punk-rock-clothed rebel "bohemians" to find the music that they've only heard rumors about, and bring back ROCK AND ROLL. This leads to one of those curious paradoxes: a rock musical that features a bunch of people singing rock songs about how there is no rock music any more. Cast all sing fine (though no one will ever replace Freddy) and overact to within an inch of their lives. The show has some funny moments, but not enough to make the two hours (without intermission) go by quickly enough to get to what everyone came for the first place, "Bohemian Rhapsody." In Paris Las Vegas, 3655 Las Vegas Blvd. South. ☎ 877/ROCK-SHOW or 702/946-4567. Tickets $45–$100. Mon–Wed and Fri 7 and 10:30pm; Sat–Sun 2 and 8:30pm.

Zumanity

It's shocking how much goodwill Cirque du Soleil has squandered with this ill-conceived show. Purportedly dedicated to celebrating human sexuality, it's the least subtle show on the Strip (no easy feat, that), an erotic cabaret of the sort that stopped being shocking in *fin de siecle* Paris, not that that stops the crowd from eating up a bevy of acts which are all meant to be lewd or alluring or both. But if you pay attention, they are mostly just basic Cirque acts (and, worse, just basic striptease acts, which you can see anywhere in town for a great deal less money), though instead of giving the illusion of near-nakedness, they give the illusion of total nakedness (an illusion that works better the farther you sit from the stage). As they contort and writhe and feign pleasure or apathy, we feel sympathy for all the parents who spent money on gymnastics and ballet lessons over the years, only to have their poor kids end up in this. See, Cirque is naturally sexy and erotic, so all this is gilding the lily until it chokes from lack of oxygen and dies. Save your money for *La Femme* across the street or just go to Sapphire and tip the best dancer there. In New York–New York, 3790 Las Vegas Blvd. South. © **866/ 606-7111** or 702-740-6815. Ages 18 and over only. Tickets $65–$125, including tax. Fri–Tues 7 and 10pm.

2 Headliner Showrooms

Vegas entertainment made its name with its showrooms, though its glory days are somewhat behind it, gone with the Rat Pack themselves. For a long time, Vegas headliners were something of a joke; only those on the downhill side of fame were thought to play there. But with all the new performance spaces—and high fees—offered by the new hotels, Vegas suddenly has credence again, especially in, of all things, the rock scene. Both the Hard Rock Hotel's The Joint and the House of Blues are attracting very current and very popular acts that find it hip, rather than humiliating, to play Sin City. However, the classic Vegas showroom itself does seem headed for the way of the dinosaurs; many of the hotels have shuttered theirs. As for the remainder, one is pretty much like the other, with the exception of the Hard Rock and HOB (hence their detailed descriptions), and in any case, audiences go based on the performer rather than the space itself. Check with your hotel or those free magazines in your room to see who is in town when you are.

Hard Rock Hotel's The Joint 🎸 Formerly just about the only game in town in terms of good rock bookings, The Joint, with a 1,400-seat capacity, now faces some stiff competition from the House of Blues. For example, when Alanis Morrissette came to town, she played The Joint, but her opening act, Garbage, played the House of Blues. On the other hand, it was here the Rolling Stones chose to do a show during their arena tour—this was the smallest venue the band had played in years, and, as you can imagine, it was one hot ticket.

The venue is not a preferred one, however; it's worth going only if a favorite performer is playing or if it's an opportunity to see a big artist play a smaller-than-usual room. Though there's sometimes table seating, it's usually festival style, making personal space at a premium during a crowded show, and though the floor is slightly raked, this still makes for poor sightlines. The balconies upstairs, if you can get to them, aren't much better, as once the bodies are packed in about two deep, the stage is completely obscured. Unless you want to brave the crush at the very front (sure, you should—it's a rock show!), we suggest standing at the rail toward the back, which not only elevates you slightly above the crowd, but also at least protects one side of your body from the crowd.

Showroom policies: Smoking permitted for some shows; seating is either preassigned or general, depending on the performer. **Price:** $20 to $100, depending on the performer (tax and drinks extra). **Show Times:** 8:30pm (nights of performance vary). **Reservations:** You can reserve up to 30 days in advance. In Hard Rock Hotel & Casino, 4455 Paradise Rd. ℂ **800/693-7625** or 702/693-5000.

House of Blues ℛℛ   The House of Blues goes head-to-head with The Joint at the Hard Rock Hotel, which has translated into much better rock bookings overall, thanks to the competition. On its own merits, the House of Blues is a good, intimate room with a cozy floor surrounded by a bar area, and an upstairs balcony area that has actual theater seating. (The balcony might actually be a better place to see a show since the sightlines are unobscured, unlike down below, where posts and such can obstruct the view.) It's probably the most comfortable and user-friendly place to see a rock show in Vegas.

The House of Blues has rock and blues shows just about every night, with nationally recognized acts flocking to the place, including Bob Dylan, Seal, X, Garbage, Taylor Dane, Etta James, Al Green, James Brown, the Go-Gos, and the Neville Brothers.

Showroom policies: Smoking permitted; seating is either preassigned or general, depending on the performer (some shows are all general admission, with everyone standing on the floor). **Price:** $18 to $100, depending on the performer. **Show Times:** Vary, but usually 8pm. **Reservations:** You can buy tickets as soon as shows are announced; lead time varies with each artist. In Mandalay Bay, 3950 Las Vegas Blvd. South. ℂ **877/632-7400** or 702/632-7600.

3 Comedy Clubs

Comedy Club   The Riviera's comedy club, on the second floor of the Mardi Gras Plaza, showcases four comedians nightly. Once a month, usually on the last weekend, the club hosts a late-night *XXXTREME Comedy Showcase* for shock and X-rated comedians. In Riviera Hotel & Casino, 2901 Las Vegas Blvd. South. ℂ **800/634-6753** or 702/734-9301. Tickets $18. Daily 8:30 and 10:30pm, with occasional Fri–Sat late-night shows at 11:45pm.

Comedy Stop   Similar to the other comedy clubs in town, Comedy Stop features three nationally known comedy headliners nightly. In Tropicana Resort & Casino, 3801 Las Vegas Blvd. South. ℂ **800/468-9494** or 702/739-2411. Tickets $20 (includes tax, tip, and 2 drinks). Daily 8 and 10:30pm.

The Improv ⓡ These are talented performers—the top comics on the circuit, whom you're likely to see on Leno and Letterman. In Harrah's Las Vegas, 3475 Las Vegas Blvd. South. ⓒ **800/392-9002** or 702/369-5111. Tickets $25. Tues–Sun 8:30 and 10:30pm.

4 A Coffeehouse/Wine Bar

Jazzed Cafe & Vinoteca ⓡⓡⓡ *Finds* This genuine European-style (well, by way of California) cafe/wine bar is owned and operated by the charming and friendly Kirk, a choreographer who lived in Italy for 10 years. Originally just an itty bitty location on Flamingo, it's now a larger, but still intimate (seating only 40), venue on Sahara, an even farther drive for the average tourist, but well worth it if you want something less Vegas-pretentious. Featuring candlelight and cool jazz most nights, with hot art on the walls, they try to serve eclectic and unusual wines, along with multiple coffee drinks (be sure to try the terrific Illy, a renowned Italian brand) and average wine. There's a small but satisfying food menu featuring inexpensive authentic Italian specialties, all made by Kirk on the spot. It's a great respite from the maddening crowds (and a cheap place to eat well), though it fills up after the shows let out with the owner's show-and-dance pals. Open Sunday through Thursday 5 to 10pm, and Friday and Saturday 5pm to 3am. 8615 W. Sahara (at Durango St). ⓒ **702/233-2859.**

5 Gay Bars

Hip and happening Vegas locals know that some of the best scenes and dance action can actually be found in the city's gay bars. And no, they don't ask for sexuality ID at the door. All are welcome at any of the following establishments—as long as you don't have a problem with the people inside, they aren't going to have a problem with you. For women, this can be a fun way to dance and not get hassled by overeager lotharios. (Lesbians, by the way, are just as welcome at any of the gay bars.)

If you want to know what's going on in gay Las Vegas during your visit, pick up a copy of the *Q Vegas*, a free gay-oriented newspaper that's available at any of the places described below. Or call ⓒ **702/650-0636** or check out the online edition at **www.qvegas.com**. You can also find gay nightlife listings on the Web at **www.gaylasvegas.com** or **www.gayvegas.com**.

The Buffalo ⓡ Close to Gipsy, this leather/Levi's bar is popular with motorcycle clubs. It features beer busts (all the beer you can drink for $5) Friday night from 9pm to midnight. Pool tables, darts, and music videos play in an otherwise not-striking environment. It's very cheap, however, with long necks going for around $2, and it gets very, very busy, very late (3 or 4am). Open 24 hours. 4640 Paradise Rd. (at Naples Dr.). ℂ 702/733-8355.

The Eagle ℛ Off the beaten track in just about every sense of the phrase, The Eagle is the place to go if well-lit bars make you nervous. It's dark and slightly seedy but in that great '70s gay bar kind of way. All in all, it's a refreshing change from the overprocessed slickness that is Las Vegas. The crowd, tending toward middle age, is mostly male and is of the Levi's/leather group. There is a small dance area (calling it a dance floor would be generous), a pool table, video poker, and a nice-size bar. Drinks are inexpensive, and special events make them even more so. For instance, The Eagle is rapidly becoming famous for its twice-weekly underwear parties (if you check your pants, you receive draft beer and well drinks for free—that's right: free). Open 24 hours. 3430 E. Tropicana Ave. (at Pecos Rd.). ℂ 702/458-8662.

Gipsy ℛ For years, Gipsy reigned supreme as the best gay dance place in the city, and for good reason: great location (Paradise Rd., near the Hard Rock), excellent layout (sunken dance floor and two bars), and very little competition. A few years ago, some fierce competition stole some of its spotlight, along with a good portion of the clientele, and so the Gipsy fought back with a $750,000 renovation that seemed to recapture past glories. But apparently they aren't willing to rest on their laurels. Drink specials along with special events, shows, male dancers, and theme nights have always made this place a good party bar. Open daily 10pm to 6am. 4605 Paradise Rd. (at Naples Dr.). ℂ 702/731-1919. Cover varies but is usually $5 and up on weekends, less or even free on weekdays.

Good Times ℛ This quiet neighborhood bar is located (for those of you with a taste for subtle irony) in the same complex as the Liberace Museum, a few miles due east of the MGM Grand. There's a small dance floor, but nobody really uses it, the crowd preferring instead to take advantage of the cozy bar area. A small conversation pit is a perfect spot for an intimate chat. Of course, there's the omnipresent pool and video poker if you're not interested in witty repartee. We remember this place as being a lot more crowded than it was during our most recent visit (but perhaps we were there on an off night). It makes a nice respite after the Liberace Museum (after

Moments   Lounge Lizard Supreme

All those faux-hipster artists doing woeful lounge act characters in Hollywood and New York only wish they could be
Mr. Cook E. Jarr, whose sincerity and obvious drive to
entertain puts mere performance artists to shame. With
George Hamilton's tan, Cher's first shag haircut (it's certainly not his factory original coif), and a bottomless, bor-
derless catalog of rock, pop, soul, swing, and standard
favorites, he's more Vegas than Wayne Newton.

Cook has a cult following of blue-collar casino denizens
and the youthful cocktail set, who listen enraptured as he
plays human jukebox, complete with karaoke-style back-
ing recordings, terrible jokes, an array of disco-era lights,
and (his favorite) a smoke machine. He's actually a solid,
throaty singer with a gift for vocal mimicry as he moves
from Ben E. King to Bee Gees to Tony Bennett turf. And his
tribute to the night Sinatra died—a version of "My Way"
in which he voiced, alternatively, Sammy, Dino, and Elvis
welcoming Ol' Blue Eyes to Heaven—was priceless.

You can catch him at **Harrah's Carnaval Court Lounge** at
3475 Las Vegas Blvd. South (© **702/369-5222**). Don't miss
him! (And if he has left there by the time you read this, try
to track him down.)

which you may very well need a stiff drink). Open 24 hours. In the
Liberace Plaza, 1775 E. Tropicana Ave. (at Spencer St.). © **702/736-9494.**

6 Other Bars

In addition to the venues listed below, consider hanging out, as the
locals quickly began doing, at **Aureole, Red Square,** and the **House
of Blues,** all in **Mandalay Bay** (p. 36). There's a separate bar at
Aureole, facing the wine tower, where your wish for wine sends
comely lasses flying up four stories, courtesy of "Peter Pan"–style
harnesses, to fetch your desired bottle. At Red Square, keep your
drink nicely chilled all night long on the ice bar, created from water
that's freshly poured and frozen daily. Or hang out and feel the blues
at the small bottlecap-bedecked bar in the corner of the House of
Blues restaurant, which gets quite lively with off-duty locals after
midnight. **Zuri** in the MGM Grand is the best of the casino-hotel

bars that don't charge admission (although the drinks are expensive), probably because of its construction—a semicurtained enclave just off the elevators (as opposed to a space just plunked down right off, or right in the middle of, a casino). Amid swooping wood and red velvet couches, you can actually hear your partner's whispered sweet nothings.

You might also check out the incredible nighttime view at the bar atop the **Stratosphere**—nothing beats it.

There's also the **Viva Las Vegas Lounge** at the Hard Rock Hotel, where every rock-connected person in Vegas will eventually pass through.

And the **Petrossian Bar** in the Bellagio offers class along with its cocktails (to say nothing of caviar and other delicacies)—but come for the cocktails, as those in the know claim it's not only the best bar in Vegas for such matters, but maybe the best bar in the West.

Caramel 𝒌𝒌   It's small but worlds away from the Bellagio-business-as-usual just outside its doors. How happy the 20-somethings are that there is this hip-hop spinning, glowing, caramel-and-chocolate-coated drink glasses, glowing bar, nonthreatening (and non-Euro-stodgy), scene-intensive hangout in the middle of Bellagio. How much does this prove Bellagio is trying to lure the Ghost Bar crowd away from the Palms? Not that this will do it, but if you are here and young, it's where you should be. Open daily 5pm to 4am. 3600 Las Vegas Blvd. South. (in Bellagio). © 702/693-7111.

Champagnes Cafe 𝒌𝒌   Wonder where old Vegas went? It ossi-fied right here. Red-and-gold-flocked wallpaper and other such trappings of "glamour" never die—in fact, with this ultra-low-key lighting, they will never even fade. A seedy old bar with seedy old scary men leering away. They even serve ice-cream shakes spiked with booze—two indulgences wrapped into one frothy package, and quite a double addiction delight. Some might run screaming from the place, while others will think they've died and gone to heaven. Just remember—this is the kind of place director Quentin Tarantino, or this year's alt-cult hit movie, will make famous. It can't be long. And then it will be overrun with hipsters. Beat the rush, go there now, and brag that you knew about it back before it was so cool it became passé. Again. Open 24 hours. 3557 S. Maryland Pkwy. (between Twain Ave. and Desert Inn Rd.). © 702/737-1699.

Coyote Ugly 𝒌   You've seen the movie, now go have some of that prepackaged fun for yourself. Oh, come on—you don't think those bartender girls really dance on the bar and hose down the crowd just because they are so full of spontaneous rowdy high spirits, now do you? Not when the original locale built a reputation (and inspired a bad movie) for just such behavior, creating a success strong enough to start a whole chain of such frat boy fun places? Open daily from 6pm until 4am. In New York–New York, 3790 Las Vegas Blvd. South. (at Tropicana Ave.). ℭ 702/740-6969. Cover varies, usually $10 and up on weekends.

The Dispensary ℜ   Stuck in a '70s time warp (the waterwheel and the ferns are the tip-off, though the songs on the Muzak confirm it), this is a fine place for a nice, long, quiet drink. One that lasts decades, perhaps. It's very quiet, low-key, and often on the empty side. Things pick up on weekends, but it still isn't the sort of place that attracts raucous drunks. (Of course, if it were on the Strip instead of being tucked away, it probably would.) "We leave you alone if you don't want to be bothered," says the proprietor. (We still worry about what happens if you sit here long enough.) If you are a hepcat, but one on the mild side, you'll love it. Open 24 hours. 2451 E. Tropicana Ave. (at Eastern Ave.). ℭ 702/458-6343.

Double Down Saloon ℜℜ *Finds*   "House rule: You puke, you clean." Okay, that about sums up the Double Down. Well, no, it doesn't really do the place justice. This is a big local hangout, with management quoting an old *Scope* magazine description of its clientele: "Hipsters, blue collars, the well-heeled lunatic fringe." Rumored to have been spotted there: director Tim Burton and Dr. Timothy Leary. Need to know more? Okay, trippy hallucinogenic graffiti covers the walls, the ceiling, the tables, and possibly you if you sit there long enough. Decor includes Abby Rents–type chairs and thrift-store battered armchairs and sofa, a couple of pool tables, and a jukebox that holds everything from the Germs and Frank Zappa to Link Wray, Dick Dale, and the Rev. Horton Heat. On Wednesday night, they have a live blues band, while other nights might find local alternative, punk, or ska groups performing. There's no cover unless they have some out-of-town band that actually has a label deal. Open 24 hours. 4640 Paradise Rd. (at Naples Dr.). ℭ 702/791-5775. www.doubledownsaloon.com.

Drop Bar ℜ   Smack in the middle of the Green Valley Ranch Resort casino, with '60s-inspired go-go girls dancing away. Open 24 hours. In Green Valley Ranch Resort, 2300 Paseo Verde Pkwy., Henderson. ℭ 702/221-6560. Cover varies, usually $10 and up.

Eiffel Tower Bar ℜ   From this chic and elegant room, in the restaurant on the 11th floor of the Eiffel Tower, you can look down on everyone (in Vegas)—just like a real Parisian! (Just kidding, Francophiles.)

But really, this is a date-impressing bar, and, since there's no cover or minimum, it's a cost-effective alternative to the overly inflated food prices at the restaurant. Drop by for a drink, but try to look sophisticated. And then you can cop an attitude and dismiss everything as gauche—or droit, depending on which way you are seated. Open Sunday to Thursday nights until midnight, Friday and Saturday nights until 1am. In Paris Las Vegas, 3655 Las Vegas Blvd. South. © **702/948-6937.**

40 Deuce 🎯🎯   Imported from Los Angeles, where it's a highly successful nightlife spot (and regular hangout for every hot young celebrity you can think of, and so very likely to be so in Vegas as well), this is part of the trend of new "burlesque" clubs—a bar with regular performances. Every 90 minutes or so, scantily clad girls come out and skillfully shake their groove thangs, stripping down to pasties, teeny boy shorts, and G-strings. There's both a bar (with obscenely expensive drinks) and a proper cabaret space—performers utilize both stage and bar top—where DJs spin in between performance spots. On weekends, you can't fit a piece of paper inside. Open Sunday and Wednesday 10pm to 4 am, Friday and Saturday 10pm to 6am. Shows start at 11pm. In Mandalay Bay, 3950 Las Vegas Blvd. South. © **702/632-7000.** Cover varies.

Ghost Bar 🎯🎯   Probably the most interesting aspect of this desperate-to-get-into-the-gossip-pages-as-the-trendy-bar-of-the-moment place (decorated in that '60s mod/futuristic silver gleam look) is that though much is made of the fact that it's on the 55th floor, it's really on the 42nd. Something about the number 4 being bad luck in Asian cultures. Whatever, the view still is fabulous, which is the main reason to come here, that and to peer at those tousled-hair beauties copping an attitude on the couches and see if any of them have the kind of names that will make tomorrow's gossip pages. It may be the hot bar of the moment by the time you get there (dress up), or everyone may have moved on. Open daily from 7pm until the early hours of the morning. In Palms Resort & Casino, 4321 W. Flamingo. © **702/942-7778.** Cover varies, usually $10 and up.

Gordon-Biersch Brewing Company 🎯   This is part of a chain, and while it does feel like it, it's better than the average such entry. The interior is both contemporary and rustic, warmer than its semi-industrial look might usually deliver. It's roomy, so you don't feel stacked up on top of other customers. The house lager (they specialize in German brews) is tasty and the noise level acceptable. A good place to go hoist a few. Open Sunday through Thursday from

11:30am until 2am, Friday and Saturday until they feel like closing. 3987 Paradise Rd. (just north of Flamingo Rd.). © 702/312-5247.

Peppermill's Fireside Lounge 🉐 *Finds* Walk through the classic Peppermill's coffee shop (not a bad place to eat, by the way) on the Strip, and you land in its dark, plush, cozy lounge. A fabulously dated view of hip, it has low, circular banquette seats; fake floral foliage; low neon; and electric candles. But best of all is the water and fire pit as the centerpiece—a piece of kitsch thought long vanished from the Earth, and attracting nostalgia buffs like moths to a flame. It all adds up to a cozy, womblike place, perfect for unwinding a bit after some time spent on the hectic Strip. The enormous, exotic froufrou tropical drinks (including the signature bathtub-size margaritas) will ensure that you sink into that level of comfortable stupor. Open 24 hours. 2985 Las Vegas Blvd. South. © 702/735-7635.

Pink E's 🉐 Sick of the attitude at Club Rio? (And well you should be.) Escape directly across the street to Pink E's, where the theme is pink. (You were expecting, maybe, seafoam?) Anyway, at least one regular described this as "the only place to go if you are over 25 and have a brain." And like pink. Because everything here is: the many pool tables, the Ping-Pong tables, the booths, the lighting, the lava lamp on the bar, and even the people. In its own way, it's as gimmick-ridden as The Beach dance club (see "Dance Clubs," later in this chapter), but surely no one would put out a pink pool table in all seriousness? Yeah, it's a ludicrous heresy, but don't you want to play on one? Anyway, Pink E's offers retro diner food and a DJ on weekends. The dress code basically translates to "no gangsta wannabe wear." Go, but wear all black just to be ornery. Open 24 hours. 3695 W. Flamingo Rd. (at S. Valley View Blvd.) © 702/252-4666.

Risque 🉐 Ready to put the *ooh la la* back in Vegas (like it needed it, but never mind), this is Paris Las Vegas's most recent lounge (a bar with a dance floor, in this case), which has '80s lingerie-clad girls practicing lurid versions of their yoga poses, with a detached and yet erotic attitude, perched on a ledge for you to gawk at as soon as you walk in the door. More scantily dressed gals work the top of the bar, while a DJ spins discs in this industrial-nightclub-meets-modern-day-strip-bar. Of course, for every dipped-in-black club kid beauty there is a denim-wearing tourist, but still, you can get your jollies. Open Thursday through Sunday from 10pm to 4am. In Paris Las Vegas, 3655 Las Vegas Blvd. South. © 702/946-7000. Cover varies but usually men $20, women $10.

Sand Dollar Blues Lounge ☆   This is the kind of funky, no-decor (think posters and beer signs), atmosphere-intensive, slightly grimy, friendly bar you'll either wish your town has or hope it never does. Just up the road from Treasure Island, this is a great antidote to artificial Vegas. Attracting a solid mix of locals and tourists (employees claim the former includes everything from bikers to chamber of commerce members), the Sand Dollar features live blues (both electric and acoustic, with a little Cajun and zydeco thrown in) every night. We wondered how Vegas had enough blues bands to fill out a whole weekly bill. The answer? All the musicians play in multiple bands in different configurations. The dance floor is tiny and often full. The minimal cover always goes to the band. Depending on your desires, it's either refreshingly not Las Vegas or just the kind of place you came to Vegas to escape. Go before someone has the idea to build a theme hotel based on it. Open 24 hours. 3355 Spring Mountain Rd. (at Polaris Ave.). ☎ 702/871-6651. Cover varies but is usually no more than a few bucks.

Sky Lounge ☆   It may not have quite the view offered by the Stratosphere's bar, but it's pretty darn good and a lot easier to get to. You see too much of the Holiday Inn Boardwalk directly across the street and not quite enough of the MGM Grand to the left, but otherwise there are no complaints. The decor is too modern (heavy on '80s black and purple), but overall the place is quiet (especially during the day) and civil. A jazz vocal/piano act performs at night, when the views are naturally best. The atmosphere produced by all this is classic Vegas in the best sense (with only a slight touch of necessary kitsch). It's worth a trip for an escape from the mob, though you won't be the only tourist fighting for window seats. Open 8am until whenever they feel like closing. At Polo Towers, 3745 Las Vegas Blvd. South. ☎ 702/261-1000.

Triple 7 Brew Pub ☆ *Finds*   Yet another of the many things Main Street Station has done right. Stepping into its microbrew pub feels like stepping out of Vegas. Well, maybe, except for the dueling piano entertainment. It has a partial modern warehouse look (exposed pipes, microbrew fixtures visible through exposed glass at back, and a very high ceiling), but a hammered tin ceiling continues the hotel's Victorian decor; the overall effect seems straight out of San Francisco's North Beach. It's a bit on the yuppified side but escapes being pretentious. And frankly, it's a much-needed modern touch for the Downtown area. This place has its own brewmaster, a number of microbrews ready to try, and an oyster and sushi bar, plus fancy burgers and pizzas. It can get noisy during the aforementioned piano duel act, but otherwise casino noise stays out. Since all of Downtown is too heavy on the old Las Vegas side (which is fine, but not *all* the time), this is good for a suitable breather. Open Sunday through Thursday from 11am until 3am, Friday and Saturday from 11am until 4am. In Main Street Station, 200 Main St. ✆ 702/387-1896.

Whisky Sky 🀄🀄 This is probably your best bet for a trendy place that might actually have either beautiful locals or out-of-town celebs looking for a cool time but wanting a lower profile, thanks to its very off-the-Strip location and also its creator, hip-bar-master Rande Gerber (Cindy Crawford's hubby). Think beds instead of couches, and you've got a sense of the gestalt. Open daily from 4pm until 4am. In Green Valley Ranch Resort, 2300 Paseo Verde Pkwy., Henderson. ✆ 702/221-6560. Cover varies, usually $10 and up.

A KARAOKE BAR

Ellis Island Casino—Karaoke 🀄 Admit it. You sing in the shower. And when the acoustics are just right, you fancy you could give a Vegas lounge singer a run for his money. Here's your chance to test this theory without the comfort of tile acoustics. In this small, smoky den filled with leather and candles, any number of people from all walks of life get up and act out their lounge singer fantasies. You can join them. With more than 6,000 titles, including multiple Engelbert Humperdinck, Mac Davis, and Tom Jones selections, there are plenty of cheesy numbers just perfect for this kind of environment. And if you stay here long enough, you'll hear them all. Karaoke is offered daily 9pm to 3am. 4178 Koval Lane (off Flamingo Rd., behind Bally's). ✆ 702/733-8901.

7 Dance Clubs

In addition to the options listed below, country music fans might want to wander on over to **Dylan's,** 4660 Boulder Hwy. (✆ 702/451-4006). It offers country music (live and otherwise) and line dancing, with free dance lessons. Dylan's is casual and basic, with a definite roadhouse vibe. Also look for the rise of the new "burlesque clubs"—think really classy, sexy, and expensive strip shows—like Tangerine at Treasure Island, the Pussycat Dolls at Pure in Caesars Palace, and 40 Deuce, listed above.

The Beach 🀄 If you're a fan of loud, crowded, 24-hour party bars filled with tons of good-looking fun-seekers, then bow in this direction, for you have found Mecca. It's a two-story affair with five separate bars downstairs and another three up.

Just in case walking the 20 feet to the closest bar is too much of an effort, they also have bikini-clad women serving beer out of steel tubs full of ice (they also roam the floor with shot belts). The drinks are on the pricey side, but the unfailingly gorgeous, 4% body-fat bartenders (both men and women) are friendly and offer rotating drink specials that might keep you from busting your budget.

Downstairs is the large two-story dance floor, which dominates the center of the room and is built around a full-service bar at one end. And let's not forget those Jell-O shot contests where club-goers try to eat shaky cubes of alcohol-spiked gelatin off each other's partially bared bodies.

The crowd is aggressively young and pretty, more men than women (70/30 split), and about 60% tourist, which is probably why the place can get away with charging up to $10 (and even sometimes more) cover. Party people look no further. There's free valet parking, and if you've driven here and become intoxicated, they'll drive you back to your hotel at no charge. Open daily from 10pm until the wee hours. 365 S. Convention Center Dr. (at Paradise Rd.). ⓒ 702/731-1925. www.beachlv.com. Cover $5 and up.

Bikinis ⓡ By now, you should be getting the format for the most recent trend in clubs and lounges in Vegas: liberal use of dancing girls who wear very, very little. What makes this different from an honest strip bar, we don't know (but you can read some thoughts on the matter below, in our review of Sapphire), but it does show how mainstream strip bars have become. How else to explain the go-go dancers here, who wear thong bikinis and little wisps of gauze as they dance, with various degrees of enthusiasm and talent, on stages with strippers' poles, and then sometimes get into tanks of water to gyrate? There is a dance floor for you to shake your thang to hip-hop and house, while the interior Lava Lounge plays old-school funk. Open Thursday to Sunday from 10pm to late into the night. In Rio, 3700 W. Flamingo Rd. ⓒ 702/777-7777. Cover varies.

Cleopatra's Barge Nightclub ⓡ This is a small, unique nightclub set in part on a floating barge—you can feel it rocking. The bandstand, a small dance floor, and a few (usually reserved) tables are here, while others are set around the boat on "land." It's a gimmick, but one that makes this far more fun than other, more pedestrian, hotel bars. Plenty of dark makes for romance, but blaring volume levels mean you will have to scream those sweet nothings.

Check out the bare-breasted figurehead on the ship's prow who juts out over the hallway going past the entrance. She could put someone's eye out. Open nightly from 10:30pm until 4am. In Caesars Palace, 3570 Las Vegas Blvd. South. ✆ **702/731-7110.** No cover, 2-drink minimum.

Club Rio ☕ This is one of the hottest nightspots in Vegas, but apparently made so by people who don't mind long lines, restrictive dress codes, attitudinal door people, hefty cover charges, and bland dance music. Waits can be interminable and admittance denied thanks to the wrong footwear or shirt.

Once inside, you find a large, circular room, with a spacious dance floor taking up much of the space. Giant video screens line the upper parts of the walls, showing anything from shots of the action down below to catwalk footage. Comfy circular booths fill out the next couple of concentric circles; these seem mostly reserved, and when empty, they leave the impression that the place isn't very full—so why the wait? Music on a recent visit included a Madonna medley and the perennial "Celebration," not the most au courant of tunes. The total effect is of a grown-up, not terribly drunken, frat and sorority mixer. The club opens at 11pm Thursday through Saturday and stays open until about 4am. In Rio, 3700 W. Flamingo Rd. ✆ **702/252-7777.** www.riovegasnights.com. Cover varies.

Drai's After Hours ☕ Young Hollywood film execs and record company types are likely to be found here, schmoozing and dancing it up to house, techno, and tribal music. Open Wednesday through Sunday from midnight until dawn. In the Barbary Coast, 3595 Las Vegas Blvd. South. ✆ **702/737-0555.** Cover varies, usually $20.

Ice ☕ Housed in the former Drink space (one of our favorite Vegas clubs; we miss it), this is along the same lines (hence, doubtless, the linked name); though there is one main multistory dance floor, there are also several themed rooms, so the effect is of several clubs rolled into one massive space. Very good for a group where someone wants to hear house music in all its many varieties and someone else wants acid jazz and someone else wants R&B. It's all state-of-the-art, and very chic. The intimate smaller rooms include the "Fur Room," where S&M fantasies are teased. There are even platforms for performance artists. The new hot (or cool) destination, it's far more interesting than most of the clubs at the big hotels. Open Tuesday and Thursday through Sunday 11pm until 5am. 200 E. Harmon Ave. (at Koval Lane) ✆ **702/699-9888.** Cover $20.

Light ☕☕ In contrast to the metallic high gloss that characterizes most trendy nightspots, this is a grown-up nightclub (sister to an establishment in New York City)—fitting, since it's in the grown-up Bellagio—all wood and velvet and polite attitudes from the staff. Music tends toward both modern and old-school hip-hop and pop, with dancers (real ones) clad in not skimpy garments but rather modest costumes, and even touches such as a live sax player jamming along to the music. Guests are probably all tourists, but tourists of the heir-to-the-hotel fortune sort—and yet, the club doesn't feel exclusive but rather like one big open party. A nifty and tricky feat to pull off. Note that a dress code of no jeans, no sneakers, and shirts with collars is strictly enforced. Open Thursday through Sunday from 10:30pm until 4am. In Bellagio, 3600 Las Vegas Blvd. South. (C) **702/693-8300.** Cover varies, usually $20.

Monte Carlo Pub & Brewery 𝄞 *(Finds* After 9pm nightly, this immense warehouselike pub and working microbrewery (see details in chapter 5) turns from a casual restaurant into something of a dance club. Rock videos blare forth from a large screen and 40 TV monitors around the room, while on stage, dueling pianos provide music and audience-participation entertainment. The Pub is cigar-friendly and maintains a humidor. There's a full bar, and, of course, the house microbrews are featured; you can also order pizza. Open until 3am Sunday to Thursday, until 4am Friday and Saturday. In Monte Carlo Resort & Casino, 3770 Las Vegas Blvd. South. (C) **702/730-7777.** No cover.

Pure 𝄞 The biggest new nightclub—two levels, 36,000 square feet—is a celebrity financial venture owned in part by Celine Dion, Shaquille O'Neal, Andre Agassi, and Steffi Graf (does anyone get a connection among these four?). It's expected to be a four-story indoor/outdoor club with bars, private cabanas, a waterfall, a fire pit, another dance floor, and what is being billed as "incredible panoramic views" of the Strip. A few months after the opening of Pure, the Pussycat Dolls Lounge will open adjacent to the main nightclub and will feature a nightly, adult-flavored cabaret show and more drinking and partying space. In Caesars Palace, 3570 Las Vegas Blvd. South. No other information yet.

Ra 𝄞 Named Las Vegas's best nightclub by *Las Vegas Weekly* in 2002, the futuristic Egyptian-themed Ra is part of the new generation of Vegas hot spots. It has that Vegas "we're a show and an attraction" vibe but is still not overly pretentious. The staff is friendly, which is a rare thing for a hot club. You'll find heavy gilt decor, a major light show, cigar lounges off the disco, draped VIP booths, and plenty of little nooks and crannies. Current dance music (mostly techno) is on the soundtrack. The later you go, the more likely the mid- to upper 20s clientele will be entirely local. Open Wednesday through Saturday from 10pm until 4am. In Luxor Las Vegas, 3900 Las Vegas Blvd. South. ✆ 702/262-4000. www.ralv.com. Cover $10–$20.

Rain ✦✦✦   The hottest nightclub in Vegas—at least, until everyone moves to the next one. Which means you (and us—don't think we aren't standing there with you, shoulder to shoulder in solidarity) will probably spend most of your time trying to convince someone, anyone, to let you in. But we also have to be honest: If you can brave the wait, the crowds, and the attitude, you will be inside a club that has done everything right, from the multilevel layout that allows them to pack the crowds in and allows those crowds to peer up and down at their brethren, to DJs who play the right house and techno cuts (at a pulse-thumping tempo, so don't expect for your good pickup lines to be overheard), to the scaffolding that holds pyrotechnic and other mood-revvers, to the ubiquitous-of-late go-go girls dressed like strippers. If this is your choice, then note that they start lining up way before the 11pm opening time. Open Thursday to Saturday from 11pm until dawn. In the Palms, 4321 W. Flamingo Rd. ✆ 702/940-7246. Cover $20 and up.

Rumjungle ✦✦   Now, normally our delicate sensibilities wince at such overkill, and we tend to write off efforts such as this as just trying a bit too hard. But surprisingly, rumjungle really delivers the great fun it promises. The fire-wall entrance gives way to a wall of water; a two-story bar is full of the largest collection of rum varieties anywhere, each bottle illuminated with a laser beam of light; go-go girls dance and prance between bottles of wine, to dueling congas; and the food all comes skewered on swords. It's all a bit much, but it works, really it does. Get there early (before 10pm) to avoid lines/guest lists/the cover charge, and consider having dinner (served 'til 11pm); it's costly, but it's a multicourse, all-you-can-eat feast of flame-pit-cooked Brazilian food. For the amount of food and the waiving of the cover charge, dinner is a good deal. Then dance it off all night long (the club is open 'til 4am Fri–Sat nights and 2am the rest of the week). In Mandalay Bay, 3950 Las Vegas Blvd. South. ✆ 702/632-7408. Cover $25–$30.

Studio Club ✦   In the main rotunda of MGM Grand, which once housed the *Wizard of Oz* walk-through diorama, this is the biggest and best of the free hotel lounges, which are these days otherwise best known for their enthusiastic but not notably talented cover bands (you just know most of the singers are the sort who didn't get past the first couple auditions for *American Idol*). It has an enormous and elaborate stage and band, but since it's in the middle of an area you have to cross if you are passing through from the Strip, it can be hard to navigate through on a busy weekend night. In MGM Grand, 3799 Las Vegas Blvd. South. ℂ 702/891-1111. No cover.

Studio 54   The legendary Studio 54 has been resurrected here in Las Vegas, but with all the bad elements and none of the good ones. Forget Truman, Halston, and Liza doing illegal (or at least immoral) things in the bathroom stalls; that part of Studio 54 remains but a fond memory. The snooty, exclusive door attitude, however, has been retained. Hooray. Red-rope policies are all well and good if you're trying to build a mystique in a regular club, but for a tourist attraction, where guests are likely to be one-time-only (or, at best, once a year), it's obnoxious. The large dance floor has a balcony overlooking it, the decor is industrial (exposed piping and the like), the music is hip-hop and electronic, and there is nothing to do other than dance. If the real Studio 54 had been this boring, no one would remember it today. Open Tuesday through Saturday from 10pm until 3am or later. In MGM Grand, 3799 Las Vegas Blvd. South. ℂ 702/891-1111. www.studio54lv.com. Cover 20 and up.

Tabu ℝ   This hot nightclub is, despite the name, less stripper saucy than the other new "ultra lounges" (which here means "noisy, high-priced bar"), and consequently is more grown up—and just as loud. With an interior of late-'90s high-tech/industrial meets cheesy '80s bachelor's den, it's nothing aesthetically special, though there are some nice spots for canoodling. But do find a wall or the circular couch if you want to hear yourself think. Open Tuesday through Saturday from 10pm until "early morning." In MGM Grand, 3799 Las Vegas Blvd. South. ℂ 702/891-7183. Cover varies, but about $10 for men, free for women.

VooDoo Lounge ℝ   Occupying, along with the VooDoo Cafe, two floors in the new addition to the Rio, the Lounge almost successfully combines Haitian voodoo and New Orleans Creole in its decor and theme. There are two main rooms: one with a large dance floor and stage for live music, and a disco room, which is filled with large video screens and serious light action. Big club chairs in groups form conversation pits, where you might actually be able to have a conversation. The big seller? The bartenders put on a show, a la Tom Cruise in *Cocktail*. They shake, jiggle, and light stuff on fire. Supposedly, the live music includes Cajun acts, but when it comes down to it, rock seems to rule the day. The mid- to late-20s crowd is more heavily local than you might expect; the dress code calls for "business casual," with no shorts, jeans, or shirts without collars for men. Open 5pm to 3am or later. In Rio, 3700 Las Vegas Blvd. South. ✆ **702/252-7777.** Cover $5–$10.

8 Strip Clubs

No, we don't mean entertainment establishments on Las Vegas Boulevard South. We mean the other kind of "strip." Yes, people come to town for the gambling and the wedding chapels, but the lure of Vegas doesn't stop there. Though prostitution is not legal within the city, the sex industry is an active and obvious force in town. Every other cab carries a placard for a strip club, and a walk down the Strip at night will have dozens of people thrusting flyers at you for clubs, escort services, phone sex lines, and more. And some of you are going to want to check it out.

And why not? An essential part of the Vegas allure is decadence, and naked flesh would certainly qualify, as does the thrill of trying something new and daring. Of course, by and large, the nicer bars aren't particularly daring, and if you go to more than one in an evening, the thrill wears off and the breasts don't look quite so bare.

Cheetah's ✪ This is the strip club used as the set in the movie *Showgirls,* but thanks to the magic of Hollywood and later renovations by the club, only the main stage will look vaguely familiar to those few looking for Nomi Malone. There's also a smaller stage, plus three tiny "tip stages" so that you can really get close to (and give much money to) the woman of your choice. Eight TVs line the walls; the club does a brisk business during major sporting events. The management believes that if you treat people right, they will keep coming back, so the atmosphere is friendlier than at other clubs. Lap dances are $20. Open 24 hours. 2112 Western Ave. ✆ **702/384-0074.** Topless. Cover $10–$20.

Club Paradise ✪ Until the new behemoths moved into town, this was the nicest of the strip clubs. Which isn't to say it isn't still nice—it's just got competition. The interior and atmosphere are rather like those of a hot nightclub where most of the women happen to be topless. The glitzy stage looks like something from a miniature showroom: The lights flash and the dance music pounds, there are two big video screens (one featuring soft porn, the other showing sports!), the chairs are plush and comfortable, the place is relatively bright by strip-club standards, and they offer champagne and cigars. Not surprisingly, they get a very white-collar crowd here. The result is not terribly sleazy, which may please some and turn others off. Lap dances are $20. Open Monday to Friday 5pm to 6am, and Saturday and Sunday 6pm to 6am. 4416 Paradise Rd. © 702/734-7990. Topless. $10–$20 cover, 2-drink minimum (drinks $4.50 and up). Unescorted women allowed.

Crazy Horse, Two *(Overrated)*   We've omitted the address of this place on purpose. It's full of so much obnoxious attitude, with overly aggressive girls soliciting lap dances, that even the other clubs in town sneer at them. There are plenty of strip bars—pass this one by.

Déjà Vu Showgirls ✷✷   Owned by the same people as Little Darlings (see below), this place both deeply perturbs us and amuses the heck out of us. The latter because it's one of the rare strip clubs where the women actually perform numbers. Instead of just coming out and taking off an article or two of clothing and then parading around in a desultory manner before collecting a few tips and running off to solicit lap dances, each stripper comes out and does an actual routine—well, okay, maybe not so much, but she does remove her clothes to personally chosen music, shedding an outfit tailored to her music selection. And so it happened that we have now seen a punk rock chick strip to "Anarchy in the UK." Lap dances are $20 to $30. Open Monday through Saturday from 11am to 6am, and Sunday from 6pm to 4am. 3247 Industrial Rd. © 702/894-4167. Totally nude. $10–$25 cover. Unescorted women allowed.

Glitter Gulch ✷   Right there in the middle of the Fremont Street Experience, Glitter Gulch is either an eyesore or the last bastion of Old Las Vegas, depending on your point of view. Given its convenient location, this is the perfect place for the merely curious—you can easily pop in, check things out, goggle and ogle, and then hit the road, personal dignity intact. Table dances are $20. Open daily 1pm to 4am. 20 Fremont St. © 702/385-4774. Topless. No cover, 2-drink minimum (drinks $7.75 and up).

Jaguar's   At press time, all kinds of we-thought-this-only-happened-in-the-movies things were going on with this club. Short version: racketeering charges. The point is that the last we heard, there was some struggle to keep operating. This may be over with by the time you read this, or new ownership may have happened and the place could be different, or you could show up and everything is exactly as follows: This was going to be the largest strip club in town—25,000 square feet—and then someone built something much bigger. So they had to settle for being perhaps the prettiest. It is sort of the Bellagio of strip clubs, by which we mean two-story over-the-top marble Italian palace style (think the glory days of Caesars Palace), with high-tech gizmos (such as fingerprint identification for certain VIP rooms) for the well-heeled (and willing to spend it on seminaked girls). Lap dances are $20. Open daily 4:30pm to 4am. 3355 S. Procyon St. ✆ **702/732-1116.** Topless. Cover $20. Unescorted women allowed.

Little Darlings ☜   They call themselves the "Pornocopia of Sex," and given the number of services they offer, you can see why. In addition to a fully stocked adult store, they have private nude dances in booths. This is one of the few clubs where the women are not allowed any physical contact with the customers. There are also rooms where you can watch a nude woman take a shower (in theory doing erotic things with soap), and "Fantasy Rooms" where a glass pane separates you from a woman performing still more erotic stunts. Despite all the nude offerings, the resultant atmosphere is not especially dirty, just rowdy. Totally nude private dance in booth $20, Fantasy Room $30. Open daily 11am to 6am. 1514 Western Ave. ✆ **702/366-0145.** Totally nude. Cover $20. No unescorted women.

Olympic Gardens Topless Cabaret ☜   Once the largest of the strip clubs, this almost feels like a family operation, thanks to the middle-aged women handling the door. It also has a boutique that sells lingerie and naughty outfits. The crowd is a mix of 20s to 30s blue-collar guys and techno geeks. As the place fills up and the chairs are crammed in next to each other, it's hard to see how enjoyable or intimate a lap dance can be when the guy next to you is getting one as well. Oh, and by the way, they also have male strippers most nights of the week, so you ladies don't feel left out. Lap dances are $20, more in VIP room. Open 24 hours. 1531 Las Vegas Blvd. South. ✆ **702/385-8987.** Topless. Cover $20. Unescorted women allowed.

Palomino Club ☜   Once the nicest strip club in town, this place now edges into the seedy end of things. It's also a bit out of the way. On the other hand, it does offer total nudity in a classic red-walled setting. And its location outside the Vegas city limits means that it's one of the only clubs that offers both total nudity *and* alcohol. Topless lap dances are $20, totally nude dances are $40. Open daily 5pm to 5am. 1848 Las Vegas Blvd. North. ✆ **702/642-2984.** Totally nude. Cover $15–$30. Unescorted women allowed.

Sapphire Gentleman's Club ☜☆☜   Ladies and Gentlemen, particularly the latter, Las Vegas, home of the largest everything else, now brings you—drum roll—the largest strip club *in the world!*

That's right, 71,000 square feet of nakedidity. Of course, you have to see it—and, of course, that's what they are counting on. But let's say this: While really, it's nothing you haven't seen before, strip-club wise, if you haven't seen a strip club, this is the place to start because it's modern and clean, although, frankly, it's not all that different, looks-wise, from Rain, the superhot nightclub at the Rio. Lap dances are $20. Open 24 hours. 3025 S. Industrial Rd. ✆ **702/796-0000.** Topless. Cover $20 after 6pm. Unescorted women allowed.

Spearmint Rhino ✿   Did you know that even strip bars come in chains? They do, and this is a familiar brand to those in the know or who read billboards close to airports. The runway (where some of the dancers get a little personal with each other) is actually in a separate back area, so it is possible to have a drink at the front (where there are many TVs and other manly accouterments) and never see a naked girl (save for the smaller stage and pole nearby). On a busy night, it's crammed with grown-up frat boys enjoying a clubby space. There can be a veritable factory assembly line of lap dances during these busy periods, which, frankly, seems the opposite of a turn-on to us. Lap dances are $20. Open 24 hours. 3444 Highland Dr. ✆ **702/796-3600.** Topless. Cover $20. Unescorted women allowed.

Strip Tease Cabaret ✿   Redone to eliminate the rather disturbing "fantasy rooms" (where lap dances could occur in private), replacing them with generic "classy" gentlemen's club look, all shiny runways and stage (three total) plus the "shower" stage. One of the bouncers was in *Ocean's 11* as a thug menacing George Clooney. Live DJs, girls far more interested in working the lap dance angle than dancing, it's a fine safe first-time strip bar experience, but not one to make you see what all the fuss is about. Lap dances are $20 and up. Courtesy limo pickup. Open daily 24 hours. 3750 S. Valley View Blvd. ✆ **702/253-1555.** Topless. Cover up to $20. Unescorted women allowed, couples encouraged.

9

Side Trips from Las Vegas

You might not know it to look at the brochures, but there is a big wide world outside of Vegas, and some of it is extraordinary—especially if your aesthetic sensibilities favor the stark and surprising mysteries of desert landscapes. There is every bit as much to marvel at out there as there is within the confines of Vegas, and the two settings make for a curious contrast of the entirely artificial and the wholly natural.

But apart from simple admiration, there is ample to do, from touring the true architectural marvel that is Hoover Dam, to hiking Red Rock Canyon, to swimming and boating on Lake Mead. You'll get a dose of much-needed fresh air—possibly even some exercise—and your kids can get their ya-yas out.

The excursions covered in this chapter, with the exception of the Grand Canyon trips mentioned below, will take you from 20 to 60 miles out of town. Every one of them offers a memorable travel experience.

GRAND CANYON TOURS

Generally, tourists visiting Las Vegas don't drive 300 miles to Arizona to see the Grand Canyon, but dozens of sightseeing tours do depart from the city daily. In addition to the Coach USA tours described in chapter 6, the major operator, **Scenic Airlines** (© **800/ 634-6801** or 702/638-3300; www.scenic.com), runs deluxe, full-day guided air-ground tours for $219 per person ($189 for children 2–11); the price includes a bus excursion through the national park, a flight over the canyon, and lunch. All scenic tours include flight-seeing. The company also offers both full-day and overnight tours with hiking.

Scenic also offers tours to other points of interest and national parks, including Bryce Canyon and Monument Valley. Ask for details when you call.

Excursions from Las Vegas

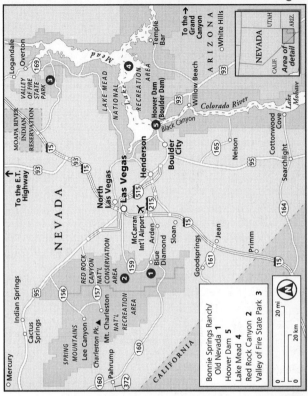

Map legend:
- Bonnie Springs Ranch/ Old Nevada **1**
- Hoover Dam **5**
- Lake Mead **4**
- Red Rock Canyon **2**
- Valley of Fire State Park **3**

1 Hoover Dam & Lake Mead

30 miles SE of Las Vegas

This is one of the most popular excursions from Las Vegas, visited by 2,000 to 3,000 people daily. Why should you join them? Because Hoover Dam is an engineering and architectural marvel, and it changed the Southwest forever. Without it, you wouldn't even be going to Vegas. Kids may be bored, unless they like machinery or just plain big things, but expose them to it anyway, for their own good. (Buy them an ice cream and a Hoover Dam snow globe as a bribe.) Obviously, if you are staying at Lake Mead, it's a must.

The tour itself is a bit cursory and commercialized, but you do get up close and personal with the dam. Wear comfortable shoes; the tour involves quite a bit of walking. Try to take the tour in the morning to beat the desert heat and the really big crowds. You can have lunch out in Boulder City and then perhaps drive back through the **Valley of Fire State Park** (described later in this chapter), which is about 60 magnificently scenic miles from Lake Mead (purchase gas before you start!). Or you can spend the afternoon in Lake Mead pursuits—hiking, boating, even scuba diving in season—or perhaps taking a rafting trip down the Colorado River.

GETTING THERE

Drive east on Flamingo or Tropicana to U.S. 515 south, which automatically turns into I-93 south and takes you right to the dam. This will involve a rather dramatic drive, as you go through Boulder City, come over a rise, and Lake Mead suddenly appears spread out before you. It's a beautiful sight. At about this point, the road narrows down to two lanes, and traffic can slow considerably. On busy tourist days, this means the drive can take an hour or more.

Go past the turnoff to Lake Mead. As you near the dam, you'll see a five-story parking structure tucked into the canyon wall on your left. Park here ($5 charge) and take the elevators or stairs to the walkway leading to the new visitor center.

If you would rather go on an **organized tour,** check out **Coach USA** (© 800/828-6699; www.coachusa.us), which offers a Hoover Dam package that includes admission and a tour of the dam. When you're in Las Vegas, look for discount coupons in the numerous free publications available at hotels. The 4-hour **Hoover Dam Discovery Tour** departs daily at 1:30pm and includes pickup and drop-off; the price is $44 for adults, $35 for children 2 to 12.

HOOVER DAM 𝘢𝘢𝘢

There would be no Las Vegas as we know it without the Hoover Dam. Certainly not the neon and glitz. In fact, the growth of the entire Southwest can be tied directly to the electricity created by the dam.

Until the Hoover Dam was built, much of the southwestern United States was plagued by two natural problems: parched, sandy terrain that lacked irrigation for most of the year, and extensive flooding in spring and early summer, when the mighty Colorado River, fed by melting snow from its source in the Rocky Mountains, overflowed its banks and destroyed crops, lives, and property. On the positive side, raging unchecked over eons, the river's turbulent, rushing waters carved the Grand Canyon.

In 1928, prodded by the seven states through which the river runs during the course of its 1,400-mile journey to the Gulf of California, Congress authorized construction of a dam at Boulder Canyon (later moved to Black Canyon). The Senate's declaration of intention was that "A mighty river, now a source of destruction, is to be curbed and put to work in the interests of society." Construction began in 1931. Because of its vast scope and the unprecedented problems posed in its realization, the project generated significant advances in many areas of machinery production, engineering, and construction. An army of more than 5,200 laborers was assembled, and work proceeded 24 hours a day. Completed in 1936, 2 years ahead of schedule and $15 million under budget (it is, no doubt, a Wonder of the Modern Fiscal World), the dam stopped the annual floods and conserved water for irrigation and industrial and domestic use. Equally important, it became one of the world's major electrical generating plants, providing low-cost, pollution-free hydroelectric power to a score of surrounding communities. Hoover Dam's $165-million cost has been repaid with interest by the sale of inexpensive power to a number of California cities and the states of Arizona and Nevada. The dam is a government project that paid for itself—a feat almost as awe inspiring as its engineering.

The dam itself is a massive curved wall, 660 feet thick at the bottom and tapering to 45 feet where the road crosses it at the top. It towers 726 feet above bedrock (about the height of a 60-story skyscraper) and acts as a plug between the canyon walls to hold back up to 9.2 trillion gallons of water in Lake Mead, the reservoir created by its construction. Four concrete intake towers on the lake side drop the water down about 600 feet to drive turbines and create power, after which the water spills out into the river and continues south.

All the architecture is on a grand scale, and the design has beautiful Art Deco elements, unusual in an engineering project. Note, for instance, the monumental 30-foot bronze sculpture, *Winged Figures of the Republic,* flanking a 142-foot flagpole at the Nevada entrance. According to its creator, Oskar Hansen, the sculpture symbolizes "the immutable calm of intellectual resolution, and the enormous power of trained physical strength, equally enthroned in placid triumph of scientific achievement."

The dam has become a major sightseeing attraction, along with Lake Mead, America's largest artificial reservoir and a major Nevada recreation area.

Seven miles northwest of the dam on U.S. 93, you'll pass through **Boulder City,** which was built to house managerial and construction workers. Sweltering summer heat (many days it is 125°F/52°C) ruled out a campsite by the dam, and the higher elevation of Boulder City offered lower temperatures. The city emerged within a single year, turning a desert wasteland into a community of 6,000. By 1934, it was Nevada's third-largest town.

TOURING THE DAM

The very nice **Hoover Dam Visitor Center,** a vast three-level circular concrete structure with a rooftop overlook, opened in 1995. You'll enter the Reception Lobby, where you can buy tickets; peruse informational exhibits, photographs, and memorabilia; and view three 12-minute video presentations (about the importance of water to life, the events leading up to the construction of Hoover Dam, and the construction itself, as well as the many benefits it confers). Exhibits on the Plaza Level include interactive displays on the environment, habitation, and development of the Southwest; the people who built the dam; and related topics.

Yet another floor up, galleries on the Overlook Level demonstrate, via sculpted bronze panels, the benefits of Hoover Dam and Lake Mead to the states of Arizona, Nevada, and California. The Overlook Level additionally provides an unobstructed view of Lake Mead, the dam, the power plant, the Colorado River, and Black Canyon. (There are multiple photo opportunities throughout this trip.)

You can visit an exhibit center across the street where a 10-minute presentation in a small theater focuses on a topographical map of the 1,400-mile Colorado River. It also has a cafeteria. Notice, by the way, how the restrooms in the center have only electric dryers, no paper towels. A tribute?

Self-guided tours commence at Reception Lobby between 9am and 4:45pm daily, except Thanksgiving and Christmas, although since it takes a couple of hours to do the tour justice, they recommend you get there no later than 3pm so you can do it all before they close at 5pm. Admission is $10 for adults, $8 for seniors 62 and over, and $5 for children 7 to 16; free for children under 7. Although it's not compulsory, it's not a bad idea to call in advance to reserve a place on the tour (© **866/291-TOUR** or 702/597-5970). Tours, by the way, are "not recommended for claustrophobics or those persons with defibrillators."

Note: At this writing, thanks to post–September 11, 2001, security measures, tours of the dam keep changing format. Currently, visitors go to the exhibit center, see a movie, check out views of the dam from various locations, and enter an elevator to descend partly into the bowels of the thing. Guides and docents are posted along the way to answer questions and offer still more information. The whole thing can take up to 2 hours to do, if you go through it carefully. Purses and backpacks are not allowed, though lockers are provided for storage. Obviously, those measures could at any moment be lifted, or further tightened. We include a description of the usual tour by way of illustrating what you could get if matters ever return to normal. You may want to call in advance to see what state the tour is in, but apparently, even with the new measures, it's still most (if not even more) informative.

The tour begins with a 561-foot elevator descent into the dam's interior, where an access tunnel leads to the Nevada wing of the power plant. (You cross to Arizona only on the hard-hat tour.) In the three stops on the regular tour, you see the massive turbines that generate the electricity using the water flow, go outside on the downriver side of the dam, looking up at the towering structure (which is pretty awesome), and then go into one of the tunnels that contains a steel water diversion pipe that feeds the turbines. (It's one of the largest steel water pipes ever made—its interior could accommodate two lanes of automobile traffic.)

Some fun facts you might hear along the way: It took 6½ years to fill the lake. Though 96 workers were killed during the construction, contrary to popular myth, none were accidentally buried as the concrete was poured (it was poured only at a level of 8 in. at a time). Look for a monument to them outside—"they died to make the desert bloom"—along with one for their doggy mascot who was also killed, although after the dam was completed. Compare their wages of 50¢ an hour to those of their Depression-era peers, who made 5¢ to 30¢.

For more information on the dam, and sometimes discount coupons, visit **www.usbr.gov/lc/hooverdam**.

LAKE MEAD NATIONAL RECREATION AREA 🐾🐾

Under the auspices of the National Park Service, the 1.5-million-acre Lake Mead National Recreation Area was created in 1936 around Lake Mead (the reservoir lake that resulted from the construction of Hoover Dam) and later Lake Mohave to the south (formed with the construction of Davis Dam). Before the lakes emerged, this desert region was brutally hot, dry, and rugged—unfit for human habitation. Today it's one of the nation's most popular playgrounds, attracting about 9 million visitors annually. The two lakes comprise 291 square miles. At an elevation of 1,221 feet, Lake Mead itself extends some 110 miles upstream toward the Grand

Canyon. Its 550-mile shoreline, backed by spectacular cliff and canyon scenery, forms a perfect setting for a wide variety of water sports and desert hiking.

The **Alan Bible Visitor Center,** 4 miles northeast of Boulder City on U.S. 93 at NV 166 (© **702/293-8990**), can provide information on all area activities and services. You can pick up trail maps and brochures here, view informative films, and find out about scenic drives, accommodations, ranger-guided hikes, naturalist programs and lectures, bird-watching, canoeing, camping, lakeside RV parks, and picnic facilities. The center also sells books and videotapes about the area. It's open daily 8:30am to 4:30pm except Thanksgiving, Christmas, and New Year's Day.

For information on accommodations, boat rentals, and fishing, call **Seven Crown Resorts** (© **800/752-9669** or 702/293-3484; www.sevencrown.com). You can also find Lake Mead info on the Web at **www.nps.gov/lame**.

The **entry fee** for the area is $5 per vehicle, which covers all passengers.

OTHER OUTDOOR ACTIVITIES

This is a lovely area for scenic drives amid the dramatic desert scenery. One popular route follows the Lakeshore and Northshore Scenic Drives along the edge of Lake Mead. From these roads there are panoramic views of the blue lake, set against a backdrop of the browns, blacks, reds, and grays of the desert mountains. Northshore Scenic Drive also leads through areas of brilliant red boulders and rock formations, and you'll find a picnic area along the way.

BOATING & FISHING   A store at **Lake Mead Resort and Marina,** under the auspices of Seven Crown Resorts (© **800/752-9669** or 702/293-3484; www.sevencrown.com), rents fishing boats, ski boats, personal watercraft, and patio boats. It also carries groceries, clothing, marine supplies, sporting goods, water-skiing gear, fishing equipment, and bait and tackle. You can get a fishing license here ($69 a year, or $18 for 1 day plus $7 for each additional day; discounts for children under 15 are available; additional fees apply for special fishing classifications). The staff is knowledgeable and can apprise you of good fishing spots. Largemouth bass, striped bass, channel catfish, crappie, and bluegill are found in Lake Mead; rainbow trout, largemouth bass, and striped bass in Lake Mohave. You can also arrange here to rent a fully equipped houseboat at **Echo Bay,** 40 miles north.

Other convenient Lake Mead marinas offering similar rentals and equipment are **Las Vegas Boat Harbor** (𝒞 **702/565-9111;** www.lasvegasbaymarina.com), which is even closer to Las Vegas, and **Callville Bay Resort & Marina** (𝒞 **800/255-5561** or 702/565-8958; www.callvillebay.com), which is the least crowded of the five on the Nevada Shore.

Note: Several years of drought have drastically reduced the size of Lake Mead and moved its shoreline. As a result, several of the lake's marinas are threatened with relocation or even closure, and some activities on and around some areas of the lake have been restricted. Be sure to call ahead to verify the latest lake conditions.

CAMPING Lake Mead's shoreline is dotted with campsites, all of them equipped with running water, picnic tables, and grills. Available on a first-come, first-served basis, they are administered by the **National Park Service** (𝒞 **702/293-8990;** www.nps.gov). There's a charge of $10 per night at each campsite.

CANOEING The **Alan Bible Visitor Center** (see above) can provide a list of outfitters that rent canoes for trips on the Colorado River. There's one catch, however: A canoeing permit ($10 per person) is required in advance for certain areas near the dam and is available from the **Bureau of Reclamation.** Call 𝒞 **702/293-8204** or visit **www.usbr.gov/lc** for information.

HIKING The best season for hiking is November to March (it's too hot the rest of the year). Some ranger-guided hikes are offered via the **Alan Bible Visitor Center** (see above), which also stocks detailed trail maps. Three trails, ranging in length from .75 miles to 6 miles, originate at the visitor center. The 6-mile trail goes past remains of the railroad built for the dam project. Be sure to take all necessary desert-hiking precautions (see "Desert Hiking Advice" in chapter 6).

LAKE CRUISES A delightful way to enjoy Lake Mead is on a cruise aboard the **Lake Mead Cruises** boat *Desert Princess* 𝒜 (𝒞 **702/293-6180;** www.lakemeadcruises.com), a Mississippi-style paddle-wheeler. Cruises depart year-round from a terminal near **Lake Mead Lodge** at 322 Lake Shore Rd. in Boulder City. It's a relaxing, scenic trip (enjoyed from an open promenade deck or one of two fully enclosed, climate-controlled decks) through Black Canyon and past colorful rock formations known as the "Arizona Paint Pots" en route to Hoover Dam, which is lit at night. Options include buffet breakfast cruises ($33 adults, $15 children under 12), narrated midday cruises ($20 adults, $9 children), cocktail/dinner cruises ($44 adults, $21 children), and sunset dinner/dance cruises with live music ($54 adults, children not allowed). Dinner is served in a pleasant, windowed, air-conditioned dining room. There's a full bar onboard. Call for departure times.

SCUBA DIVING   October to April, there's good visibility, which lessens in summer months when algae flourishes. A list of good dive locations, authorized instructors, and nearby dive shops is available at **Alan Bible Visitor Center** (see above). There's an underwater designated diving area near Lake Mead Marina.

BOULDER CITY

You might want to consider poking around Boulder City on your way back to Vegas. Literally the company town for those building Hoover Dam, it was created by the wives who came with their husbands and turned a temporary site into a real community, since aided by the recreational attractions and attendant businesses of Lake Mead. It doesn't look like much as you first approach it, but once you are in the heart, you'll discover that it's quite charming. There are some antiques and curio shops, and a number of family-style restaurants, burger and Mexican joints, including **Totos,** a reasonably priced Mexican restaurant at 806 Buchanan Blvd. (© **702/ 293-1744**); it's in the Von's shopping center. Or you could try the **Happy Days Diner,** 512 Nevada Hwy. (© **702/293-4637**), which is right on the road to and from the dam. A '50s diner in looks and menu, it has the usual burgers, shakes, and fries, plus complete breakfasts, and is quite inexpensive ($3 for a turkey burger on a recent visit), friendly, and a good place to take the kids.

2 Valley of Fire State Park ★★

60 miles NE of Las Vegas

Most people visualize the desert as a vast expanse of undulating sands punctuated by the occasional cactus or palm-fringed oasis. But the desert of America's Southwest bears little relation to this Lawrence of Arabia image. Stretching for hundreds of miles around Las Vegas in every direction is a seemingly lifeless tundra of vivid reddish earth, shaped by time, climate, and subterranean upheavals into majestic canyons, cliffs, and ridges.

The 36,000-acre Valley of Fire State Park typifies the mountainous red Mojave Desert. It derives its name from the brilliant sandstone formations that were created 150 million years ago by a great shifting of sand, and continues to be shaped by the geologic processes of wind and water erosion. These are rock formations like you'll never see anywhere else. There is nothing green; just fiery flaming red rocks, swirling unrelieved as far as the eye can see. No wonder various sci-fi movies have used this as a stand-in for another planet—it has a most otherworldly look. The whole place is very mysterious, loaded with petroglyphs, and totally inhospitable. It's not hard to believe that for the Indians it was a sacred place, where the men came as a test of their manhood. It is a natural wonder that must be seen to be appreciated.

Although it's hard to imagine in the sweltering Nevada heat, for billions of years these rocks were under hundreds of feet of ocean. This ocean floor began to rise some 200 million years ago, and the waters became shallower. Eventually the sea made a complete retreat, leaving a muddy terrain traversed by ever-diminishing streams. A great sandy desert covered much of the southwestern part of the American continent until about 140 million years ago. Over eons, winds, massive fault action, and water erosion sculpted fantastic formations of sand and limestone. Oxidation of iron in the sands and mud—and the effect of ground water leaching the oxidized iron—turned the rocks the many hues of red, pink, russet, lavender, and white that can be seen today. Logs of ancient forests washed down from faraway highlands and became petrified fossils, which can be seen along two interpretive trails.

Human beings occupied the region, a wetter and cooler one, as far back as 4,000 years ago. They didn't live in the Valley of Fire, but during the Gypsum period (2000 B.C.–300 B.C.) men hunted bighorn sheep (a source of food, clothing, blankets, and hut coverings) here with notched sticks called *atlatls* that are depicted in the park's petroglyphs. Women and children caught rabbits, tortoises, and other small game. In the next phase, from 300 B.C. to A.D. 700, the climate became warmer and dryer. Bows and arrows replaced atlatls, and the hunters and gatherers discovered farming. The ancestral Puebloan people began cultivating corn, squash, and beans, and communities began replacing small nomadic family groups. These ancient people wove watertight baskets, mats, hunting nets, and clothing. Around A.D. 300, they learned how to make sun-dried ceramic pottery. Other tribes, notably the Paiutes, migrated to the area. By A.D. 1150, they had become the dominant group. Unlike the ancestral Puebloans, they were still nomadic and used the Valley of Fire region seasonally. These were the inhabitants whom white settlers found when they entered the area in the early to mid-1800s. The newcomers diverted river and spring waters to irrigate their farmlands, destroying the nature-based Paiute way of life. About 300 descendants of those Paiute tribespeople still live on the Moapa Indian Reservation (about 20 miles northwest) that was established along the Muddy River in 1872.

GETTING THERE

From Las Vegas, take I-15 north to exit 75 (Valley of Fire turnoff). However, the more scenic route is to take I-15 north, then travel Lake Mead Boulevard east to Northshore Road (NV 167), and proceed north to the Valley of Fire exit. The first route takes about an hour, the second 1½ hours.

There is a $5 per vehicle admission charge to the park, regardless of how many people you cram inside.

Plan on spending a minimum of an hour in the park, though you can spend a great deal more time. It can get very hot in there (there is nothing to relieve the sun beating down on all that red and reflecting off it) and there is no water, so be certain to bring a liter, maybe two, per person in the summer. Without a guide, you must stay on paved roads, but don't worry if they end; you can always turn around and come back to the main road again. You can see a great deal from the car, and there are also hiking trails.

Numerous **sightseeing tours** go to the Valley of Fire. **Coach USA** (© **800/828-6699;** www.coachusa.us) has a 6-hour tour from Las Vegas that includes Lake Mead in the morning and the Valley of Fire in the afternoon, plus lunch. Cost is $100 per person, no discounts for children. Inquire at your hotel tour desk. **Char Cruze of Creative Adventures** (see "Unique Desert Tours by Creative Adventures" in chapter 6) also offers a fantastic tour.

The Valley of Fire can also be visited in conjunction with Lake Mead. From **Lake Mead Lodge,** take NV 166 (Lakeshore Rd.) north, make a right turn on NV 167 (Northshore Rd.), turn left on NV 169 (Moapa Valley Blvd.) west—a spectacularly scenic drive—and follow the signs. The Valley of Fire is about 65 miles from Hoover Dam.

WHAT TO SEE & DO

There are no food concessions or gas stations in the park; however, you can obtain meals or gas on NV 167 or in nearby **Overton** (15 miles northwest on NV 169). Overton is a fertile valley town replete with trees, agricultural crops, horses, and herds of cattle—quite a change in scenery. On your way in or out of the teeming metropolis, do stop off at **Inside Scoop** &, 395 S. Moapa Valley Blvd. (© **702/ 397-2055**), open Monday through Saturday from 10am until 8pm and Sunday from 11am to 7pm. It's a sweet, old-fashioned ice-cream parlor run by extremely friendly people, with a proper menu that, in addition to classic sandwiches and the like, features some surprising choices—a vegetarian sandwich and a fish salad with crab and shrimp, for example. Everything is quite tasty and fresh. They also do box lunches, perfect for picnicking inside the park. We strongly recommend coming by here on your way in for a box lunch, and then coming by afterward for a much-needed ice cream.

At the southern edge of town is the **Lost City Museum** &, 721 S. Moapa Valley Blvd. (© **702/397-2193**), a sweet little museum, very nicely done, commemorating an ancient ancestral Puebloan village that was discovered in the region in 1924. Reconstructed wattle-and-daub pueblos surround the museum. Admission is $3 for adults, $2 for seniors 65 and over, and free for children under 18. The museum is open daily 8:30am to 4:30pm. Closed Thanksgiving, Christmas, and New Year's Day.

Information headquarters for the Valley of Fire is the **Visitor Center** on NV 169, 6 miles west of Northshore Road (© **702/397-2088;** http://parks.nv.gov/vf.htm). It's open daily 8:30am to 4:30pm and is worth a quick stop for information and a bit of history before entering the park.

There are **hiking trails, shaded picnic sites,** and **two campgrounds** in the park. Most sites are equipped with tables, grills, water, and restrooms. A $12 per vehicle per night camping fee is charged for use of the campground.

Petroglyphs at Atlatl Rock and Petroglyph Canyon are both easily accessible. In summer, when temperatures are usually over 100°F (38°C), you may have to settle for driving through the park in an air-conditioned car.

3 Red Rock Canyon ★★★

19 miles W of Las Vegas

If you need a break from the Vegas hubbub, Red Rock Canyon is balm for your overstimulated soul. Less than 20 miles away—but a world apart—this is a magnificent unspoiled vista that should cleanse and refresh you. You can drive the panoramic 13-mile **Scenic Drive** (open daily 7am–dusk) or explore it in more depth on foot, making it perfect for both athletes and armchair types. There are many interesting sights and trail heads along the drive itself. The

National Conservation Area (www.redrockcanyon.blm.gov) offers hiking trails and internationally acclaimed rock-climbing opportunities (especially notable is the 7,068-ft. Mt. Wilson, the highest sandstone peak among the bluffs). There are picnic areas along the drive and in nearby **Spring Mountain Ranch State Park** (http://parks.nv.gov/smr.htm), 5 miles south, which also offers plays in an outdoor theater during the summer. Since Bonnie Springs Ranch (see the next section) is just a few miles away, it makes a great base for exploring Red Rock Canyon.

GETTING THERE

Just drive west on Charleston Boulevard, which becomes NV 159. Virtually as soon as you leave the city, the red rocks begin to loom around you. The visitor center will appear on your right.

You can also go on an **organized tour. Coach USA** (© 800/828-6699; www.coachusa.us), among other companies, runs bus tours to Red Rock Canyon. Inquire at your hotel tour desk.

Finally, you can go **by bike.** Not very far out of town (at Rainbow Blvd.), Charleston Boulevard is flanked by a bike path that continues for about 11 miles to the visitor center/scenic drive. The path is hilly but not difficult if you're in reasonable shape. However, only exceptionally fit and experienced bikers should attempt to explore Red Rock Canyon by bike.

Just off NV 159, you'll see the **Red Rock Canyon Visitor Center** (© 702/515-5350), which marks the actual entrance to the park. There, you can pick up information on trails and view history exhibits about the canyon. The center is open daily 8:30am to 4:30pm. A visit to Red Rock Canyon can be combined with a visit to Bonnie Springs Ranch.

WHAT TO SEE & DO

Begin with a stop at the **visitor center;** not only is there a $5 per vehicle fee to pay, but you can pick up a variety of helpful literature: history, guides, hiking trail maps, and lists of local flora and fauna.

Tips Wild Weather

Although it can get very hot in Red Rock during the summer, it can also get very cold there during the winter. A recent trip in March to Red Rock and Bonnie Springs found the latter closed—due to snow!

You can also view exhibits that tell the history of the canyon and depict its plant and animal life. You'll see a fascinating video here about Nevada's thousands of wild horses and burros, protected by an act of Congress since 1971. Furthermore, you can obtain permits for hiking and backpacking. Call ahead to find out about ranger-guided tours as well as informative guided hikes offered by groups like the Sierra Club and the Audubon Society. And, if you're traveling with children, ask about the free *Junior Ranger Discovery Book* filled with fun family activities.

The easiest thing to do is to **drive the 13-mile scenic loop** 🕸🕸. It really is a loop, and it goes only one way, so once you start, you are committed to driving the whole thing. You can stop the car to admire any number of fabulous views and sights along the way, or have a picnic, or take a walk or hike. As you drive, observe how dramatically the milky-white limestone alternates with iron-rich red rocks. Farther along, the mountains become solid limestone, with canyons running between them, which lead to an evergreen forest— a surprising addition to the desert.

If you're up to it, however, we can't stress enough that the way to really see the canyon is by **hiking.** Every trail is incredible—glance over your options and decide what you might be looking for. You can begin from the visitor center or drive into the loop, park, and start from points therein. Hiking trails range from a .7-mile-loop stroll to a waterfall (its flow varying seasonally) at Lost Creek to much longer and more strenuous treks. Actually, all the hikes involve a certain amount of effort, as you have to scramble over rocks on even the shorter hikes. Unfit or undexterous people should be aware. Be sure to wear good shoes as the rocks can be slippery. You must have a map; you won't get lost forever (there usually are other hikers around to help you out, eventually), but you can get lost. It is often tough to find a landmark, and once you're deep into the rocks, everything looks the same, even with the map. Consequently, give yourself extra time for each hike (at least an additional hour), regardless of its billed length, to allow for the lack of paths and getting disoriented, and simply to slow down and admire the scenery.

Biking is another option; riding a bicycle would be a tremendous way to travel the loop. There are also terrific off-road mountain biking trails, with levels from amateur to expert.

After you tour the canyon, drive over to Bonnie Springs Ranch (details in the next section) for lunch or dinner. See chapter 6 for further details on climbing.

4 Bonnie Springs Ranch/Old Nevada ⋆⋆⋆

About 24 miles W of Las Vegas, 5 miles past Red Rock Canyon

Bonnie Springs Ranch/Old Nevada is a kind of Wild West theme park with accommodations and a restaurant. If you're traveling with kids, a day or overnight trip to Bonnie Springs is recommended, but it is surprisingly appealing for adults, too. It could even be a romantic getaway, offering horseback riding, gorgeous mountain vistas, proximity to Red Rock Canyon, and temperatures 5° to 10° cooler than on the Strip.

For additional information, you can call **Bonnie Springs Ranch/ Old Nevada** at ✆ **702/875-4191** or visit them on the Web at www.bonniesprings.com.

If you're **driving,** a trip to Bonnie Springs Ranch can be combined easily with a day trip to Red Rock Canyon; it is about 5 miles farther on. But you can also stay overnight.

Jeep tours to and from Las Vegas are available through **Action Tours.** Call ✆ **888/288-5200** or 702/566-7400 (http://actiontours. com) for details.

WHAT TO SEE & DO IN OLD NEVADA

Old Nevada (✆ **702/875-4191**) ⋆⋆ is a re-creation of an 1880s frontier town, built on the site of a very old ranch. As tourist sights go, this is a good one; it's a bit cheesy, but knowingly, perhaps even deliberately so. It's terrific for kids up to about the age of 12 or so (before teenage cynicism kicks in) but not all that bad for adults fondly remembering similar places from their own childhood. Many go expecting a tourist trap, only to come away saying that it really was rather cute and charming.

Certainly, Old Nevada looks authentic, with rustic buildings entirely made of weathered wood. And the setting, right in front of beautiful mountains with layered red rock, couldn't be more perfect for a western. You can wander the town (it's only about a block long), taking peeps into well-replicated places of business, such as a blacksmith shop, a working mill, a saloon, and an old-fashioned general store (cum gift shop) and museum that has a potpourri of items from the Old West and Old Las Vegas: antique gaming tables and slot machines, typewriters, and a great display of old shoes, including lace-up boots. There is also a rather lame wax museum; the less said about it, the better.

Country music is played in the saloon during the day, except when **stage melodramas and stunt-shootouts** take place (at frequent intervals 11:30am–5pm). These are entirely tongue-in-cheek—the actors are goofy and know it, and the plot is hokey and fully intended to be that way.

Movies (one about nearby Red Rock Canyon, one a silent film) are shown in the **Old Movie House** throughout the day from 10:30am to 5pm. You can tour the remains of the **old Comstock lode silver mine,** though there isn't much to see there.

Admission to Old Nevada is charged by vehicle—$7 per car weekdays for up to 6 people in the car and $10 per car on the weekend. The park is open daily 10:30am to 5pm November to April, and until 6pm the rest of the year.

WHAT TO SEE & DO AT BONNIE SPRINGS RANCH

There are several things to do here free of charge, and it's right next door to Old Nevada. It's quite a pretty place, in a funky, Western kind of way, and in season, there are tons of flowers everywhere, including honeysuckle and roses. The main attraction is the small **zoo** ✿ on the premises. Now, when we say "zoo," unfortunately we mean in addition to a petting zoo with the usual suspects (deer, sheep, goats, and rabbits) and some unusual animals (pot-belly pigs and snooty, beautiful llamas) to caress and feed, there is also a maze-like enclosure of a series of wire mesh pens that contain a variety of livestock, some of which should not be penned up (though they are well taken care of), including wolves and bobcats. Still, it's more than diverting for kids.

Less politically and ecologically distressing is the aviary, housing peacocks, Polish chickens, peachface and blackmask lovebirds, finches, parakeets, ravens, ducks, pheasants, and geese. Keep your eyes peeled for the peacocks roaming free; with luck, they will spread their tails for a photo op. With greater luck, some of the angelic, rare white peacocks will do the same. It may be worth dropping by just in the hopes of spotting one in full fan-tailed glory.

Riding stables offer guided hour-long trail rides into the mountain area on a continuous basis throughout the day (9am–3:15pm spring–fall, until 5:45pm in summer). Children must be at least 6 years old to participate. Cost is $25 per person. For more information, call ✆ **702/875-4191.**

Scenic 20-minute **stagecoach rides** are offered weekends and holidays; they cost $5 for adults, $3 for children under 12.

Index

See also Accommodations, and Restaurant indexes below.

FROMMER'S® COMPLETE TRAVEL GUIDES

Alaska
Alaska Cruises & Ports of Call
American Southwest
Amsterdam
Argentina & Chile
Arizona
Atlanta
Australia
Austria
Bahamas
Barcelona, Madrid & Seville
Beijing
Belgium, Holland & Luxembourg
Bermuda
Boston
Brazil
British Columbia & the Canadian Rockies
Brussels & Bruges
Budapest & the best of Hungary
Calgary
California
Canada
Cancún, Cozumel & the Yucatán
Cape Cod, Nantucket & Martha's Vineyard
Caribbean
Caribbean Ports of Call
Carolinas & Georgia
Chicago
China
Colorado
Costa Rica
Cruises & Ports of Call
Cuba
Denmark
Denver, Boulder & Colorado Springs
England
Europe
Europe by Rail
European Cruises & Ports of Call

Florence, Tuscany & Umbria
Florida
France
Germany
Great Britain
Greece
Greek Islands
Halifax
Hawaii
Hong Kong
Honolulu, Waikiki & Oahu
India
Ireland
Italy
Jamaica
Japan
Kauai
Las Vegas
London
Los Angeles
Maryland & Delaware
Maui
Mexico
Montana & Wyoming
Montréal & Québec City
Munich & the Bavarian Alps
Nashville & Memphis
New England
Newfoundland & Labrador
New Mexico
New Orleans
New York City
New York State
New Zealand
Northern Italy
Norway
Nova Scotia, New Brunswick & Prince Edward Island
Oregon
Ottawa
Paris
Peru

Philadelphia & the Amish Country
Portugal
Prague & the Best of the Czech Republic
Provence & the Riviera
Puerto Rico
Rome
San Antonio & Austin
San Diego
San Francisco
Santa Fe, Taos & Albuquerque
Scandinavia
Scotland
Seattle
Shanghai
Sicily
Singapore & Malaysia
South Africa
South America
South Florida
South Pacific
Southeast Asia
Spain
Sweden
Switzerland
Texas
Thailand
Tokyo
Toronto
Turkey
USA
Utah
Vancouver & Victoria
Vermont, New Hampshire & Maine
Vienna & the Danube Valley
Virgin Islands
Virginia
Walt Disney World® & Orlando
Washington, D.C.
Washington State

FROMMER'S® DOLLAR-A-DAY GUIDES

Australia from $50 a Day
California from $70 a Day
England from $75 a Day
Europe from $85 a Day
Florida from $70 a Day
Hawaii from $80 a Day

Ireland from $80 a Day
Italy from $70 a Day
London from $90 a Day
New York City from $90 a Day
Paris from $90 a Day
San Francisco from $70 a Day

Washington, D.C. from $80 a Day
Portable London from $90 a Day
Portable New York City from $90 a Day
Portable Paris from $90 a Day

FROMMER'S® PORTABLE GUIDES

Acapulco, Ixtapa & Zihuatanejo
Amsterdam
Aruba
Australia's Great Barrier Reef
Bahamas
Berlin
Big Island of Hawaii
Boston
California Wine Country
Cancún
Cayman Islands
Charleston
Chicago
Disneyland®
Dominican Republic
Dublin

Florence
Frankfurt
Hong Kong
Las Vegas
Las Vegas for Non-Gamblers
London
Los Angeles
Los Cabos & Baja
Maine Coast
Maui
Miami
Nantucket & Martha's Vineyard
New Orleans
New York City
Paris

Phoenix & Scottsdale
Portland
Puerto Rico
Puerto Vallarta, Manzanillo & Guadalajara
Rio de Janeiro
San Diego
San Francisco
Savannah
Vancouver
Vancouver Island
Venice
Virgin Islands
Washington, D.C.
Whistler

FROMMER'S® NATIONAL PARK GUIDES

Algonquin Provincial Park
Banff & Jasper
Family Vacations in the National
  Parks

Grand Canyon
National Parks of the American
  West
Rocky Mountain

Yellowstone & Grand Teton
Yosemite & Sequoia/Kings
  Canyon
Zion & Bryce Canyon

FROMMER'S® MEMORABLE WALKS

Chicago
London

New York
Paris

San Francisco

FROMMER'S® WITH KIDS GUIDES

Chicago
Las Vegas
New York City

Ottawa
San Francisco
Toronto

Vancouver
Walt Disney World® & Orlando
Washington, D.C.

SUZY GERSHMAN'S BORN TO SHOP GUIDES

Born to Shop: France
Born to Shop: Hong Kong,
  Shanghai & Beijing

Born to Shop: Italy
Born to Shop: London

Born to Shop: New York
Born to Shop: Paris

FROMMER'S® IRREVERENT GUIDES

Amsterdam
Boston
Chicago
Las Vegas
London

Los Angeles
Manhattan
New Orleans
Paris
Rome

San Francisco
Seattle & Portland
Vancouver
Walt Disney World®
Washington, D.C.

FROMMER'S® BEST-LOVED DRIVING TOURS

Austria
Britain
California
France

Germany
Ireland
Italy
New England

Northern Italy
Scotland
Spain
Tuscany & Umbria

THE UNOFFICIAL GUIDES®

Beyond Disney
California with Kids
Central Italy
Chicago
Cruises
Disneyland®
England
Florida
Florida with Kids
Inside Disney

Hawaii
Las Vegas
London
Maui
Mexico's Best Beach Resorts
Mini Las Vegas
Mini Mickey
New Orleans
New York City
Paris

San Francisco
Skiing & Snowboarding in the
  West
South Florida including Miami &
  the Keys
Walt Disney World®
Walt Disney World® for
  Grown-ups
Walt Disney World® with Kids
Washington, D.C.

SPECIAL-INTEREST TITLES

Athens Past & Present
Cities Ranked & Rated
Frommer's Best Day Trips from London
Frommer's Best RV & Tent Campgrounds
  in the U.S.A.
Frommer's Caribbean Hideaways
Frommer's China: The 50 Most Memorable Trips
Frommer's Exploring America by RV
Frommer's Gay & Lesbian Europe
Frommer's NYC Free & Dirt Cheap

Frommer's Road Atlas Europe
Frommer's Road Atlas France
Frommer's Road Atlas Ireland
Frommer's Wonderful Weekends from
  New York City
The New York Times' Guide to Unforgettable
  Weekends
Retirement Places Rated
Rome Past & Present